CRAFT:
THE EXPEDITION OF BUSINESS

CRAFT:
THE EXPEDITION OF BUSINESS

Proven tools and insights for leaders of small and mid-sized businesses

BY ZACK TOMLIN

A guide for those mastering the craft of building an exceptional business

Published by Harnessing Energy LLC
Raleigh, NC
https://harnessing.energy

First edition, March 2026
10 9 8 7 6 5 4 3 2 1

ISBN (paperback): 979-8-9999688-1-4
ISBN (hardcover): 979-8-9999688-2-1
ISBN (ebook): 979-8-9999688-3-8

DEDICATION

To all those working hard to be better,
on the journey to master their craft.

To John Stewart.
The kind of dad I strive to be.
The father-in-law that left us far too soon.

CONTENTS

1 | *Author's Note: The Road Ahead*
5 | *Orientation*

PART 1: DESTINATION

17 | *Ch. 1 - The Perfect Business*
23 | *Ch. 2 - The Mountain of Why*
33 | *Ch. 3 - Pyramids of Decisions*
41 | *Ch. 4 - Levers of Control*

PART 2: CREW

51 | *Ch. 5 - Paddle Downstream*
61 | *Ch. 6 - Vantage Points*
71 | *Ch. 7 - Undercurrents (G.E.A.R.)*
79 | *Ch. 8 - Wired for Survival*
89 | *Ch. 9 - Made Different*
97 | *Ch. 10 - Internal Maps*
107 | *Ch. 11 - Narrow Trails*
115 | *Ch. 12 - Harnessing Energy*

PART 3: LEADER

127 | *Ch. 13 - Business Leadership Defined*
141 | *Ch. 14 - What Leaders Provide*
153 | *Ch. 15 - Why Leaders Are Chosen*
163 | *Ch. 16 - Who Leaders Are*
187 | *Ch. 17 - The Cost of Leadership*

PART 4: EXPEDITION

197 | *Ch. 18 - Rule #1: Don't Die Along the Way*
209 | *Ch. 19 - Coalitions and Caravans*
229 | *Ch. 20 - Tell the Tale*
255 | *Ch. 21 - Setting North*
281 | *Ch. 22 - Navigation and Reconnaissance*
301 | *Ch. 23 - Lines of Communication*
317 | *Ch. 24 - Supply Lines*
333 | *Ch. 25 - Beachheads*
351 | *Ch. 26 - Anchor Before Setting Sail*

361 | *Onward*

AUTHOR'S NOTE: THE ROAD AHEAD

Like many others, I found myself leading a company despite no formal business training. As the child of blue-collar parents and an engineering undergraduate who was forced into entrepreneurship by the Global Financial Crisis, I was left to learn how to lead an organization on my own—a classic case of "building the plane while flying it."

In hindsight, I wouldn't have it any other way. But I am also under no delusion that traditional business education fully prepares anyone for the trials and tribulations of running an organization. For all business leaders, there is some element of figuring it out for ourselves.

Regardless of circumstances, curiosity sits behind our hunger for knowledge. And when answering our most pressing questions has a material effect on our livelihood and the ability we have to provide for our family and employees, our need to know grows larger.

And so, I am grateful to live in a time when information and possible answers to those questions are readily accessible. I would not have achieved the growth and success I've enjoyed if not for all the thinkers and authors I had access to via a library card, bookstores, or my online shopping basket. To all of them, I say, "Thank you."

I never planned on adding "Author" to my résumé, yet here we are. Writing a book is no simple task—but like running a business, there are plenty of others to help you along. The best advice I received in writing this book clarified the goal: *Non-fiction books answer questions.*

There are already thousands of books that attempt to answer the question, *"How to build a great business."* My aim is to answer a question that is slightly different in wording but significantly different in meaning: *"How to be a better builder of a great business."* Or—perhaps better said, *"How to master the craft of business."*

Answering that question and becoming a better builder is a journey, and along the way there are dozens of other questions to be addressed—many of them are listed in the map that follows, an outline of the road ahead.

The pace of the book will be intentionally quick. There is a lot of ground to cover, and I would prefer to err on the side of speed—knowing that a reader can always back up and cover the same terrain again if needed.

How fast you proceed doesn't matter. Nor do you need to agree with my assessment of the questions at hand. What's important is that the ideas resonate, that they spur your curiosity, and that having a better version of **your** answer to the questions would help you on your journey.

If that is true, then this book is for you.

FIELD NOTES FROM THE EXPEDITION OF BUSINESS

The books we read and the journeys we undertake change us. But their benefit is far greater when we take the time to reflect on what we've experienced.

The greatest explorers carried journals, not just as personal records, but as essential tools. They recorded their observations, their questions, and what they discovered along the way. Writing helped them make sense of unfamiliar terrain and chart the path forward.

This book attempts to answer certain questions. It provides frameworks and principles to help you think more clearly about your business.
The journal is where you craft your own answers. Use it to capture what stands out, clarify what matters most, and define your next steps.

SCAN THE QR CODE OR VISIT THE LINK BELOW TO ACCESS YOUR COMPANION JOURNAL
WWW.THEEXPEDITIONOFBUSINESS.COM/JOURNAL

THE JOURNEY TO MASTERY ON THE EXPEDITION OF BUSINESS

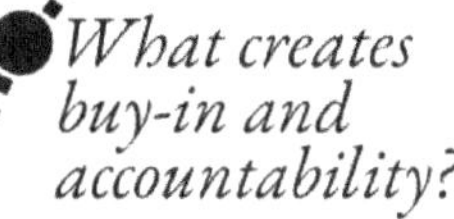

ORIENTATION

What is the journey that's brought you to where you are today?

When did you set off, and with what goal in mind?

What obstacles have you had to overcome, and how have you changed along the way?

To an extent, we're all on the same journey—an expedition from where we are today to where we want to be. Navigating the route between the two is rarely easy, and the person we were at the start often has no chance of reaching the intended destination. Achieving our goals means learning, growing, and changing during the pursuit. The experience becomes as much about who we are and what we believe as where we're going and what we hope to accomplish.

On most expeditions, a leader directs their crew on a journey toward the intended destination, while at the same time they are on a quest all their own—one of finding the wisdom, discipline, and discernment necessary to become a great leader. In the process, they learn from their mistakes and those sages they meet along the way. They put into practice the principles they've come to rely on, and slowly they become masters of their craft.

The expedition of business and the journey of its leader are no different, and one core question is common to both.

Maps, trail markers, north stars, buoys, beacons, and a compass in your hands—financial reports, employee surveys, customer satisfaction scores, and industry reputation: they all answer questions about where you've been, where you are, and perhaps even where you're going next.

But only you can answer the most important question about the journey you're on:

Why are you going?

———◦———

When I was around eight years old, most Sunday afternoons my mom would load my sister and me into the car, and we'd drive over to see Dad. Sunday was visiting day at the Catawba County Correctional Center.

It wasn't the first occasion, nor the last, that Dad would find himself as a guest of the State. At the time, I found it none too surprising that he was in prison. For all of my life, and for the rest of his, Dad would battle substance abuse of one form or another. It would be a struggle that harmed relationships, sabotaged opportunities, and inevitably landed him in legal trouble. However, there were always stretches of sunshine between the clouds.

When he was on the right side of the prison gates and away from the bottle, things were good. Riding shotgun at the golf course, following our favorite sports teams, fishing farm ponds out in the country (I was told those "No Trespassing" signs were "*for other people*"): they were times any boy wants to spend with his dad. At a young age, you just enjoy the good, not dwelling on what you wish was different.

The questioning comes later: questions like how an otherwise capable and intelligent man could let his escapes cost him a marriage, a business, time with his kids, and more than once, his personal freedom. And questions of human potential: how people of similar talent, intellect, and abilities can find markedly different levels of success.

They are questions I would return to more than once. First, in my efforts to escape the cycle of instability of my youth. Next, when building a career and family. And then later, when running a business and wanting to get the best out of myself and my team.

The latter brought the questions into sharper focus. In business, nearly everything revolves around people—our customers, our competition, our staff—but as leaders, our influence is strongest on those within our organization. So, we focus our efforts on recruiting, hiring, and developing people the best we can. Next, we turn to defining responsibilities, strategies, and goals. And while knowing more and clarifying our aim brings better success, our efforts are less effective if we overlook our most important thought—what we think of ourselves.

The people and leaders who comprise our businesses can have all the potential in the world, but it matters little if they make the journey overloaded with self-doubt.

For some, the load to carry is lighter. Whether it's a product of past successes, the encouragement of others, or intentional effort to control their thoughts—the climb to being their best may not be easy, but it is more achievable. Others are not so fortunate. Circumstances beyond their control or conditions which they have yet to learn to navigate leave them looking for a foothold on the ascent of realizing their potential.

In hindsight, it's easier to see the load Dad was carrying and the struggle to find his footing. He alone was responsible for his actions, and I have no interest in providing excuses, but with time I can see why facing the world under the influence lessened the strain of doing so sober.

Explaining the anchors that held Dad back would be less difficult if there weren't so many ways he was exceptional. There's a long list of what Dad did well, but years later one stands out:

Work. His work. His craft.

Dad worked in all types of construction and could rarely be choosy about the next job, but working alongside him often, I knew the work that he liked best. Even now, when I enter a new room, my eyes inevitably move toward the finish work—the door trim, the window casings, the baseboards, and the crown molding that moves a room from being purely utilitarian to a place we enjoy being just a little bit more. It's a small piece of civilized living that we take for granted.

For those who have never done it, it's tougher than it looks—getting the angles right, working with the grain of the wood, knowing how paint or stain would take, hiding the seams even when the wood would expand or contract. He was good at it; he knew it, and he was proud of it. He liked talking about it and admiring when others did it well. I just enjoyed watching him do it.

In a world where it's easy to get down on yourself, there's something uplifting to be found in work, in improving, and in doing something well. And we thrive in situations that allow us to do just that: to learn, to grow, to have a craft, and to master it. This alone may not be enough, but for many of us, it lightens the load and allows us to reach our intended destination.

For the business leader, providing such an opportunity for their people is altruistic, but it is also a strategic choice.

The zeitgeist of business includes popular lore around "A Players" and "Rockstars." And while some individuals simply possess more talent and ability, there's not a person on Earth who doesn't perform better in the right environment.

All leaders see people as they are; the ones who find success on the expedition of business also see people as who they could become.

——◆O◆——

The path to business leadership is different for everyone. Maybe you started a company from scratch, or with a partner or two. Maybe you were promoted through a large organization or hired from the outside to take a leadership role. Maybe you're the next generation in a family-owned business. Regardless of the path, you didn't get there by accident. You've been good—very good—at something before. You know what it's like to have a craft that is challenging but rewarding when done well.

Now you have a different craft: leading a business. While your past success or failure may have been mostly in your control, now you're beholden to a team of people and their performance. Like any expedition, you're all in it together. And how well they're mastering their craft has much to do with how well you're mastering yours.

I spent years doing my best to be a master of mine. A core belief that came from watching Dad served me well during that time. It serves me now as I work with other business leaders on similar journeys. ***The work we do, and how well we do it, matters.***

Your craft matters. It matters to the world and to the people you serve and create for—to customers and clients who come back again and again and refer you to others. It matters to your staff and employees. And the environment it creates for them to perform at their best separates great businesses from average ones. Your craft matters to you, and it determines whether leading a business is an experience of doubt and struggle or one of growth and success.

This book is for business leaders who take pride in their work, who want to see their staff and employees do the same. It is for business leaders who are on their journey to mastery, on an expedition of always looking to learn and improve.

I founded and successfully ran my own business for 12 years. Like most, I didn't start that journey with all the answers. Nor do I pretend to have them all now, but the world of business advice is only so big. Nearly two decades of relentlessly looking for answers is enough time to cover most of the terrain of business books, podcasts, and gurus.

Unfortunately, *the* answer is not out there, but along the way you learn how to think about business better, how to make sounder decisions, and you discover the first principles that you hold to be true.

Many leaders are looking to do the same, and that is why I'm on my current journey. I left my prior business and career to help others on their own expedition of business.

It is important and meaningful work.

They and leaders like you are the creators of opportunity. Yes, of economic growth, innovation, and prosperity, but more importantly, the opportunity for millions of hard-working people to be part of an organization that helps them to grow and to learn—to master their own craft, to feel like Dad at the moments he was doing his best work, to feel proud of their efforts and good about themselves.

The average adult spends most of their waking hours at work. How that experience goes, and the opportunity they have to succeed, may be the biggest factor in their quality of life.

Having the ability to earn a living, to provide for their family, and to come home at night feeling appreciated, engaged, and capable: that changes a person. They become the person who is likely to be a better spouse, a better parent, and a better neighbor. That's the person who makes the world a better place for all of us. It's also the person who—when you have enough of them—takes your business from average to remarkable.

Like it or not, being a business leader comes with great responsibility: to provide that opportunity and to make a real impact in the lives of others. But doing so provides an opportunity for yourself: to meet the challenge head-on, to go on the journey of becoming a master of your craft, and to have the world be better for it. It's hard work, but learning from one's mistakes, keeping the goal in mind, and making each attempt better than the last gets us to the destination we seek.

⁘⊰⊙⊱⁘

Craftsmanship is often, and unfairly, associated with works produced by hand. The woodworker, the tanner, the potter: these are synonymous with craftsmanship, but they and folks like them don't have a monopoly on excellence. I grew up around working-class people of all types, and my working career has been no different. All had their work to do, some with their hands, others with their intellect, and many did it well.

Whether it be trim carpentry or leading a business, craftsmanship is performing a task at a high level, making decisions based on a deep understanding of core principles, and producing an outcome of exceptional quality.

Learning those principles, putting in the time and practice to master them: these aren't the efforts of someone content with being average. No, it speaks of someone who went out beyond their current limits and blazed a trail through the wilderness of ignorance—someone who thought more was possible and went on an expedition to learn how to be better at their craft.

There are two ways we make progress through such terrain. First, we try and fail, try and fail, try and fail, until eventually we succeed. These are lessons of experience, self-teaching, and practice. Second, we listen to others who have done the same before us—learning by example. If we're lucky, their stories reveal insight and real understanding. If we're wise enough, we figure out when to apply them to our own journey.

Like the expeditions that take men and women up tall mountains, across vast oceans, and deep into parts unknown, the journeys we find ourselves on in business consist of four parts—as does the rest of this book:

The **Destination** we seek—**Part 1**:

No expedition begins without a goal in mind. But reaching the intended destination is a combination of our efforts and external factors. We may be beholden to the storms, the unknowns, and the bad luck which awaits us, but one thing is always in our control: the decisions we make along the way. Part 1 is about how to make better ones—climbing from the imitation of others to the first principles unique to you and your organization, understanding the weight each decision carries, and identifying the four levers that control any business.

The **Crew** that we're going with—**Part 2**:

We can't make the journey alone, but the people we lead aren't parts in a machine or mere resources to be deployed—they're humans running on ancient wiring, each one different, each one telling themselves a story about the work they do, each one navigating different challenges, and each one primed to delight, confuse, or drive us crazy at any moment. Part 2 is about developing a mental model that many leaders lack: understanding what drives the individuals who comprise their teams—and how to put that insight to work.

The **Leader** they follow—**Part 3**:

Someone must be out in front, but why should anyone follow? Leaders succeed when they provide clarity in a sea of confusion and establish the order that keeps chaos from brewing. And while there are many paths that lead to the summit of effective leadership, each is overgrown with clichéd advice and examples that don't apply to the specific demands of business. Cutting through means understanding who leaders are, why they are chosen, and the costs of leadership that too often go uncounted.

And the **Expedition** we set off on in pursuit of our goal—**Part 4**:

Business and expedition leaders are both tasked with directing their crews into unknown terrain—places filled with potential but only reachable by charting a new course. It takes a vision of the final destination, but also the infrastructure and routines that keep everyone moving forward—even when we can't be by their side. Part 4 is the operational core: knowing the challenges we're up against, selecting who to bring along, and telling the story of where we've been, where we're going, and how we will get there—all without drifting off course.

There will be many bends in the trail between here and the finish line. At times the terrain will appear similar; at others, we'll find ourselves in unfamiliar territory. Some ideas and insights will be specific and tactical, while others may feel more philosophical and harder to place. But there is a method to the musing.

Execution can't happen without defined tactics. Tactics are just a collection of tricks without sound strategy. And the best strategies support a clear goal while arising from solid first principles.

The best first principles, and the ones that gave rise to the book that follows, are rooted in truths that don't change with the next crop of buzzwords, the latest technology trends, or whatever "Gen" is slated to enter the workforce next.

Instead, they allow one to build on what stays the same: every decision comes with opportunity costs, complexity compounds, constraints clarify possibilities, and a drift toward disorder is the natural current of the universe. But the most important principles relate to people: how our brains work, how we learn in the most fundamental way, how we make sense of the world, how we navigate uncertainty, and the quirks, traits, and limitations that—at times—make us our own worst enemy.

All are patterns that show up whether we're leading a team today or an expedition in 1905, and they are the foundations on which we can design, operate, and lead a great business.

To do so, you will need to cross terrain that is as unique as the business you lead. No one has gone exactly that way before. The decisions you make and how well you execute them along the way are part of mastering the craft of business. And while the responsibility is solely yours, no one has to make the journey alone.

I hope the pages that follow will help you on your way. They provide plenty of principles, insights, and frameworks that I benefited from and that my clients have found helpful. I trust you'll have the wisdom of knowing when to apply those ideas, when to listen to others, and when to go your own way.

That's what craftsmanship is after all: knowing what to do, when to do it, and then doing it well. Doing it your way. Doing it for your why.

PART 1

DESTINATION

CHAPTER 1

THE PERFECT BUSINESS

Imagine two locations on a map. One is the current state of your business. The other is the perfect business. Chances are you never expected perfection, and I applaud your realism. But undoubtedly you have goals, a vision of the organization you would like to have in the future. And that business lies somewhere between those two points, on the route between today and perfection.

The same is true for any craft. The woodworker starts with the perfect chair in mind, the chef with the perfect meal, and the surgeon with the perfect outcome. Having an idea of perfection provides a mental model—one that helps distill the complexity of the outcome into a framework of manageable parts.

"Why is it perfect?" becomes the illuminating question. To the craftsman, a chair can't be just a "chair," nor a meal a "meal," nor a surgery a "surgery." More depth is required: a knowledge of the parts that make up the whole and the interplay between them. It's that insight that allows us

to consider the quality of one's work, but also to determine which step to take next.

Without a vision of the perfect business, we have no lodestar for our travels—no beacon to guide us on the expedition of business, and no way of determining if our next step is one in the right direction. It's all wandering in the wilderness until we know where we're going. And if where we're going is somewhere between our business of today and the perfect business of the future, then it all begins with one question: how do we define perfection?

In 2009, Tom Watson—regarded as one of the best golfers of all time—found himself in a familiar spot. He was once again in the lead and standing in the fairway on the last hole of a major championship. All that was between him and the title was hitting a solid second shot onto the green. From there, he could easily close out the hole and the championship.

But there was something unusual about this situation, and it had caught the attention of fans around the world. The average age of winners of major golf tournaments is 32. That day, Tom Watson was 59—making him 11 years older than any prior major champion. To put it mildly, he would be an unexpected winner. And it would take something close to perfection to best a field of the world's best (and much younger) golfers.

Prior to the shot, he consulted with his caddy, understood the distance to the hole, considered the wind, and visualized the slopes of the green on which the ball would land. He was a master of his craft, considering all the variables in play. The shot itself reflected the same: the right club aimed in the right direction. Watson would say after the round: *"When that ball was in the air, I said, 'I like it.'"*

The golf world held its breath as the ball hit the green, and as Watson would later say, it *"landed right where I wanted it to."*

A feeling of inevitable victory quickly spread through the air, only to retreat just as fast. The ball didn't stop as expected. Groans came from the crowd as it rolled through the green, leaving him with a very difficult third shot—one that would cause him to finish the round in a tie with another golfer and subsequently lose the tournament in a playoff.

Years later, Tom Watson gave an interview about that shot on the last hole. He recounted several spectators telling him that as the ball hit the green, a gust of wind from the same direction blew through. The wind almost certainly propelled the ball a little farther than intended and turned a perfect decision and a perfect swing into an outcome that was less exceptional.

No one would blame Tom Watson for being disappointed after the loss. But I hope he takes solace knowing he made a great decision and executed just as he wanted. If there is craftsmanship in golf, he put it on display, and it may very well have been perfection. But even within the controlled confines of sport, forces beyond his control dictated the outcome.

In business, the difficulty is that much greater. Leaders are tasked with leading organizations through a world of complexity and in the face of both unknown and unknowable outside forces.

A fast-growing donut chain has its sales plummet after the low-carb Atkins diet craze emerges. A regional manufacturer signs the biggest deal in their history only to have port strikes in Long Beach force them to idle production for two weeks. The wettest summer on record puts a construction contractor a month behind schedule on a high-profile project. And I spend months hiring the perfect candidate for an open role, only to have their spouse get a promotion and need to move the family out of state.

How do we respond?

In the moments when things go awry, we need firm beliefs to fall back on, and none may be as important as how we judge our decisions and our efforts.

We're all entitled to our own definition of perfection. Here's mine, and though I don't claim it to be original, it was among the most useful lessons learned on my journey of leading a business:

Perfection isn't the result; it's the highest mark for the quality of our decisions and the performance of our execution. Everything else is outside our control.

Global pandemics, unexpected election outcomes, new competitors moving to town, a hurricane cutting power to my office for two weeks (true story): what was the last unfortunate event that derailed your perfect plan?

These things happen. Just like Tom Watson's fateful second shot that day, sometimes circumstances spoil one's best effort. A useful vision of the perfect business can't be based on outcomes. It must reflect the quality of decisions made by its leaders and how everyone involved executes the plans that result.

Making the best decisions we can and carrying them out to the best of our ability: that's the craft and expedition of business. It's the best we can do. And while it may not result in the perfect business, it puts us on the path that leads there and toward the business you are aiming to build.

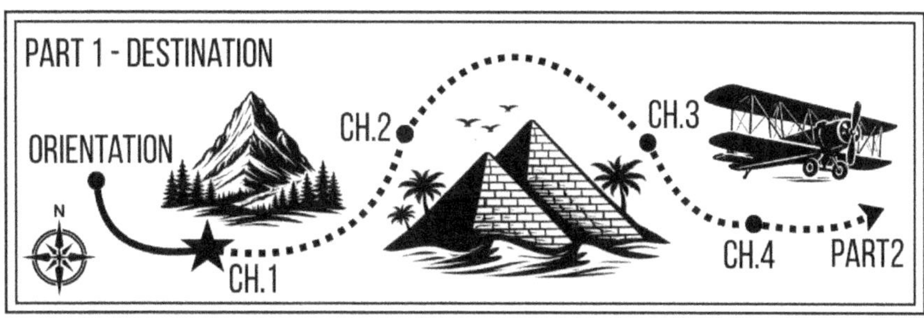

Tom Watson had the benefit of the golf world, the play of those before him, and years of data on his own swings to help judge his decisions. In business and in leadership, once again things are more complex. So, how do we rate the quality of our decisions?

The easiest path is to judge them by outcomes alone. But as we've seen, charting a straight line from decision to result ignores the realities of the terrain. The better path is more challenging and requires ascending through different levels of our thinking. Along the way, we learn that part of the craft of business is the decisions we make, but just as important is how we think about the problem in the first place.

CHAPTER 2

THE MOUNTAIN OF WHY

I grew up in the rural South and in a time before smartphones, the internet, or cable TV. Summer days were long, hot, and often boring. You did what you could to pass the time—some place with air conditioning, if by God's mercy.

My great-uncle's house was just such a place. I never knew him that well, and he wasn't exactly warm and inviting to a noisy seven-year-old kid. His name was Dallas, but he went by "Bubba." Fitting, for someone as blue-collar as they come—a career semi-truck mechanic who sported his rental uniform work shirt every day but Sunday.

Bubba's preferred activity to pass the time was solitaire. These days the game consists of swiping images across a screen, but back then it was sorting 52 actual cards into four piles on his living room coffee table.

If the game itself sounds boring, being a spectator is that much worse. But it was someplace cool and better than midday soap operas.

One day my spectating must have gone on for some time, because at one point I found the courage to interrupt his play—one of the best decisions I ever made.

A red seven of hearts came up on the "stock" pile. It looked like Bubba was going to flip the next card when I, with some mix of childhood excitement and trepidation, pointed out a black eight of spades on the board. It was an opportunity to move the card over.

What followed was a whipsaw of emotions that I can still feel every second of.

Bubba said, "*Now I'm playing solitaire...*"—and my heart sank. I knew the joke that was to come: some form of "*solitaire, a game meant for one.*" Some unspoken sentiment of "*Why don't you leave me the hell alone.*" But that's not what happened.

Bubba started articulating a multi-step thought process about why he didn't play that card. Yes, he could make that move, but there was a good chance it would sabotage his game. A possibility you could only see by looking five or six steps down the road. Bubba was some sort of card game savant, a master craftsman of sorting solitaire piles. And I, a novice receiving sage instruction, was dumbfounded.

It was the first time in my life that a critique of my decision-making wasn't "*right or wrong,*" but "*you're not even thinking about this the right way.*" Bubba was making decisions on a higher plane than I even knew existed.

He was the type of guide we all hope to meet on a journey—not someone who simply points the way or regales you with anecdotes and rules of thumb, but someone who shares a deep understanding of how things work and knows how to use that information to get where you want to go.

Running a business obviously involves more risk than deciding where to put that red seven of hearts, but it still comes back to the decisions we make.

Do we bring on a CFO and build an accounting team in-house or stay lean and use an outsourcing group? Does "work from home" become permanent after COVID, or do we require people to return to the office? Does it make sense to have a commissioned sales team, or should we have a salaried business development group?

Decisions like these are forks in the trail on the expedition of business, and the craft is how we go about picking which path to take. Do we have a process? Clear intentions and principles that we believe matter most? Are we prepared to explain "why" to our team, our shareholders, or to ourselves? And, maybe most importantly, can we live with the results regardless of the outcome?

The deeper and more thorough the decision-making, the more confident we can feel, and the closer we are to the perfect business.

But how do we judge the quality of our decisions?

The answer involves a climb up what I've come to call The Mountain of Why, an ascent undertaken by entrepreneurs of all ages.

A few years ago, my family and I moved into a new neighborhood—a kid-friendly place with large trees, sidewalks, and parks nearby. And so, it is not surprising that there are many examples of the most quintessential American enterprise: the lemonade stand.

Why does a kid set up their first lemonade stand? Simple: the same reason we get started in any craft. They saw someone else do it, and why shouldn't they do the same? It's the easiest path to follow on the first leg of any journey, the path that's already there.

LEVEL 1 - MIMICRY

On the Mountain of Why, there are five campsites where you can pitch your tent on the ascent to the summit. **Mimicry** is the first and represents **Level 1** decision-making: the default when you don't have the information or mental models to make a more advanced decision.

We make decisions this way often, and advertisers know it. Drink Gatorade, wear Nike shoes, *"Be like Mike"*; choose Dos Equis, the "most interesting man in the world" does. And most of the time this level of decision-making is fine; life is short, be a champion, eat your Wheaties, and move on. But let's not pretend that only trivial decisions are made this way.

Ask most business leaders why they have a 40-hour work week, why they do "Annual Reviews" with their employees, or the last book they read. If you do, you're likely to find a decision that was made solely based on following in the footsteps of someone before them. It's how we all get our first lemonade stand up and going, but there's room for improvement.

LEVEL 2 – HEURISTICS

I see a lot of lemonade stands. Some get an "A," many are "B's" or "C's," but a few are "F's"—just terrible. I've seen stands set up in the cold or on rainy days. Stands with no sign, or even worse these days, "cash only." These kids deserve an "A" for effort; they're learning.

Over time, you see things improve. Kids do what we all do to learn: they try, observe, iterate, and try again. The older kids get an idea to move their stand from their house to the park nearby, the signs get better, someone figures out customers can send a Venmo to their mom: sales improve. They start to make **Level 2** decisions and use **Heuristics**. It's the simplest of decision-making: "*Did it work before?*"

It's a furniture store having another "going out of business sale" because "*it worked last time.*" It's a COO hiring a department manager who played college soccer because that's what their other manager did, and "*he's great.*" It's a sales rep doing all his cold calling between 9:30 and 11 because that's "*when they answered last week.*"

In a way, making a Level 2 decision is mimicry of our past self—an attempt to recreate what proved successful at least once before. If it keeps working, we might be on to something, but more often we find the results inconsistent. We're missing some key variables, and we go out scouting for a better understanding of the problem at hand.

LEVEL 3 – FRAMEWORKS

I love talking to these kids about their lemonade stands. The conversations with the younger kids are mostly encouragement and basic questions, but nothing too illuminating. The conversations with the older kids are more interesting. They are still out hustling for a few extra dollars, and it's not just lemonade. They've figured out there's a market for cookies, homemade bracelets, and apparently hand-painted rocks are a big seller.

With the older kids, I see **Level 3** decision-making. They're using **Frameworks** and are better able to generalize the requirements for making a sale. One girl, savvy enough to know most people walk with dogs, sells dog treats alongside lemonade at her table. She is developing a model of customer-product fit. One boy knows when they hold soccer practice at the park nearby. He sets up shop there but also runs home to set up his table when school lets out. He can articulate to me that traffic drives his sales. The complexity of their decisions is going up, but so is the quality.

It's like Tom Watson considering the distance to the green but also the wind, the slope of the terrain, and even how much adrenaline he's feeling. A framework is a set of factors that predict the outcome better than any single factor alone.

It's a gym franchise considering parking availability, area demographics, and competition density before signing a new lease. It's bringing a new product to market based on focus group responses, but also existing factory tooling and supplier relationships.

It is also at this level where more business advice becomes "productized" and distributed through books and other media. Level 3 brings us SPIN Selling, Porter's Five Forces, EOS, Scaling Up, The 4 Disciplines of Execution, and similar programs. They all help break large, messy, and complex questions into more manageable pieces.

However, all are general in their approach. Their design is for the average business, not necessarily *your* business. To find better tailored solutions, we need to climb yet higher on The Mountain of Why.

LEVEL 4 – SYNTHESIZED STRATEGIES

If lemonade stands are the most popular "side hustle" for kids in our neighborhood, coming in a close second is the selling of Girl Scout cookies. For a few weeks every year, it's hard not to be offered as many boxes of Thin Mints and Caramel deLites as your wallet—and waistband—can withstand. During that time, a microcosm of commerce is on display once again.

But what happens when circumstances change? When the product changes from lemonade, typically sold at sidewalk folding tables, to boxes of cookies, which are more traditionally sold door-to-door?

Level 4 decisions are made, and **Synthesized Strategies** emerge.

Much of the lemonade strategy remains effective—ease of payment, a variety of options, and a fair price—but some parts break down. The cookie season is short, and depending on foot traffic alone isn't enough. You can't wait for the buyer to come to you; you must go to them.

That big "*Lemonade $0.25*" sign—no one's hauling that door to door. A new advertising campaign is needed.

And how many cookies can you really heft to each house? A new plan for supply chain and inventory management is required, but the kids figure it out.

They show up at my door with some cookies available on the spot and some available for order later. I can pay now or pay for them on delivery. If I'm not home, no problem: on Saturday, they'll have the table set up by the sidewalk—and at the park, and at the grocery store.

They're effective in selling these cookies and raising money, and it maps back to making strong Level 4 decisions on how they go about it. Excellent businesses do the same when faced with similar questions. They take generic strategies and adapt them to be more effective. And the result is better answers to hard questions.

How does a company adjust a conventional sales funnel when its success depends on a handful of long-term, repeat clients versus more transactional customers?

What should a team do when a daily "stand-up" meeting is part of their business operating system, but few things change day-to-day, and the team works across six time zones?

And should a company—at the urging of its peer group—really invest in a detailed marketing plan when referrals are keeping the phone ringing?

Better answers arise from Level 4 decision-making and creating synthesized strategies tailored to a unique situation. Such decisions bring us near the summit of The Mountain of Why. And while we're a long way from the base camp of mimicry, a look back at Levels 1, 2, 3, and 4 reveals they all have something in common.

These are decisions based on what we or someone else has observed before. There may be case studies, data from a reasonable sample size, and testimonials of satisfied users of the strategy, but they remain an exercise in faith because few of them explain ***why*** they work.

We haven't yet reached that elevation on our climb, where decisions come from a foundation of first principles. That type of discernment awaits where many travel on their search for answers: the top of the mountain.

LEVEL 5 – FIRST PRINCIPLES

Abbas Ibn Firnas was a "Renaissance Man" long before the Renaissance and always tinkering with new ideas. Around 1,200 years ago, he did something unusual—even for him. Somewhere in the Spanish countryside, he climbed a tall mountain. After finding a high ledge that was to his liking, he stopped and emptied his backpack, covered himself with feathers, strapped on a couple of homemade wings, and jumped off.

It went surprisingly well. As one historian later recounted:

"According to the testimony of several trustworthy writers who witnessed the performance, he flew a considerable distance, as if he had been a bird, but, in alighting again on the place whence he had started, his back was very much hurt, for not knowing that birds when they alight come down upon their tails, he forgot to provide himself with one."

And so went the thinking for hundreds of years: we're not flying like birds because we are not yet bird-like enough.

Firnas and aviation pioneers like him started where we all do, with analogy and with mimicry. They made their decisions based on what they had seen for themselves or heard from others; betting that with time and different iterations, they would get the results they wanted.

But it wasn't enough, and it never would be. The same is often true in business: to really move the needle, to get more impactful results, we need a brand-new approach.

It was the Wright brothers who finally got us skywards. While everyone else was asking, *"How can we fly like birds?"* they asked, *"What are the fundamental requirements for controlled flight?"*

The answer was the first principles that made their decisions more effective:

More power is meaningless without the ability to control it. Three axes of control is the minimum; two will never work. The ratio of engine weight to power produced was critical. Propellers need to be designed for air; using marine propellers was a dead end.

It was these ideas that guided their Level 5 decisions. They decided certain things must be true and built their thinking from there.

Mastering the craft of business requires a similar approach. It takes gaining the discernment and experience we need to make our stand, creating our own version of *"We hold these truths to be self-evident,"* and developing the foundational ideas that we believe will lead to success.

Jeff Bezos decided customers always wanted low prices, fast delivery, and lots of choices: Amazon was the extrapolation of those core tenets.

Netflix decided that convenience trumped everything else in entertainment and dominated their rivals.

And recently, one of my clients planted their flag on the belief that people want to feel included and hate uncertainty. The result was them adding one simple meeting in the middle of their process. It cured both ills and resulted in a substantial difference in engagement, morale, and project quality. Now they're looking for other places where they can build strategies around the same idea.

As a leader, such first principles must be yours. They reflect what you hold to be true, even if the variance and messiness of the world always leave room for doubt—and doubt is an opportunity.

Without doubt, everyone believes the same thing. If everyone believes the same thing, then everyone takes the same actions. And if everyone takes the same action, then there is no advantage to be had.

Any advantage lies with those like the Wright brothers, those who work hard to discover what they believe to be true, and those who aren't afraid of taking a new approach. It is they who reach the summit of The Mountain of Why, receive the benefit of Level 5 decision-making, and move one step closer to the perfect business.

Bubba chose not to play that red seven of hearts. Firnas believed that his best feather suit would get him skyward. And the Wright brothers elected to take a novel approach when designing their plane. We can debate where on The Mountain of Why each belongs, but it's clear they were all meaningful decisions, made in pursuit of their goal.

Yet, we would be mistaken if we considered all decisions equal in their weight. Bubba may have still found victory either way—and if not, he'd be dealing new cards out soon enough. Firnas was lucky to escape his crash landing, but there were plenty of other ways he could decide to imitate birds. The Wright brothers' decisions carried more implications; pursuing a novel approach meant decisions needed to be made not only at the strategy level, but at the level of tactics and execution as well.

As we'll see, the same is true in business. There's the question to be decided, the elevation from which we answer, but also the weight the decision carries.

CHAPTER 3

PYRAMIDS OF DECISIONS

My wife recently interviewed for a new position, a leadership role managing and overseeing a team of people. During the interview process, she was asked an interesting question:

"What would you do if you made a decision, and all 12 people on your team disagreed with you?"

Pause here and think for a minute. How would you answer?

I'm notorious for having some favorite jokes that maybe 1 out of 100 people find funny, so mass rebellion to what works in my head isn't unfamiliar territory. Nonetheless, something about that question didn't sit right.

Then it hit me...

A patient sits in a doctor's office. The doctor comes into the room and says, *"I'm sorry, you only have seven to live."* Confused, and a bit panicked, the patient responds, *"Seven what? Seven years? Seven months? Seven weeks?"* And the doctor responds, *"Six."*

The interview question assumed all decisions are equal—ironically, as one of the chief responsibilities of a leader is knowing which decisions are more important.

Seven years is preferable to seven weeks. And people getting bent out of shape about granola bars replacing potato chips in the break room is less concerning than someone redefining our ideal customer.

In the prior chapter, we talked about depth of decision-making and the five levels of The Mountain of Why. But what exactly is being decided? How do we separate granola bars from a life-or-death diagnosis? To answer that question, we can turn to a well-known framework: **Goal-Strategy-Tactics-Execution**. Together they form **Pyramids of Decisions**. And it is there that most business decisions can find a home.

For example, in my business, I decided on the **goal** of running a successful professional services company. A core **strategy** was leveraging more junior and less expensive staff to do work on par with their more senior and more expensive counterparts. One **tactic** to support that strategy was a series of checklists that created a "scaffold" for people to climb as they completed a project. Decisions around the **execution** piece included making those checklists easy to find and requiring a signed version to be turned in with each project. Many decisions, varying degrees of importance.

One beauty about these pyramids is that they are fractal in nature—a fancy word for saying these pyramids take the same shape at different scales and sizes.

Do you have a goal of being the #1 tamales producer in South Texas? A Pyramid of Decisions can help map that out. Are people archiving their leftovers in the break room fridge for weeks on end? Organizing your decisions in the same way may end the science experiments.

As a leader, it is very difficult to articulate everything you want to happen or to explain how others should make each decision. Some leaders exhaust themselves doing so, while others only communicate part of the plan.

A town manager is proud of their city parks. They're ornate and manicured, but one park is having trouble keeping kids out of the flower beds. It's a headwind against the department's **goal** of keeping the parks beautiful. Their instruction to the maintenance crew—their **strategy**: *"Keep the kids out of the flower beds."*

I saw the result when I visited the park. The flower beds were full of blossoms, a kaleidoscope of colors. Also there were the biggest, tackiest signs you can imagine: "STAY OUT OF FLOWER BEDS."

The **tactic** (the signs) supported the **strategy** (keep kids out of the flower beds), but it sabotaged the **goal** (keeping the park beautiful). One could argue this was a failure of common sense, but if the goal had been communicated along with the strategy, would the tactic have been better?

The first step is to be clear on how we categorize these decisions.

I once did an exercise with a new client. I gave each of the four members of the leadership team a stack of small sticky notes. Next, I asked them to write down what they think of when they hear the word **"Goal"**—as it relates to the company they're leading. The below is what soon covered the whiteboard.

"GOALS"

★ *Superintendents' daily reports*	★ *Employee development*
★ *Completing S.O.P.s and checklists*	★ *More ideal-fit jobs*
★ *Cross-training administrative staff*	★ *New sector marketing*
★ *Employee growth and training*	★ *Improving systems*
★ *Improve safety*	★ *Better project hand-offs*

All of these were worthy objectives, and I wouldn't call any of their answers "wrong," but are they all **goals**? Or are some **strategies**? And are a few **tactics** or the **execution** of them?

Until we're clear on how we define each, it becomes an argument of semantics.

GOAL

A goal is what we're trying to accomplish. It's the outcome we want—the specific result we're working toward. Running a successful professional services company, becoming the #1 tamales producer in South Texas, ending the science experiments in the break room fridge: goals can be big or small. What matters is their relative position in the pyramid.

A goal is the target—it doesn't support anything else; everything else supports it. It's the answer to "Where are we going?" And because these pyramids are fractal in nature, a goal at one level can become a strategy or tactic at another. Keeping parks beautiful is the town's goal, but keeping kids out of flower beds is just one strategy to get there. Without clarity on what the actual goal is in any given context, every decision becomes arbitrary because there's no way to know if we're moving in the right direction.

STRATEGY

My favorite definition of strategy comes from the book "This is Strategy" by Seth Godin: *"Strategy is our philosophy of becoming."*

Strategy is the core of what we believe will get us to our goal. It's the fundamental bet we're making about how to succeed.

Will we compete on price or quality? Grow through new customers or deeper relationships with existing ones? Build expertise in-house or partner with specialists? Strategy answers *"What's our approach?"* And it sets the direction for everything below it.

A good strategy reflects a clear point of view about what matters most and what we're willing to trade off. It's the bets that we're willing to place, and—as we'll see in Part 4—it's very much part of the story of our organizations.

When our strategy is sound, decisions on tactics and execution have a north star to guide them. When it's unclear, even great decisions lower down the pyramid don't add up to much.

TACTICS

Tactics are the specific initiatives and actions we take to make our strategy a reality. If our strategy is leveraging junior staff to do senior-level work, our tactics might include training programs, mentorship pairings, and quality review processes. Tactics answer *"What will we actually do?"* They're more tangible than strategy and more flexible—we can adjust tactics as we learn what works without changing our overall approach. Or, in the context of my wife's interview, there's less reason for concern if we get some dissent.

The key is to ensure each tactic supports the relevant strategy. When there's alignment, tactics reinforce each other and build momentum. When there isn't, we end up with a list of disconnected activities that don't add up to progress.

EXECUTION

Execution is how well we do what we said we'd do. It's the quality of the work, the consistency of follow-through, and the attention to getting details right. Making those checklists easy to find and ensuring they actually get used, having the training happen on schedule and making it worth people's time: execution answers the question *"How well are we doing this?"*

This is where most businesses win or lose—not in having the perfect strategy or clever tactics, but in doing the work that reinforces the base of our Pyramids of Decisions.

Being clear on these definitions and having the rest of our team follow suit isn't an academic exercise. It's an effort to build one of the essential reference points in an organization. What are we trying to do? What decisions are we making? And how do those decisions integrate with one another? Having good answers is at the heart of effective delegation and high performance.

If we could program every instruction and ensure the correct decisions are always made by our staff, then we wouldn't need them. We would have a legion of robots, computers, or some other form of algorithms cycling through decision trees. We know that's not real life; inevitably we must trust people to make their own choices.

But sending our teams into the wilderness with no guidance would end in disaster. Part of the expedition of business is providing a map. One that distills things down to key landmarks and doesn't lose people in excessive detail. Our Pyramids of Decisions do that and make for a guide when the path forward isn't always obvious.

So, my answer to the interview question…

Just what decision are we talking about? If it's on the **tactics** or **execution** level, then my job is to explain—hopefully with a Level 5 "Why" of first principles—how it supports the relevant **goal** or **strategy**. If it's a decision about our **goal** or a key **strategy**, then I'm on a fool's errand trying to accomplish either with a full mutiny brewing.

In the end, there's a depth to the decisions we make (The Mountain of Why), and a purpose and function for each (Pyramids of Decisions). There's also the question of who's responsible for making each decision—something we will visit in Part 4.

Making those decisions well, communicating them clearly, and ensuring the intent is known are all parts of the craft of business.

The summit is in sight now. We can see decisions judged not by outcomes alone, but by the elevation from which they're made—from mimicry to first principles. The weight of each choice understood—goals separated from strategies, tactics from execution. Our vision of the perfect business is coming into focus.

But while we're getting a clearer view of the parts, the picture of the whole is yet to be assembled. The Wright brothers didn't just make better decisions about wing angles and propeller design for the hell of it—they knew exactly what those decisions were meant to accomplish. Every adjustment, every lever pulled, moved them closer to controlled flight.

The same is true in business. All these frameworks, all this careful thinking, all the ascending of The Mountain of Why and building Pyramids of Decisions—they exist to move something, to make a change. And it turns out there are only four things any leader is really trying to control—four levers that every decision ultimately pulls.

Energy, Unity, Resistance, and Yield: they are the Levers of Control and the final piece of the perfect business.

CHAPTER 4

LEVERS OF CONTROL

The Wright brothers—our friends from Chapter 2—tinkered and toiled with mechanisms, gadgets, and gizmos of all types before finally setting their sights on airplanes. A short five years later, they were ready to make history on the Outer Banks of North Carolina.

It was a December morning, cold, windy, and miserable—but the conditions were perfect for flight. Wilbur had won a coin toss to be first in the saddle, but his attempt to be "The First in Flight" had ended with a crash a few days prior. Orville would be at the controls.

The motor was humming, the wind was blowing, and once the restraining wire was cut, the plane started bouncing down the launch rail. Speed increased, wind rolled across the wings, skids lifted off the rails, and there it was: Orville was in flight.

We can all relate to some version of toil and struggle before finally, success. I thought and schemed for some time before launching my first business. Landing those first clients, seeing the first checks roll in, hiring the first staff—no one is going to commemorate my story on a license plate, but these feelings seem parallel to Orville's as things finally got off the ground.

I don't know his specific reaction, but as he was soaring above the ground in their homemade contraption, part of me suspects his reaction was like mine and many other business leaders new at the controls: *"Oh shit, now what?"*

For Orville, that answer lay in the levers he had at his disposal: a lever for the speed of the engine, a lever for the angle of the wing, and levers for the pitch, roll, and yaw of the plane.

For me, the answer was in levers as well. The four levers that any business is trying to control—to get their organization soaring.

One for **Energy**—Hire it, grow it, buy it, cultivate it.

Another for **Unity**—Everyone aligned and moving in the same direction.

The third for **Resistance**—Lowering obstacles, working smarter, finding the best path.

And the last for **Yield**—Selling results for maximum return.

Success on the expedition of business is about those four **Levers of Control** and finding the right balance between them.

ENERGY	UNITY	RESISTANCE	YIELD
Hire it, grow it, buy it, or cultivate it.	*Getting everyone aligned, moving in the same direction.*	*Lowering obstacles, working smarter, finding the best path.*	*Marketing and selling results for maximum returns.*

Every business is adjusting these levers as they make their way forward on a similar path. They are all paid to do work, something their customer or client can't or would prefer not to do themselves. The business exists because it can amass the **energy** needed to do the work, **unify** it in a single direction, lower the **resistance**, and finally, maximize the **yield** received for a job well done.

These four variables create an infinite number of paths to success, and each business crafts a different one.

A local plumbing company builds its...

Energy and their team by targeting recent high school graduates, partnering with a local community college to train them in the trade, and creating a profit-sharing plan to boost engagement.

They **Unify** that energy via their creed: "*Treat every home like your own.*" Clear job descriptions and documented SOPs: efforts to get everyone focused and aligned.

Resistance is lowered via larger trucks re-stocked daily with parts to avoid return trips, customers being able to upload photos and videos of their plumbing issues—giving technicians the chance to prepare better before they arrive. It all makes the work easier.

And **Yield** increases by offering preventative maintenance plans after a repair, asking for online reviews and testimonials, and by tracking the install dates of water heaters—that way customers can be contacted when it's time for a new one. A single customer, multiple benefits.

The question isn't whether a business is pulling each of these levers, but how?

There are limitless ways, and an equal number of suggestions as to what's best. Books, courses, podcasts, consultants, coaches, and gurus: there is a river of information, but it all flows toward pulling one of the four levers.

"*Hire slow, fire fast*"—**Energy**

"*Everyone rowing in the same direction*"—**Unity**

"*Work smarter, not harder*"—**Resistance**

"*Land and expand*"—**Yield**

Best practices, effective strategies, common tactics, and even the clichés; they all find a home here. It's our job as leaders to sift through all the information we come across, to figure out how it best serves us when sitting at the controls, and it starts with a thorough understanding of each.

ENERGY

Energy is the capacity to do work—the hours and effort that get things done. It's the fuel that powers everything. A restaurant needs enough cooks to handle the dinner rush. A law firm needs enough attorneys to take on new clients. A construction company needs enough crew members to finish the job on time.

Energy is why businesses hire when demand outpaces capacity, why they lose sleep over retention when key people leave, why burnout becomes a crisis when the team is running on fumes. Energy answers the question *"Do we have enough to get this done?"*

UNITY

When unity is high, you need less total energy to accomplish the same work because effort compounds instead of canceling out. Five people aligned outperform ten people working with different intents. Decisions happen faster because everyone understands the direction. And teams collaborate without constant coordination from above.

When unity is low, we end up needing more people just to overcome the inefficiency of misalignment: the sales team promises features the product team hasn't built, marketing targets customers operations can't serve, and leadership debates strategy while the front line improvises. Unity answers the question *"Are we all working toward the same thing?"*

RESISTANCE

Resistance is everything that makes work hard; it's also why we get paid to do our job. Some is inherent to the work itself, but much is self-imposed: approval processes that add days but no value, software systems that don't talk to each other, and weekly meetings where nothing changes. It's the new hire who can't find templates and reinvents the wheel, the technician who drives back for parts because the truck wasn't stocked, or the service rep who spends $50 in time finding approval for a $20 refund.

Lowering the resistance provides a buffer for energy and unity. When we lower the resistance, we can do the same with less: fewer people, less alignment, less time, less money. Resistance answers the question *"What's getting in our way?"*

YIELD

Yield is how we're compensated for our work. Two businesses can do the same job, the same way, with the same people, yet the one that has a plan to maximize their yield comes out better.

It's the waiter who pushes dessert after your meal, the consultant who records advice once and sells it a hundred times, and the coffee shop that adds a loyalty program—turning occasional visitors into daily regulars.

Yield often gets less attention because it's not as visible as adding people or fixing processes, but it's often free money just waiting for us to pick it up. Yield answers the question *"Are we leaving anything on the table?"*

❖

Pulling each of the four levers to our benefit is a product of how we assemble our Pyramids of Decisions. Effectively constructing the strategies, tactics, and execution that support our goal of more energy, greater unity, lower resistance, and higher yield comes back to how high up The Mountain of Why we are climbing.

Each decision is an individual block—some are from Level 1 of Mimicry, others are from Level 2 of Heuristics, fewer are from Level 3 of Frameworks, and only a handful are from Level 4 of Synthesized Strategies. But the rarest, and the hardest blocks to form, stem from the first principles we hold to be true. Together these blocks support the decisions above them and form our Pyramids of Decisions.

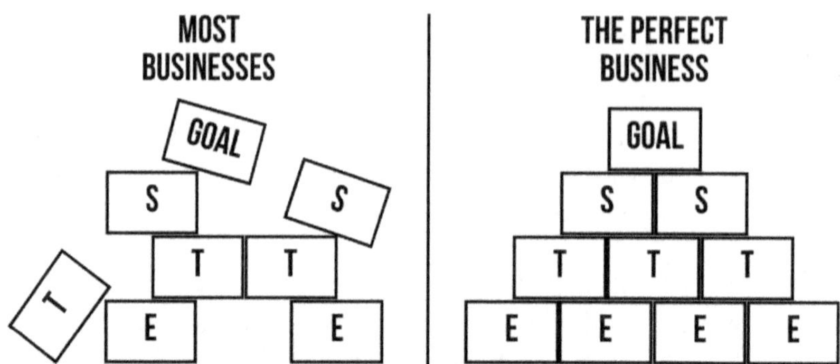

The Pyramids of Decisions for most organizations are missing a few blocks, while some decisions are unrelated to the goal at hand. A perfect business builds its Pyramids of Decisions with high quality decisions from top to bottom.

The result is a model that allows us to judge our business and our efforts independently of results. How organized are our decisions? How well are they thought through? Do they move one or more of the Levers of Control? The answers to these questions tell us how close we are to the perfect business.

The journey of my business stopped before perfection was reached; yours will too, and it will be the same for all that follow. Perfection is too high a bar—as we said at the beginning, we only pursue the perfect business because it orients us for the expedition ahead. If each step of the journey moves us in that direction, then eventually, somewhere along the path, we will find the business that we set out to build.

You might disagree with my definition of "Perfection." Perhaps you'd like to judge your business differently. Your metrics could be financial or the impact on your community and employees. Maybe it's about providing the lifestyle you want for you and your family. Fortunately, it all works the same.

Whatever business you are after, the craft of business is about learning, making better decisions, and executing our best-laid plans. If we continue the journey long enough, we find ourselves closer to mastery and leading the business we always knew was possible.

With the North Star of the perfect business now set to guide us, we can proceed undistracted by elements outside our control. We can move on to the next part of the expedition, knowing that our full attention belongs to the decisions we make.

However, before we begin, we need a plan. Not just where we are going, but also how to get there. In business, the "how" centers on people. They are the medium all leaders work with in their craft, the teams that propel expeditions across tough terrain, the followers a leader can't do without, and the crew that we will discuss in Part 2.

As we'll see, they are an organization's greatest asset, but also its greatest liability. They are often the biggest variable and source of uncertainty, and many leaders find themselves resorting to decisions about their staff which are far from the summit of The Mountain of Why. Not out of laziness or indifference, but because they have not yet progressed far enough on the journey to mastery.

Fortunately, we already know more about people than we likely realize. And by considering what we know to be true about those we rely on, we can craft the first principles that will make for solid Pyramids of Decisions in our pursuit of the perfect business.

PART 2

CREW

CHAPTER 5

PADDLE DOWNSTREAM

The annals of business success stories are filled with a certain type of tale. They are accounts of individuals pushing themselves beyond normal limits in their pursuit of greatness.

They are stories we're familiar with: Elon Musk sleeping on the production floor and living at his factory, Steve Jobs setting impossible deadlines and obsessing to no end over every detail of new products, Jerry Jones going $50 million in debt before finally striking it rich buying the Dallas Cowboys.

They are stories that cause many to equate the expedition of business to Ernest Shackleton and his team being adrift on the Antarctic ice, 300 Spartans holding off a massive army, and—of course—David slaying Goliath.

There's a problem though: the metaphors are wrong.

I learned this the hard way. For the first several years of leading a business, my answer to most challenges was to work harder—*"First in, last out,"* *"Grind now, sleep later," "Make your hay while the sun shines."* Eventually, you learn that the gas pedal stops at the floorboard, and keeping it there only gets you to one place fast: burnout.

Next, the panacea was to be more efficient: *"Time blocking," "No email Fridays," "Meeting-free Wednesdays," "Deep work."* But they were all "S-curves" of results; the first 20% gets you 80% of the benefit, and beyond that improvement is marginal.

Unfortunately, my experience isn't unique, and the metaphors do reflect many businesses. There are those organizations where people are pushed to their limit—long hours, unreasonable deadlines, stress on top of stress—until "*Yes!*" The goal is achieved.

Most business leaders I work with are in search of something else. They are not scared of hard work, nor are they under any delusion that it or the need for efficiency can be avoided entirely. And while building a great business over years and decades is more akin to the stories of heroic accomplishment, in the day-to-day, and the week-to-week—the timeframes in which we all experience work and our jobs—they are looking for a way forward that feels like less of a struggle.

The problem is that we resort to what has worked for businesses in the past. Business leaders before us figured out that they and their team had a limited amount of energy. And to get better results—to power through the resistance of their work—they needed more of it.

First, they found that energy by putting animals to work: mules to drive plows, horses to pull wagons, or oxen to turn millstones. Then they discovered all the energy contained in natural resources: wood, coal, and even the inside of an atom. They built machines that would let them use these new sources of energy to overwhelm whatever stood in the way.

The bigger the challenge, the more energy thrown at it, whether animals, fuel, or human labor. It was the model for the industrial age. Like Henry Ford's production line, the input was often more people, easily replaceable human cogs in the industrial machine.

Today we're in a new age; the need for physical human labor has been drastically reduced, and the energy to run our machines is readily available and affordable. The competitive advantage of a business has become the performance of its people. The old model of "*powering through*" is falling apart, and with good reason.

But humans provide a challenge that the energy sources of old did not. While a horse that underperformed could be—literally—reined in, replaced, or spurred along, and a chunk of coal couldn't care less how it was used, people come with agency, the ability to act independently, and are heavily influenced by their environment. Someone may be "employee of the month" material on Monday, only to have us ready to fire them on Tuesday. They and all of us are far less uniform or predictable than the energy sources of old, and that makes the old way of brute force, grit, and determination less reliable.

So, what's the answer? Some new metaphors and a new approach.

Morihei Ueshiba founded the martial art of Aikido. He stood five feet two inches tall and weighed around 120 lbs., but was described by many as "unmovable," with an almost supernatural ability to throw much larger opponents to the ground.

Joel Salatin runs Polyface Farm in Virginia. Despite using no chemical fertilizers or pesticides, and investing far less capital in equipment and infrastructure, his farm produces financial results on par with more conventional competitors.

Roughly 250 people operate the Hoover Dam—a dam that generates enough power for 1.3 million people.

Ueshiba, Salatin, the Hoover Dam—all should be the envy of many business leaders, and for one specific reason: they get maximum results with minimal effort.

In Chapter 4, we considered that every business is spending its limited **energy**, in a **unified** fashion, to overcome the **resistance** of the work at hand, and trying to maximize the **yield** that results—the Levers of Control. The champions of our new metaphors are masters of this framework.

Ueshiba developed Aikido around the idea of redirecting and unifying the strength and energy of the opponent to your benefit. By not opposing the force directly, the resistance to the intended outcome is lowered. Salatin uses the natural tendencies and energy of cows and chickens to replace the work typically done by machines, humans, or chemicals. He is selective about the crops he plants—favoring more native species to lower the resistance they would face from unfavorable weather and terrain. And the Hoover Dam harnesses the energy of the Colorado River, unifying it through massive turbines to meet the energy needs of businesses and households across three different states. A river that—poetically—is the unified flow of countless creeks and streams, following the path of least resistance. The end result for all: yields more easily attained.

Gravity, wind, and sun. A few of the many ways we find to work with, and not against, what happens naturally.

These stories and these metaphors offer better parallels to the businesses that I see leaders wanting to create—businesses that can do more with less, businesses that harness and unify the energy available to them, and businesses that find ways to lower the resistance that stands between them and the yield of their efforts.

How is that done? We can find the answer in The Levers of Control and how, unfortunately, much of our struggle with resistance is a product of competition.

As discussed in Chapter 4, all businesses provide value by overcoming the resistance that stands between a customer and the product or service that the customer desires. Businesses sell their work, and work—in the most fundamental sense—is force applied to overcome resistance.

You've probably heard the phrase *"If it were easy, we wouldn't get paid for it."*

There is not a business on Earth that offers to grow weeds in your front yard, to put wrinkles in your skin, to remove hair from the top of your head, or to have a dog chew up your furniture. These things happen naturally; there is no resistance to overcome, and as a result, the only market demand is to keep them from happening.

Successful businesses capture yield—their revenue and their profit—because someone out there will pay them for a product or service. Customers choose to pay the business over two alternatives:

1. Spending their own energy, unified as best they can, to overcome the resistance of making the product or service a reality. Or...

2. Paying a competitor—one who had to overcome similar resistance for a comparable result.

That's it—that's the marketplace for a good or service. A customer does it themselves, gets it from you, gets it from one of your competitors, or they don't get it at all. There are no other options, but there are always these possibilities, and that's why resistance is such a problem.

If we could charge any price we liked for the goods or services our businesses provide, how many of our problems would go away?

Most businesses are far from having that luxury. The big tech companies or other corporate behemoths may have giant moats or structural competitive advantages. Some start-ups may grab the headlines with new innovations, deep pockets, and powerful patent protection. But for most businesses, competition does what competition is supposed to do in a free market: it puts downward pressure on prices.

There's always someone out there who will do the same work for less profit, cut more corners, or bend more rules. They are one of the Four Horsemen we will discover in Part 4, and they make business difficult. It may not change the resistance of doing our actual work, but it certainly reduces the price we can charge—and thus the yield we receive for our efforts.

To get ahead, we must find a way—like our new metaphors—to get maximum results for our efforts.

It is simple in concept, but not easy to do. The possible paths forward are many, and too often business leaders get lost along the way. They lose sight of one of the simpler truths of business: that a primary responsibility of a leader is to deploy a company's limited resources in the most productive way possible. And by resources, I mean money.

Businesses have nothing by nature. Everything they have at their disposal is either bought or rented. People, equipment, goodwill, reputation, or brand: they are all a product of money spent. All is equally true of the competition.

Thus, any advantage becomes tied to what money a business spends and what it gets in return. But more specifically, and more importantly, what money are they spending and what are they getting for it **compared to their competition**?

Stop and think for a second. What are you spending money on that your competition is as well?

Utilities, equipment, software, supplies, real estate, insurance, accounting, legal services, marketing: do any of these make the list?

More importantly, do most—if not all—seem very commoditized? In other words, does competition in those marketplaces keep price, quality, and service tightly clustered? In most cases, the answer is "Yes."

What about salaries, benefits, or bonuses? Of course, every business spends money on these, but how commoditized do employees seem? Are performance and reliability consistent at each price point?

The data on just how much employee productivity can vary from person to person is hard to summarize into a single number—but making the claim that one employee could be between 25% and 200% more productive than a peer in similar circumstances is reasonable.

That's a 25% to 200% difference in what a business gets for the money it spends—money that likely comprises 20% to 70% of its total expense structure. No other expense category comes close, while no other value received fluctuates as wildly. The rent doesn't suddenly double, nor do software platforms suddenly perform at 50% of capacity.

If we're looking for a competitive advantage—a way to maximize our efforts and our ROI on money spent—then there's no better place to look than people. Our team. Our crew.

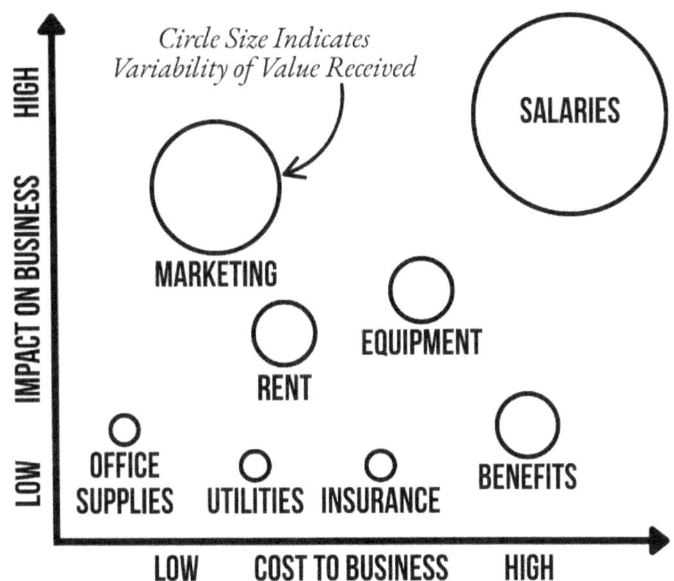

When considering cost, impact, but also variability or value, people and the salaries a business pays clearly dominate.

People are a business's greatest asset, but also its greatest liability. Getting everyone to perform at a high level, their energy unified, is paramount.

Patrick Lencioni famously said, *"If you could get all the people in an organization rowing in the same direction, you could dominate any industry, in any market, against any competition, at any time."*

But the key words in that statement are *"If you could."*

Building that alignment, getting everyone *"rowing in the same direction,"* that is a task that comes with its own resistance. And finding better solutions requires a climb up The Mountain of Why.

Novice business leaders spend too much of their time fighting that resistance. They find themselves pleading, bribing, threatening, and writing complicated rules and policies to get their team moving in a chosen direction. True masters of the craft don't spend much time thinking about how to get people to do what they want them to do. Instead, they have their first principles; they know what people want to do, and they make decisions and design a business that works with—and not against—that desire.

Creating that design is the mark of a true craftsman, and like being the master of any craft, it requires a deep understanding. Ueshiba was an expert in understanding leverage and one's center of gravity. Salatin knows as much as anyone about certain farm animals, plants, soil, and all the worms and critters that can do much of the heavy lifting. And the engineers of The Hoover Dam understood one thing very well: rivers flow to the sea.

People are more complex, but with the right insights and frameworks, a useful understanding is possible. One that allows a savvy business leader to work with the natural tendencies of their team and to lower the resistance of building alignment.

That alignment allows a business to set goals, develop strategies, build tactics, and execute them in a way that generates more energy, unifies it better, overcomes resistance more easily, and ultimately captures more of the yield they've worked hard for.

They avoid the trap of working harder being the answer to every problem. They make use of the Levers of Control and the first principles that drive their decisions to be the Aikido masters, Polyface Farm, and Hoover Dam of business. Their competitive advantage becomes working with, and not against, the natural drive of their people.

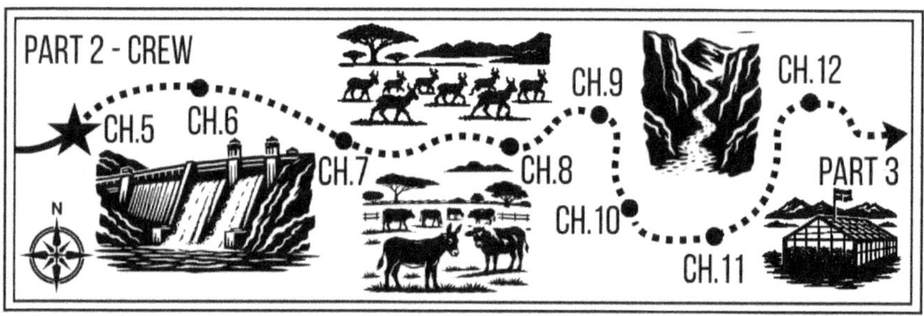

Getting our organizations to paddle downstream takes something that many business leaders lack: a cohesive mental model of why people do what they do. We all begin at the base of The Mountain of Why and assume others will behave as we do—some form of mimicry. In time, we climb higher and our predictions lean on the heuristics of past experience. Some then ascend to frameworks that consider more context and clues. But few develop a first-principles approach, taking what we assume to be true about the forces that influence us all and building from there.

The chapters to come will introduce the G.E.A.R. framework, and look at how genetics, enduring traits, adopted narratives, and real-time constraints are the undercurrents that propel the human vehicle. It's a model for aligning how someone will likely respond to a set of circumstances with the response that you, your strategy, and your business need to be successful. It's a model for getting "everyone rowing in the same direction" by tapping into the insight that people are very good at doing what they want to do and what they want to do is often predictable.

However, there's something foundational to cover first. Any model is only as good as the inputs that are provided. With the G.E.A.R. model, as with any behavioral model, that input is one's perception of reality, and as we know, we often find others living in a different reality than our own.

The first step in dealing with anyone is making sure that you begin with a shared understanding, occupy the same reality, and that you're seeing the world in a similar way. When we take that step, the ones that follow become easier on the expedition of business.

CHAPTER 6

VANTAGE POINTS

"Mr. Tomlin, I've been trying to reach you for weeks. I'm out of patience and am turning this issue over to my attorney."

It wasn't the voicemail I wanted to find when I returned from lunch, nor was it a message that I could make much sense of. I knew the number and the voice. He was a client, and two or three weeks prior we had met to resolve an issue on a project. A meeting that I thought had put matters to rest. I had not heard from him since then, and I was as perplexed as I was concerned.

My return call clued me in on a few pieces of information. He had my email address wrong; those messages I had *"ignored"* never made it to me. His phone calls that I *"didn't return"*—until that day they never ended with a voicemail. I did not know that he had called.

Now I had clarity on the *"out of patience"* part of his message, but *"my attorney"*? I thought this was resolved. It turns out he did too—until he talked with his boss. He had different ideas as to who bore responsibility.

The entire episode had started months prior when they contracted us to provide some design services. They presented *"what they had budgeted"* to my project manager, and my project manager saw his task as giving them the design *"they asked for."*

I'm not sure the client disagreed until the piece of equipment didn't work. *"We should have raised our concerns"* was my take on the situation, but I was still unclear on just what had happened.

There was much to understand. Why the voicemail? How did this design come to be? Why the change of heart? It took a while, but once I could understand everyone else, I could finally be understood, and a resolution could be reached.

Understanding is the first step in getting people aligned within an organization. What is their starting point? What is their perception of reality? Those are the foundations needed to build a usable model. One that explains what someone might want and how they are likely to respond. Without that foundation, the world can be a strange, confusing, and frustrating place.

⸺◆⸺

You're probably familiar with the classic party game "Telephone." Someone starts the game by whispering a message to the person next to them. That person does the same, and by the time you've reached the end, you're left with some altered version of the original message.

A more modern take on the game, and a better analogy for our struggles related to perception, is the game Telestrations. In that game, players alternate between drawing a picture of the *"secret word"* and writing a description of the previous player's drawing.

As you might imagine, hilarity often ensues. What started as *"A rabbit wearing a top hat"* turns into *"Richard Nixon taking a bubble bath."* Unfortunately, with business and getting our teams aligned, we often get the confusion but rarely the comedy.

There is no *"secret word"* in business. Instead, we're awash in information: calls, emails, tone, body language, and there's more. At any moment, we're also processing our entire field of view: the sounds around us, the feeling of the air and objects we're in contact with, and whatever smells our noses may be picking up.

In effect, all that incoming information is the world and our immediate place in it. To keep it from being overwhelming, our brains filter out nearly all of it. What we're left with is the small slice we focus on: our attention. What we pay attention to gets filtered through our perception, and that becomes our reality.

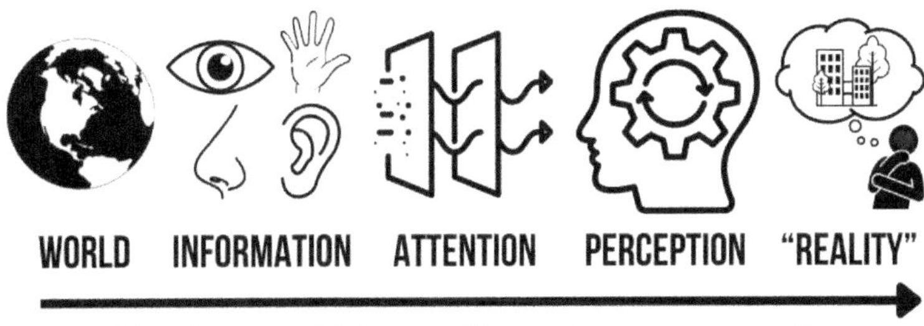

There's one world but we all experience our own reality.
Getting realities to match is the first step in getting people aligned.

Without attention and perception, it would all be noise. With them, we create a mental model to approximate reality. We can't absorb all of reality at once, so we develop a low-resolution view to make sense of that small slice of reality we pay attention to. And that perception becomes one's reality.

Unfortunately, in business, this chain of approximations often becomes our own game of Telestrations, and it's not as much fun.

Like me, you receive an angry phone call from a customer. Now the words they use aren't random; there's a long road that leads to your eardrums. It starts with the customer's perception, a product of the slice of reality they paid attention to. Maybe they're right to be upset, maybe they're not. But in the moment, their approximation of reality takes shape in their mind, and the resulting action is to give you an earful.

They then make yet another approximation. They can't express 100% of what they've experienced, how they feel, and what they want you to do about it. That all exists in their head, but to convey it to you they're left to approximate the best they can. They do so with words, their tone of voice, and maybe—if they still have a landline—slamming their phone down.

So now it's your turn. You've paid attention to some slice of the information sent screaming at you. You've perceived it the best you could, constructed your own approximation of reality, and now you must do your best to approximate the situation for an employee who can fix it. An employee who is the next link in the chain of "world," attention, perception, and action. With each step, the picture, the "reality," our communication, and expectations all drift further from the truth of the situation.

Business is hard enough even if we assume everyone is operating in the same reality. When everyone perceives the same information in different ways, it gets that much more difficult. Unfortunately, we tend to overestimate how often we're on the same page.

Research has shown that nearly 60% of us overestimate how effectively we communicate. And it's a problem in both directions. A person communicating with you is likely to assume they've delivered a clearer message than they have, and you're likely to err in the same direction about your communication with someone further down the chain. It's how we get from Peter Rabbit dressed for a night on the town to the 37th President taking a dip in the tub.

There's a long list of what makes getting others to share our version of reality difficult: our varied histories and past experiences, words and their multiple meanings, the non-verbal cues that can reinforce but also derail our messages, our tendency to fill gaps in information with assumptions or our memories, and that we all are likely to focus our attention on different pieces of information.

One can spend a career researching all the different factors that influence our specific perception of reality. But for a business leader, one question is essential: "*What do I do about it?*"

Thankfully, there's a four-step process that can help us make sense of things. It's not steeped in research or anyone's proprietary model. It's just a common-sense way to get a better grasp on the situation you're dealing with—and the person involved.

1. Relate to their perspective.

2. Explore what they think is happening and why.

3. Affirm your understanding by repeating back. And then, but only then...

4. Respond.

RELATE TO THEIR PERSPECTIVE

The word "empathy" is often used when it comes to people, leadership, and management. Unfortunately, it's come to mean being warm, soft, and compassionate with others. Not necessarily bad things, but that is affective empathy, and it comes at a cost if it pushes out a second type.

Cognitive empathy is the proverbial "*put yourself in their shoes.*" Can we mentally take ourselves on a journey to see and experience the world as someone else might? To view things through the lens of their history, their experience, their abilities, their expectations, and the information that was—or was not—available to them.

We can't get it 100% right, but the bulk of the benefit comes from giving it a shot. Otherwise, we default to the idea that everyone views the world as we do—and we'll remain confused by people and their behavior.

The best practice is to start with a powerful assumption:

Their behavior makes sense given what they believe is happening.

Said more directly, people are rarely as crazy as we'd like to assume they are.

The exercise isn't about agreeing with their reality but recognizing they're acting rationally within their mental model of the situation.

Understanding another person's perspective requires setting aside our immediate judgment about whether they're right or wrong, and instead, approaching the situation with curiosity about what version of reality would make their response reasonable. The key is to use the clues we have available to map out plausible options, versions of their potential reality that would make their behavior seem normal. With those in mind, we can get their take on the situation.

EXPLORE WHAT THEY THINK IS HAPPENING AND WHY

Here's a clever trick to figure out what someone is thinking: Ask them.

As the saying goes, *"The good Lord gave us two ears but only one mouth..."*

But listening closely is easier said than done—we're impatient and our brains are always screaming at us to come to a conclusion and move on. We've got our own perception of reality to maintain, and someone acting in a way we can't understand is really gumming up the works. The most difficult part is to simply stop and investigate.

The goal isn't to interrogate them, but to genuinely try to understand their mental model. This is where you might discover that your "unreasonable" customer heard *"we'll get back to you,"* but since they were burned by other companies before, interpreted it as *"we don't care about your problem."*

A good place to start is understanding the information they're aware of:

- What's your understanding of the current situation? What have you been told so far? Where did that information come from?

Next, we can try to get at their interpretation:

- How do you see this affecting you specifically? What's your biggest concern here? What assumptions are you making about what happens next?

Then uncover their reasoning:

- Walk me through your thinking on this. What led you to that conclusion? Help me understand why that's important to you.

Ask how married they are to their conclusion:

- What would change your mind about this? What other explanations might there be? What would you need to see to feel differently?

And finally, get at any emotional drivers:

- What's most frustrating about this situation? What are you worried might happen? What would success look like from your perspective?

By the end, we're likely to have a much better handle on their perspective. There is often a "why" behind someone's "why," and once we've found it, we can take the next step.

AFFIRM YOUR UNDERSTANDING

Air traffic controllers, emergency responders, doctors, nurses, and military personnel: they're all trained to communicate in a way that repeats back and seeks confirmation of crucial information— *"Roger," "Say again," "Confirmed," "Copy," "Over."*

Chris Voss was a long-time hostage negotiator for the FBI. He believes *"That's right"* are the best words you can hear in any negotiation. In effect, the phrase is saying—I have expressed something to you, and now you have confirmed that you understand how I feel.

Me to client: *"You're irritated that your emails and phone calls have gone without a response."*

Client to me: *"That's right!"*

Affirming our understanding is about getting *"That's right"* back from the other party. It does not mean that our view of the situation must now match theirs. What it does mean is that *we* understand *their* understanding of the situation.

We don't have to agree that our customers should be upset, but once we know why they are, we can take the next step.

RESPOND

Once we understand their perspective, one of three scenarios is likely to emerge and define the path toward a better agreement of realities.

Path 1 - Information Gap: One party is missing key information. Once the gap is filled, reality changes quickly, and behavior is likely to follow.

This is the customer who's furious because their ignored complaint was actually an email that went to spam. An employee who panics about a skinny backlog, not realizing the schedule was intentionally cleared to make way for a major new contract. Share the missing information, affirm their understanding, and the perspective shifts.

Path 2 - Different Interpretation: Everyone has the same information but draws different conclusions. The customer received the order exactly as described but interpreted *"by end of day"* differently than we did. A team member sees a new policy as micromanagement when others see it as providing clearer expectations.

This requires genuine dialogue. Sometimes we realize their interpretation makes more sense. Sometimes we can convince them of ours. The key is approaching this as a conversation, not a correction.

Path 3 - Fundamental Differences: Even with the same information and similar interpretations, there's still misunderstanding.

This comes down to differences in values, priorities, or past experiences. The customer values speed over thoroughness; we prioritize quality over quick turnaround. An employee thrives on autonomy; the business requires standardized processes.

These differences can't be argued away with better information or clearer explanations. If the matter is trivial, maybe everyone can agree to disagree. But often, the situation is more consequential. Then we have three options:

    1. We make a change. Maybe that employee isn't the right person for the job. Maybe that customer is one we can do without.

2. We assert authority. Who has the final say? It's the more heavy-handed approach, but things can't remain at loggerheads forever.

3. We divert the energy. If a customer is hung up on faster delivery, we create a premium shipping option. If an employee thrives on autonomy, we fill their schedule with projects for which they alone are responsible. And if my litigious client is most concerned with getting his boss off his back, I work with him to solve that problem instead of pointing fingers.

Remember our metaphors from Chapter 5. The aikido master doesn't try to make their opponent weaker; they redirect the force to their benefit. The farmer doesn't fight the chickens' instinct to scratch; they position them where scratching serves the farm's goals. The designers of the Hoover Dam didn't resist—but embraced—the fact that water always wants to flow downstream.

Once we understand someone's perspective, our job isn't always to change their reality. More often it's working with the reality they're operating in and designing solutions that account for how they actually see and respond to the world around them.

That's the alignment that makes business less of a struggle and lets a leader do more with less. Understanding how one perceives reality is the first step in building that alignment. Step two is getting a handle on how they are likely to respond.

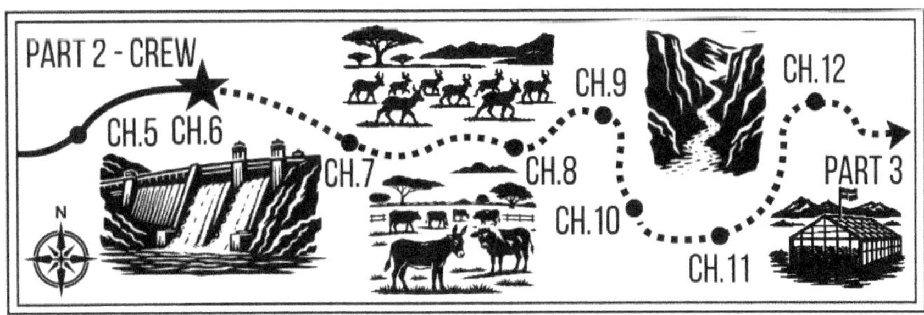

Plotting a course forward requires understanding where we currently stand. As a business leader, the terrain we're dealing with is often people and their perception. One of the most common mistakes on the expedition of

business is failing to get our bearings with an individual before we proceed. Once that position is established, then we can use the tools at our disposal to select the correct path forward.

And like the tools a master craftsman uses to work with, and not against, the natural tendencies of their medium, the chapters that follow will develop our G.E.A.R. model—a tool to help align our crew toward the intended destination.

CHAPTER 7

UNDERCURRENTS (G.E.A.R.)

I once hired a director of operations. He had great credentials, was incredibly smart, and turned out to be a true team player. He took directions and ran with them and had our company humming along. Appreciation for him was shown publicly, privately, and financially. We had a solid relationship. Eighteen months in, he was ready to quit.

Six months later, he had taken on more responsibilities, was happier than ever, and would be for years to come. What happened in between was learning what drove him and adjusting his role to be better aligned with the four undercurrents that drive us all.

When we're leading a business, we spend most of our time thinking about people.

Will the client accept our proposal? Will parents with young kids like our new back-to-school promotion? Will the candidate accept the job offer? If they do, are they going to live up to expectations? The list is endless.

In the craft of business, the medium of the work is undoubtedly people. And one of the most important properties of that medium is this:

People are very good at doing what they want to do, and not so good at doing what they don't want to do.

In his book "Creative Blindness," David Trott—a successful advertising executive—recounts the story of an army officer struggling with a difficult assignment. During the Iraq War, he was tasked with getting enlisted GIs to memorize the faces of 50 enemy officers. His clever solution was to use the faces and names of each to create a deck of playing cards. They would be issued to all enlisted GIs in the area, soldiers who wanted to play cards far more than they wanted to stare at pictures of enemy soldiers.

Trott would say about the decision, *"You don't start with what you want people to do; you start with what people want to do."*

I made the mistake of assigning my operations director only what I wanted him to do. That worked fine—until it didn't. The role didn't include enough of what he wanted to do. Together we found what was missing in his role: relatedness and a feeling of certainty.

He had a unique role in the company and, as a result, worked alone most of the time. For some, that is not an issue; for him, it was. Equally problematic, the same unique role left him without clear expectations or metrics by which to judge his performance. The uncertainty and isolation were wearing on him.

Ironically, the solution was to give him **more** responsibility. He would keep doing what he was doing, but his new tasks would have him working as part of a team. They would also give him a clearer scoreboard for his performance.

It was a case study in the power of aligning what people want with what a business wants from them. Leaders are often very clear on the latter, but the former—what their team wants—generates more confusion.

———◆○◆———

Browse through any bookstore and you'll find plenty of titles on leading, motivating, managing, and influencing people. Decade after decade, the question persists: what do people want?

Here's the problem: most people can't tell us because they themselves don't know.

In her book "Why Motivating People Doesn't Work . . . and What Does," author Susan Fowler puts it well: *"People don't understand the nature of their own motivation, so when they are unhappy at work, they ask for more money. They yearn for something different—but they don't know what it is—so they ask for the most obvious incentive: money."*

Financial motivation doesn't solve the real issue, but it's their best guess as to what will. They know something is wrong. They feel dissatisfied. But naming the actual source—that's far more difficult.

The opportunity for leaders isn't in asking people what they want; it's in understanding what drives them. A plant doesn't know it needs phosphorus-rich soil, twelve hours of sunlight, and consistent watering. It just grows or doesn't. Antelopes migrating on the savanna stop once they find clean water and plenty of grass.

Employees obviously aren't plants, and most aren't animals, but the idea is the same. We're all looking for situations that satisfy our innate desires and environments where we can thrive.

Part of the job of a leader is to architect the conditions where people flourish—the daily experience: the work itself, how it's done, and who it is done with. And we can only do so when we have a model for explaining what people really want.

Steve Jobs famously said, *"A lot of times, people don't know what they want until you show it to them."*

That is true of people in their jobs as well. As a business leader, there may be no more important task than crafting the jobs that people may not even know they want. Doing so isn't easy, but it is possible if we leverage certain principles.

Whereas plants' desire for light has them bend toward the sun and antelopes' thirst causes them to follow the spring rains, there are four forces that drive our actions. The combination of the four is the **G.E.A.R.** that drives the human vehicle.

And we will visit each in the chapters to come:

1. **Genetics** - We all have parents. They had parents. And along with the eye color or height we may have inherited, comes genetic programming that goes back millennia. And it affects our desires and behavior just as much as our appearance.

2. **Enduring Traits** - Despite that shared programming, we all have unique and deeply ingrained personalities.

3. **Adopted Narratives** - Whether a product of our parents, schooling, church, politics, or life experience, there are certain beliefs we hold dear. They are narratives that influence how we see the world and the actions we take.

4. **Real-Time Constraints** - A pressing deadline has us working late. An economic slowdown forces us to cut staff we would love to keep. Real-time constraints are just that—real. Sometimes, no matter how badly we may want to do something, we just don't have the option.

All of us are the same on a fundamental level: brain, heart, arms, legs, and some genetic programming to make it all go. Similarly, all vehicles have some form of chassis, a motor or engine, and a transmission that turns energy into motion. However, to pick the right vehicle for our needs on the expedition of business, we need a more specific model of what drives people.

It's first-principles physics that the movement of an object results from the sum of the forces placed upon that object. The flight of Tom Watson's golf ball is a product of the impact of the club, the resistance of the air it passes through, the wind that may help it along, and the gravity that inevitably pulls it back toward earth.

Similarly, it's the total of the G.E.A.R. forces that dictates what we want, and thus the likely resulting action. It was the same undercurrents that had my A+ operations director ready to change course, and the same desires that had him more engaged than ever once a few changes were made.

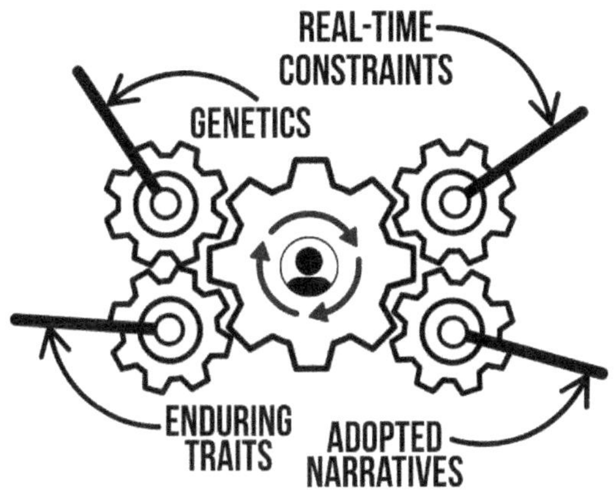

*The action an individual takes is a product of four
undercurrents, the components of G.E.A.R. that
push and pull on us all.*

I'm on the road, it's lunchtime, and I'm hungry. As I pull up to the menu, the crackled loudspeaker asks, *"Can I take your order?"*

"Yes, one second please." And the forces of G.E.A.R. in my human vehicle start playing tug of war.

The **genetic** artifacts of my food-scarce ancestors scream, *"What's the problem?! A triple bacon cheeseburger combo and a chocolate shake. We need calories, lots of them, and now!"*

Before I can speak, a "special promotion" catches my eye. "Limited time only, Nashville hot chicken sandwich"—never had one of those before. A real dangling of a carrot for someone high on the openness personality scale—an **enduring trait** of being intrigued by trying something new.

I make up my mind just in time for my "better judgment" to take over. *"I always feel terrible after eating like that, and it sure isn't healthy. I should pick something else."* **Adopted narratives** flood over me.

Fine.

"I'll have the chicken Caesar salad and an unsweet tea, please."

The speaker crackles back, *"I'm sorry, we're out of the salad."* And with that, **real-time constraints** swoop in to influence the outcome.

When was the last time you found yourself in an internal debate about just what to do—when the undercurrents within you were flowing in different directions?

We all find ourselves pulled on by the four G.E.A.R. forces when it's action time. If we get the balance of those forces moving in the right direction, we can craft a team that is motivated, engaged, and highly productive. They enjoy the job that they may not even have known they wanted, while acting with full force in the direction that both serves our business and satisfies the desires within them.

Otherwise, if those forces are in conflict, we'll find ourselves with a team like me in the drive-thru line, or my operations director with the wrong mix of tasks—hesitant and frustrated. They'll soon be antelopes without the water and grass they need, on the move and looking for better options.

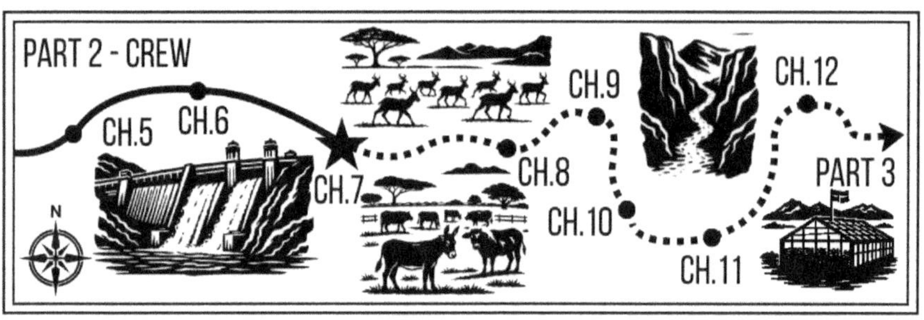

The idea for the G.E.A.R. model didn't fall from heaven or come to me in a dream. Like many things in business leadership, it was a product of necessity—of trying to run a company.

As stated in Chapter 5, people are an organization's greatest asset but also its greatest liability. And as a leader, the question of how to keep our crew more of the former and less of the latter is one of the most challenging we face.

And like most decisions, we start with mimicry and heuristics, making predictions about people based on our direct experience. But when we dig more into the sciences—psychology, sociology, biology, and even primatology—what we know about ourselves as humans, and thus of others, becomes better developed. It gives rise to decisions about people that rest closer to the summit of The Mountain of Why.

People are undeniably complex; knowing just how they are complex is illuminating but also paralyzing. I developed G.E.A.R. to make that complexity workable: detailed enough to be accurate, simple enough to be usable.

When it comes to people, we're often marketed "hammers" and told every problem is a nail. Fundamental needs, personality assessments, meaning and beliefs, or organizational design: they all have their devout advocates. But each is only one piece of the puzzle.

Craftsmanship depends on understanding all the principles in play and having a mental model that doesn't ignore variables that are significant. G.E.A.R. is such a model for the craft of business. But, like any other model, it is only as good as our understanding of the individual components involved.

In G.E.A.R. we have four to consider, and each helps us dial in the alignment between individuals, their responsibilities, and our objectives. We will cover each in the next four chapters, and we begin with the one that is the most universal, the most innate, but also the least obvious: genetics.

CHAPTER 8

WIRED FOR SURVIVAL

GENETICS: THE "G" IN G.E.A.R.

It's mid-February and by some stroke of luck, corporate sponsorship, or selling off one of your kidneys, you find yourself with a ticket to the Super Bowl.

But there's something unique about this game. The other fans in the stadium: they are your mother, and her mother, and her mother before that. They make up the line of some 80,000 direct ancestors that stretches from you back to the earliest humans. They are the headwaters of the genes you have come to inherit, the wiring that influences your appearance and longevity, but also your personality, desires, and thus actions.

Most in attendance lived a life far different from yours. By the time you reach the midpoint of your row, that person would never have ridden in a car, made a telephone call, or seen an electric light. By the end of the row, it's likely the person sitting there would never have owned or even seen a printed book. They told time by the sun and never interacted with anyone who lived more than 100 miles away.

Once you're beyond the 500 fans seated closest to you, there are ancestors who never saw written language and perhaps a few who pre-date the birth of agriculture.

The rest—the remaining 79,500 fans—are all some form of hunter-gatherers. Theirs was a life of survival in the wilderness.

All but a sliver of human history was an existence as hunter-gatherers. Even agriculture is relatively new. And modern times are a blink of an eye in comparison.

The modern world has changed more rapidly than the genes of our most innate wiring. If we move beyond the present day and consider what came well before, we can understand more of what our genes drive us to seek. Doing so provides a possible explanation of why in life and at work we are comforted by five conditions:

Certainty, Competence, Autonomy, Relatedness, and Engagement.

We are here today because of our distant ancestors. They, and at least some of their offspring, found a mate and supported the newly minted copies of their genes. It was a repeating cycle that eventually led to you and me—and many of our traits and characteristics.

In his book "Evolutionary Psychology: The New Science of the Mind," evolutionary psychologist David M. Buss argues that *"As descendants of these successful ancestors, we carry with us the adaptive mechanisms that led to our ancestors' success."*

Some of those mechanisms are more physiological: stereo vision (two eyes for depth perception), the ability to sweat, walk upright, and eat a variety of foods, while others are more patterns of the mind and the brain, or as Buss states:

"Psychological mechanisms are information-processing devices that exist in the form they do because they have solved specific problems of survival or reproduction recurrently over human evolutionary history."

The argument is that we don't choose many of our wants and desires; they reflect us being wired for survival.

Fatty, sweet, or salty foods—do you like those? Members of a certain sex catch your eye? Enjoy being too cold or too hot? How do you feel about being hungry, thirsty, or tired?

We know the answers, and it's obvious why seeking calories, a mate, and fulfilling other basic needs would have been good practice for those looking to send their genes into the future.

In business, we contend with less primal motivations, but the concept is similar: the past influences our present. And one fact about our past is particularly germane: we are tribal creatures.

Only in the last eye-blink of human history have we been able to survive on our own. Our distant ancestors didn't have developed agriculture, much less running water, air conditioning, or grocery stores. For most of human history, surviving and propagating meant being part of a pack. Or, as Buss puts it in his book:

"It is virtually impossible to hunt large game alone, at least with the tools that were available prior to the invention of guns and other weapons. In hunter-gatherer societies, large-game hunting almost invariably occurs in groups or coalitions. To be successful, these coalitions must solve an array of adaptive problems, such as how to divide the work and how to coordinate the efforts of the group, both of which require clear communication."

In other words, the challenge of getting a team to work toward a common goal is as old as humanity, but so is the solution: people seeking what they want, and leaders harnessing that energy.

Our world is one of near-infinite possibilities. Every day we go about our lives with a list of bad things that could happen hanging over our heads. Some worry about that list more than others, but in the end, we're all looking for a place where we feel comfortable—for a Tent of Comfort that can shelter us from the storm. When we find it, we tend to stay there; and when we don't, just like our antelopes in the prior chapter, we go looking elsewhere.

Businesses that build Tents of Comfort for their employees keep the talent they have, get a higher level of engagement, and attract other candidates of high potential. They are rewarded for giving people what we've always wanted: the conditions we seek to make us feel secure in our abilities, our place in the pack, and—in a primal sense—our survival.

They are the five conditions we want at work, and they're the same five desires that helped our ancestors continue the family trees that led to you and me.

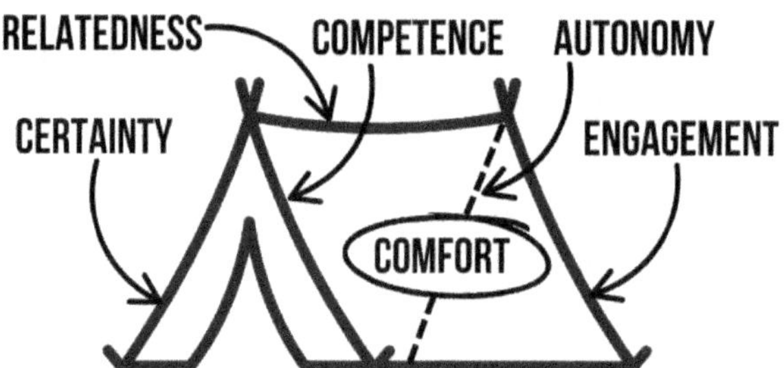

There are five poles that hold up the tent of comfort.
The structure we're all looking to establish in our lives.

CERTAINTY

We all have a different tolerance for uncertainty, but it's hard to argue that all of us don't favor knowing over not knowing. In our tribal past, uncertainty often meant danger. What was that rustling behind the tree? Would the antelope migrate as expected? If not, just where was next month's food coming from?

Uncertainty causes our brains to work overtime—our large, energy-hungry brains. Gravitating toward certainty allowed our ancestors to save calories that were often in short supply.

Today this ancient drive manifests itself as our need to know what's expected: when projects are due, how decisions are made, what is expected of someone in a role, and what success looks like.

In business, uncertainty breeds anxiety and paralysis. Employees who don't know spend energy worrying instead of working. They check and double-check, seek excessive approval, or simply avoid taking action altogether.

Leaders who provide clarity about expectations, timelines, and decision-making free their people to focus on execution rather than anxiety management. And as a result, they can feel more accomplished in their work, something we all want.

COMPETENCE

Who among us doesn't want to feel capable? And that happens more easily when we are in a workplace where we can do our best work. One where standards are clear, and we are recognized for a job well done. It also happens in a workplace where smart leaders invest in training and skill development, and match people to roles where they can excel.

For our tribal ancestors, being competent meant a lower risk of being voted off the island. So understandably, we get a little uncomfortable when we feel like we're lagging behind—possibly becoming a liability rather than an asset to our tribe.

AUTONOMY

I've looked for years, but I have yet to find an employee who likes to be micromanaged. We simply like to have control.

If you're hungry, having the freedom to search out some food is more comforting than trusting someone else will come through for you. When a customer is giving you a hard time, having the latitude to stand your ground makes work less stressful. Returning after a successful hunt or landing a big new client, both are that much more gratifying and credibility building when you get to go about it your own way.

When we do our work our way, it also generates more room for exploration, for improvement, and for mastering our craft. It circles back to competence. We want to learn and grow, and that inevitably means having the freedom to take on a challenge ourselves. It's a bit ironic, since we also love being part of something larger.

RELATEDNESS

Chances are you have a favorite sports team you pull for. A college or university you identify with. A congregation, charity, or civic group you're proud to be a part of. If none of those, then there is likely some smaller circle you enjoy: a neighborhood, friends, or family.

We are ridiculously social creatures. So social that even for the most antisocial among us, solitary confinement borders on cruel and unusual punishment.

More than anything else, relatedness is about the question, *"What (or who) is my safety net?"*

When my cave floods during a storm, when a hunting trip goes awry, when I miss a week of work tending to a sick kid, who has my back? There is a lot that can go wrong, and the consequences can be high—often life-threatening in the days of our ancestors. So of course we want someone who will be there for us.

Our need to feel connected, accepted, and valued by our group runs as deep as any other drive. If we don't find it in one workplace, we will soon find it in another. The search becomes a new challenge—something we love.

ENGAGEMENT

Our ancestors faced constant problems that required their attention and creativity: finding food, avoiding predators, adapting to changing conditions. Those with a bias toward action and improvement had an advantage. Their need to be doing something made it more likely they wouldn't be caught off guard when it came time to act.

The characteristics that drive engagement: novelty, curiosity, manageable challenge, and the opportunity to grow and receive feedback—these make up the famous "Flow" state. They are also the traits and conditions that help us learn new skills and practice them until they're mastered—a big advantage, and one our ancestors would want in navigating a more primitive world of uncertainty.

In modern times, no one wants to be bored. We like to go about our lives and our work feeling engaged. Many are correct to call their work "*boring,*" and that is why so many find something better to do while they're still on the clock.

Early in my business career, I found the book "First, Break All the Rules" by Marcus Buckingham and Curt Coffman. The quest was to see if they could use a massive collection of Gallup survey data (some 80,000 managers across 400 companies) to find the questions that best predicted a high level of employee engagement. And thus, the questions that predicted high-performing companies.

The findings consistently pointed to people needing clear expectations and a firm understanding of what success looks like (**Certainty**), the opportunity to use their strengths and be recognized for doing quality work (**Competence**), the resources, authority, and voice to do their jobs well (**Autonomy**), meaningful connections with colleagues who care about them and a shared commitment to the mission (**Relatedness**), and regular feedback, progress conversations, and opportunities to learn and grow (**Engagement**).

It's worth noting that two independent paths arrived at the same destination. Gallup's research was purely empirical—no presuppositions about human nature, just massive datasets revealing what predicted engagement and performance. Our Tent of Comfort framework took the opposite route, starting from first principles about the development of our evolutionary wiring and reasoning forward from there.

The convergence of those two trails suggests both are tapping into something real about what people need. And so, it comes as no surprise that our Tent of Comfort overlaps with many common business tactics and strategies.

BUSINESS CONCEPT	CERTAINTY	COMPETENCE	AUTONOMY	RELATEDNESS	ENGAGEMENT
PURPOSE, MISSION	✓			✓	✓
CULTURE, CORE VALUES	✓			✓	✓
GOAL SETTING	✓	✓	✓		✓
SCOREBOARDS, K.P.I.S	✓	✓	✓		✓
PERFORMANCE REVIEWS	✓			✓	
TRUST & TRANSPARENCY	✓			✓	
JOB DESCRIPTIONS	✓	✓	✓		
GROWTH PLANS		✓	✓		✓
COACHING & MENTORING		✓		✓	✓
EMPLOYEE EXPERIENCE					✓

Individual desires might be stronger in some areas than others, but when we're building our Pyramids of Decisions, seeking the first principles that can take us up The Mountain of Why, and crafting the roles for our crew on the expedition of business, we're well on our way if we can provide comfort via fulfilling the five desires people have always sought to satisfy.

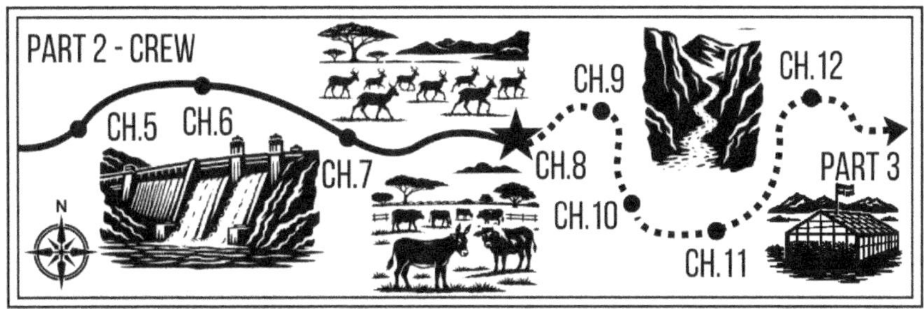

The exact details of how our distant ancestors achieved success are hard to know for certain. But the specifics are immaterial for our objective. We know it was without question a different time, and certainly one where survival was more difficult and reliance on others more essential. Equally true is that all our lineages trace back to similar conditions, or as Buss puts it in his book:

"Modern human populations show an exceptionally low amount of genetic variation, suggesting that we all came from a relatively small population of more genetically homogeneous founding ancestors."

So, when it comes to the "G" of genetics in our G.E.A.R. model, we are much more alike than different—a commonality that an astute leader can use to their advantage.

Equally advantageous is understanding how we're each made differently. While the past rewarded certain individual traits, it also rewarded a certain feature of the group: diversity in our enduring traits, the personalities that impact how we navigate the world, and the "E" of our G.E.A.R. model which we'll cover next.

CHAPTER 9

MADE DIFFERENT

ENDURING TRAITS: THE "E" IN G.E.A.R.

My niece and I once visited the cattle farm of some family friends. Mixed in with the herd of cows was a solitary donkey.

As we stood at the fence, I asked, *"Do you know why the donkey is there?"*

"No," she replied.

"To protect the cows from coyotes," I told her.

She was quiet for a minute, staring out at the pasture.

"Oh, I get it! The coyotes will eat the donkey first, right?"

I smiled.

Thankfully for the donkey, he's not there as a sacrifice. Donkeys have enduring traits of being territorial and protective. They also will bond with a herd of cattle. Combine those with a donkey's physical size, ability to bite and kick, and you have one heck of a "guard dog" for your herd.

The difference in personalities in the workplace isn't as stark, but we all know folks that are more donkey than cattle. It can be partly explained by our genes and partly by our life experiences, but to the business leader, that is irrelevant. Our concern is how we can use these differences to make better decisions.

It's not a simple question, and there's no shortage of options marketed to help you find the answer. Myers-Briggs Type Indicator, DISC, The Enneagram Institute: these are some of the more well-known personality assessments on the market. There are dozens of others, and it's easy to get overwhelmed. But to not tap into the power that lies in the "E" of our G.E.A.R. model—the enduring traits that help drive us—would be a mistake.

No master carpenter pretends all wood is the same, and a chef knows there is a difference between dried and fresh herbs. Part of the craft of business is developing a more nuanced view of individuals, then using that insight to make decisions higher up The Mountain of Why—decisions that build teams by leveraging our enduring traits.

I once hired an employee who bordered on obsessive-compulsive. Their communication style was blunt and direct—they drove people crazy at times. But they were also the best project manager and quality control person I could imagine.

Working alongside them was someone the office loved—but who drove me crazy at times. They were unpredictable and not the greatest at following directions, but they were the social engine of the organization and made work more fun.

Getting the balance right and fitting the right traits to the right role can be complicated work. Humans are by far the most complex creatures on Earth, and that extends to our personalities. And like height, hair color, or age, our enduring traits exist on a continuum with no natural breakpoints. Fortunately, we humans are good at imposing structure on continuous realities, doing so in a way that is useful without being too rigid to adapt.

The spectrum of light is continuous, but we have named colors and our friend *"ROY G BIV"* to simplify a rainbow. Sound frequencies have no discontinuities, yet we have a useful system of musical notes and scales. And perhaps the pinnacle of our structuring accomplishments: words and their infinite combinations to help describe all the intricacies of life.

Sound, temperature, time of year.
All, like personality, exist on a continuum.
All with structures that we use to understand them.

The attempts to categorize human personality may be lesser-known, but to the business leader, they can be equally useful. Which structure we use is a decision we must make for ourselves. Whereas we were born into the primary language of our family and the musical and color frameworks developed long before that time, we must decide on an approach that helps us navigate the twists and turns of human personality.

Thinking about people and their enduring traits is hard enough. We do ourselves no favors by selecting, or even paying for, a personality assessment system that we don't have an intuitive grip on. The marketers of different systems will be glad to tell you why theirs is best, and that may be true. But the greatest value comes from a system that we can ingrain in our thinking, one with terms and traits that become second nature to us when describing our crew's enduring traits.

So, my advice: select one that makes sense to *you*.

I recommend leaders consider the "Big Five" personality scale. Commonly expressed by the acronym O.C.E.A.N. (Openness, Conscientiousness, Extraversion, Agreeableness, and Neuroticism), it is the most common structure used by researchers and academics, and likely the most data-supported personality framework.

Using the dimensions of O.C.E.A.N. to describe one's personality is like using width, height, length, and weight for a package, or using the red, green, blue (RGB) color scale to break down the yellow of a banana.

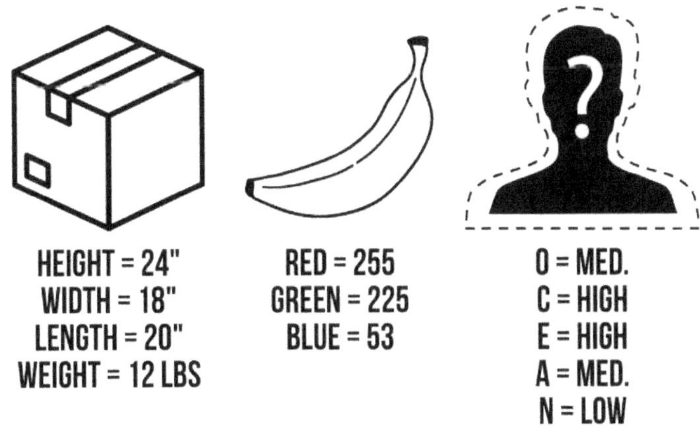

But just as we need to know what "height" and "width" actually mean to describe a package, understanding each personality dimension is essential for using O.C.E.A.N. effectively. Again, humans and their personalities are complex. So, it's not surprising that any single dimension could manifest itself in a variety of ways.

Cataloging those facets or aspects is a popular research topic. The most established approach divides each of the five dimensions into six facets, creating 30 narrow traits in total, as shown in the table that follows. This is the system used by the widely researched NEO Personality Inventory. As you move through the chart, think about yourself and the people in your life. Who comes to mind when seeing these descriptors?

OPENNESS	CONSCIENTIOUSNESS	EXTRAVERSION	AGREEABLENESS	NEUROTICISM
Fantasy	Competence	Warmth	Trust	Anxiety
Aesthetics	Order	Gregarious	Straight-Forwardness	Hostility
Feelings	Dutifulness	Assertiveness	Altruism	Depression
Actions	Achievement	Activity	Compliance	Self-Consciousness
Ideas	Self-Discipline	Excitement Seeking	Modesty	Impulsive
Values	Deliberation	Positive Emotions	Tender-Mindedness	Vulnerable

I list these traits because they are helpful in developing a grasp of each "Big Five" dimension. They list six ways that each dimension can manifest itself, but no leader wants to be tasked with remembering 30 different variables.

A newer and more user-friendly approach identifies 10 aspects. They are the result of two broader groupings within each of the five O.C.E.A.N. dimensions.

Research by DeYoung, Quilty, and Peterson found that the various manifestations of each of the "Big Five" naturally cluster into two related but distinct aspects. The table that follows shows those 10 aspects, the five

'Big' dimensions, a description of each, and guidance on applying them to individual roles. Again, as you pass through each aspect, who comes to mind? And is their current role something they are well-suited for?

PERSONALITY DIMENSION	DIMENSION ASPECT	ASPECT DESCRIPTION	WELL-SUITED FOR	LESS SUITED FOR
OPENNESS High openness thrives in innovation and change. Low openness excels in stability and proven methods.	INTELLECT	Enjoys abstract thinking, ideas, problem-solving	Strategy, research, systems design, complex problems	Highly repetitive, rule-bound work
	OPENNESS	Curious, imaginative, open to new experiences	Innovation, creative roles, change environments	Highly standardized or static roles
CONSCIENTIOUSNESS Strong predictor of performance across roles; extreme levels can lead to rigidity or burnout.	INDUSTRIOUSNESS	Persistent, goal-oriented, hard-working	Execution, operations, delivery focused roles	Unstructured roles with little feedback
	ORDERLINESS	Organized, detail-oriented, prefers structure	Compliance, QC, project management	Rapidly changing, ambiguous environments
EXTRAVERSION Extraverts excel in influence-heavy roles; introverts often thrive in deep-focus and analytical work.	ENTHUSIASM	Energetic, expressive, socially engaging	Team leadership, sales, customer-facing roles	Isolated, solitary work
	ASSERTIVENESS	Comfortable leading and influencing	Management, negotiation, decision-making	Roles requiring deference or minimal influence
AGREEABLENESS High agreeableness supports teamwork. Low agreeableness can be valuable in tough negotiations or debates.	COMPASSION	Empathetic, supportive, people-focused	Coaching, HR, caregiving, collaborative teams	Highly adversarial or competitive roles
	POLITNESS	Respectful, cooperative, conflict-avoidant	Stable teams, service roles, consensus cultures	Roles requiring frequent confrontation
NEUROTICISM Low neuroticism supports resilience. Moderate levels can improve risk awareness and vigilance.	VOLATILITY	Emotionally reactive to stress or pressure	Fast-feedback roles with emotional awareness	High-pressure, chaotic environments
	WITHDRAWAL	Sensitive to threat, prefers predictability	Risk-aware roles, planning, analysis	Constant uncertainty or public scrutiny

You could think of aspects as the "warm" and "cool" versions of each personality "primary color" or "Big Five" dimension—and there's value in the nuance.

My wife and I both score in the middle for **extraversion**. However, that is because she is high in **enthusiasm** and low in **assertiveness**—the two aspects of that dimension. I am the opposite—low in enthusiasm but high in assertiveness—and to assume we are the same would be a mistake. And it would certainly make for a bad hire.

To revisit our drive-thru example from Chapter 7, someone higher on the **openness** scale is more likely to try something new off the menu. Someone lower on the **conscientiousness** scale might struggle with an overly complex or long menu, becoming frustrated more easily by having to process so many options.

If they are higher on the **extraversion** scale, they may be more interested in chatting with the cashier, or more likely to speak up if their order is wrong—it depends on which aspect they display: **enthusiasm** and/or **assertiveness**.

Those higher on the **agreeableness** scale may be more tolerant of the restaurant being out of an item or more patient with slow service, while those higher in **neuroticism** are more likely to worry that any delay is going to make them late for their next appointment.

It is important to remember that such profiles reflect someone's natural tendencies or biases. They describe which behaviors one gravitates toward more naturally. It does not mean that someone is incapable of overcoming a propensity brought about by an enduring trait.

Leveraging our G.E.A.R. model means putting people in a position where they can more often work with—and not against—the pull of their undercurrents. Part of the craft of business is assigning people to roles where many of the 10 aspects of their personality align with the tasks at hand.

How we gather data, catalog information, and make decisions based on such characteristics of our staff is ultimately up to us. The biggest benefit comes from simply being aware of the power of our enduring traits—that each member of our crew on the expedition of business is made different, and so should be the work we ask them to do.

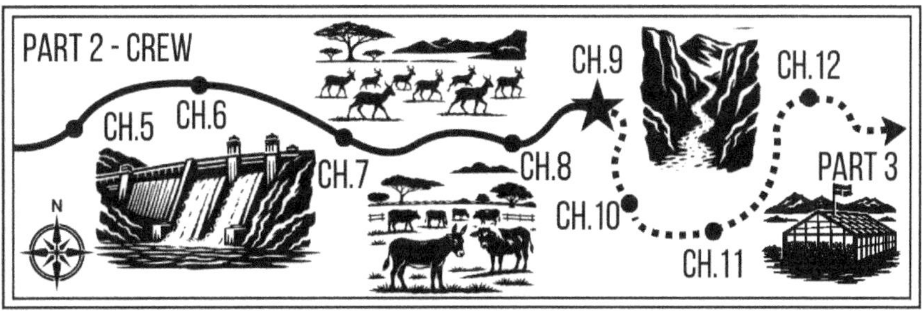

Jim Collins—made famous by his book "Good to Great"—got the business world talking about people and seats: "There are really three parts of this question of the right people. The first is the right people on the bus. Second, is the wrong people off the bus. But third is the right people in the right seats."

But once again, the value lies in the nuance. How do we define "right"? In Part 4, we'll look at two frameworks that help us answer that question, but one critical component is the enduring traits an individual possesses. They are parts of their personality that are neither "right" nor "wrong" per se—only in the context of the roles we place them in.

Enduring traits like those captured in the O.C.E.A.N. framework and the 10 associated aspects have a powerful effect on the decisions we make and the actions we take. However, those traits are a reaction to the world we find ourselves in and how we see it.

In Chapter 6, we discussed how perception is very much our reality. Some of that perception is based on facts. But much of it reflects how we make sense of the world: the stories we tell ourselves, our adopted narratives, the "A" in our G.E.A.R. model, and the subject of our next chapter.

CURIOUS ABOUT YOUR ENDURING TRAITS?

Scan the QR code or visit the link below to access a free personality assessment.
See where you are high, low, or average on the Big Five personality dimensions and the associated 10 facets.

WWW.THEEXPEDITIONOFBUSINESS.COM/ENDURING-TRAITS

CHAPTER 10

INTERNAL MAPS

ADOPTED NARRATIVES: THE "A" IN G.E.A.R.

A few days ago, I woke up and made my way down to the kitchen. An early supper the night before had me starving. I love cereal, so I grabbed a bowl and opened the pantry. Bad news: the cupboard was bare—no cereal to be had.

At about the same time, a hardware store truck was making a delivery down the street. A squirrel had a front-row seat as it munched on an acorn. A dog being walked on the opposite side of the road spotted the squirrel and darted toward it, pulling his owner in front of the oncoming hardware truck.

Fortunately, the driver saw them both and swerved in time to avoid disaster. Unfortunately, the truck rolled over in the process and dumped nails all over the street.

The next morning, I had a pantry full of cereal, but two flat tires on my car.

So, what happened?

You are likely thinking that I went to the store to buy some cereal, and on the way, I ran over some nails spilled by the hardware truck.

That's logical, reasonable, and a conclusion that lets you put the question to rest. But is it true?

As humans, we love narratives; we love stories. The pattern of first this, then that, fires up our brains. It's understandable. For much longer than the written word has been around, story has been the medium through which we explain what happened to us and hear what happened to others.

Stories are our way of explaining how things—like my flat tires—came to be. They help to reduce complexity and push the uncertainty we hate out of our minds. Unfortunately, it comes with a risk.

As for my tires, I never went to the store. I ordered my cereal from Amazon. I too would like to know why they went flat.

Anthony de Mello is famous for saying, *"The shortest distance between truth and a human being is a story."* I don't disagree, but I would add:

The shortest distance between being confidently wrong and a human being is also a story.

Our narratives, true or not, can have real consequences.

I once worked at a company for three years. To this day, I cannot tell you why the owners started the company. With no narrative to fill in the blank, I did what we're all good at doing: I made up my own. I went with the default in this situation: they must have wanted to make a bunch of money, and thus there I was, *"working for the man."*

It's a case study in how the "A" (Adopted Narratives) of our G.E.A.R. model can impact outcomes. It wasn't a bad place to work. I was good at what I did, enjoyed the people, and was compensated well, but it was very "vanilla."

Had I been given the real story—or even just a good story—I would probably have found myself more engaged, working harder, and sticking around for longer. Instead, I found myself looking for new opportunities—a better story to be a part of—and I was gone soon after. The company was left with one less capable and dependable employee, and the leaders probably created their own story as to why I departed.

Why did my tires go flat? Why did I leave my job? There are an infinite number of questions in need of answers, and thus, an equal number of narratives to be adopted. Developing influence over what we, our staff, and our customers come to believe is part of the craft of business. Identifying when narratives are out of control but still doing our best to understand them is equally important.

The first step for either is to understand when we're likely to adopt the narratives that influence our decisions.

In his paper "The Psychology of Curiosity," George Loewenstein developed what's known as information-gap theory. It's the idea that curiosity functions like a basic drive state. Similar to hunger or thirst, it creates discomfort and motivates us to seek information.

And that hunger or thirst comparison isn't just metaphorical. Research using fMRI and other brain imaging techniques has shown that potential curiosity resolution activates the brain's reward system. Potential answers to questions we're curious about create increased activity in the same brain regions that light up for food, sex, and addictive substances.

Come hell or high water, we are going to get answers to our questions. Whether they are true is a secondary concern. Information gaps influence both the "G" (genetics) and "E" (enduring traits) portions of our G.E.A.R. model. We're wired to seek certainty, and many are high in curiosity.

In business, this can be a very good thing. Letting talented people troubleshoot a difficult problem, giving creative folks free rein to develop new products, or landing on a marketing campaign that taps into our customers' innate need to know: all align what people naturally want to do with what we want them to do.

However—like most instruments of power—it can be a double-edged sword. I left a job because I assumed the worst, and I might have words with an (innocent) truck driver over my flat tires. When people's need to know works against a business, it can be harmful.

On the expedition of business, information gaps are sure to arise. If we can do a better job of anticipating them, we'll be in a better position to use them to our benefit.

Will Storr observes in his book "The Science of Storytelling" that Loewenstein's research identifies four specific mechanisms that trigger the information-seeking drive:

1. The posing of a question or the presentation of a puzzle.

2. Exposure to a sequence of events with an anticipated but unknown resolution.

3. The violation of expectations that triggers a search for an explanation.

4. Knowledge that someone else possesses information we lack.

It is these triggers that create the conditions where we're primed to seek, create, and adopt narratives to satisfy our minds—and business is rich with all of them.

Why is the tire flat? What's in the package? A juicy secret. The science says there are four types of scenarios that have us looking for answers...or cooking up our own.

A CEO starts a meeting with, "*Our competitor just launched a new product that's 30% cheaper than ours.*"

Everyone in the room processes her words, and the adopted narratives soon follow.

"We're already behind. How are we going to make it? Maybe we don't. Maybe this is the end." Some minds jump to "W*hat is the impact going to be?"*

"Well, duh. Our R&D department is a joke. Our production software is 10 years old. I've been telling you for months, it's time to upgrade." The question immediately becomes "*Who is to blame?"*

But the same information could trigger different narratives if presented in another way.

This time the CEO opens the meeting with, *"This product we have—what would allow us to produce it cheaper? Could we cut 30%? Let's hear some ideas."*

Now the force is being used for good. Narratives of fear, malice, and failure are replaced with feelings of curiosity. The reframed puzzle engages our innate problem-solving drive rather than triggering defensive resistance. The information gap and our need to know help drive people toward productive outcomes.

And unproductive ones.

A leadership team spends three hours in the conference room with the door closed. Everyone saw the consultant go in with a stack of documents. They emerged looking serious, scheduled another meeting for tomorrow, and said nothing.

The minds of the onlooking employees start racing:

"They're planning layoffs. Why else would they bring in a consultant and be so secretive? I should probably start looking for another job—just in case." The unknown becomes a threat.

"I bet they're finally addressing the Smith situation. Everyone knows he's been underperforming." The mystery becomes workplace gossip and speculation.

Imagine instead, before the meeting, a message goes out: "*This week we're working with a consultant to evaluate two potential growth opportunities that could significantly expand our business over the next few years. We're not ready to share details yet, but we wanted you to know we're excited about what we're exploring. We'll have more to share at next week's all-hands meeting."*

Now when people see the closed-door meetings, their mental narratives change. Instead of imagining threats, they're curious about opportunities. Instead of feeling excluded, they feel included in something bigger. The information gap still exists, but it's pulling people toward excitement rather than fear.

These examples show the "A" (Adopted Narratives) in our G.E.A.R. model at work. And the impact is twofold.

There is the influence of the adopted narrative itself: the story we use to make sense of the world and to fill our craving for an explanation. But also, the behavior created when we find ourselves with an information gap, the action we take in pursuit of an answer. In other words, when we get the "A" right, we can impact both thoughts and behaviors.

That said, not all narratives are created equal, and they certainly aren't equally knowable nor controllable.

—◦—

I have hired many entry-level candidates. They were—as you might imagine—young and getting their first taste of the professional world. Almost without exception, I had some version of the following conversation with them within the first year or two.

"You are going to screw up, and that is okay. It is how you learn. I expect it. It needs to happen. And whatever mess you create, we will figure it out—together."

They then knew there was a safety net and that I needed them to try new ideas. They then understood that they should trust their best judgment, and that being too cautious was bad for everyone.

These were conversations where I had a high degree of influence in shaping their adopted narratives. I could control their answers to *"What happens if I fail?" "What is expected of me?"* and *"Does anyone here care about me?"*

Their answers would dictate how engaged and committed to the organization they were. And I wanted to make sure they were true, not creations of their own imagination.

Without those conversations, they would have been left with the default: *"I'd better play it safe, go slow, double-check what 'the right answer' is, because otherwise I'm gone."*

There are situations when this is the correct approach. But when it stifles learning and diminishes productivity, that is when the astute leader knows to set things right.

Other narratives are more difficult to influence, but they still carry a high degree of impact. Questions like *"Why should I work hard?" "Should I trust others?"* and *"Can I learn new things?"*

The weight that our answers to these questions carry in the workplace is obvious. Unfortunately, they are less specific to a job, boss, or company, and more general to a lifetime of experiences, parenting, past successes, and failures.

Part of the craft of business is making the effort to understand the answers an individual has adopted to such questions.

These questions and the narratives that satisfy our "hunger" lie on a continuum. An individual's answer to each question varies in its **impact** on their actions, as does the **influence** which a leader can have on that person's answer. In the end, those variations create a 2x2 matrix like the one that follows. The questions shown are not exhaustive, and real life isn't so tidy, but there is still value in having a structure to help navigate the complexity.

LOW INFLUENCE HIGH IMPACT

Why should I work hard?
Can I learn new things?
Should I trust others?
Am I better than other people?
Does the worst always happen?

HIGH INFLUENCE HIGH IMPACT

Why do we exist as a company?
Why am I in this specific role?
What is expected of me?
Does anyone here care about me?
What happens if I screw up?

LOW INFLUENCE LOW IMPACT

Good leaders don't waste time worrying about these.

HIGH INFLUENCE LOW IMPACT

Why do we use this software?
Why are timesheets needed?
Who cleans up the breakroom?
Why are we hiring?
Why no company cars?

Notice where the real leverage is—the upper-right quadrant is where leaders earn their keep. Questions like "*Why do we exist as a company?*" and "*What happens if I screw up?*" are high impact **and** within our control. The upper-left is trickier. We can't easily rewrite someone's deeply held beliefs about trust or self-worth, but perhaps we can figure out these answers before we bring them on board. And if they are already part of the team, the answers likely serve as good reference points when navigating the minds of other people.

The questions on the bottom right seem mundane. But if we ignore enough of them, people start to wonder whether leadership is paying attention. They are some of the blocks that comprise our Pyramids of Decisions, but if left unexplained, they eventually stack up to a tower of doubt. Small explanations signal that someone is actually thinking things through, and that matters more than we tend to realize.

Success on the expedition of business means understanding the dynamics of narratives, the internal maps that our people use to navigate the unknowns of work and of life. It requires having a sense of when these explanations emerge, controlling the narratives we can, and working to understand the ones we can't. If we succeed, we will find our crew following the right path more often.

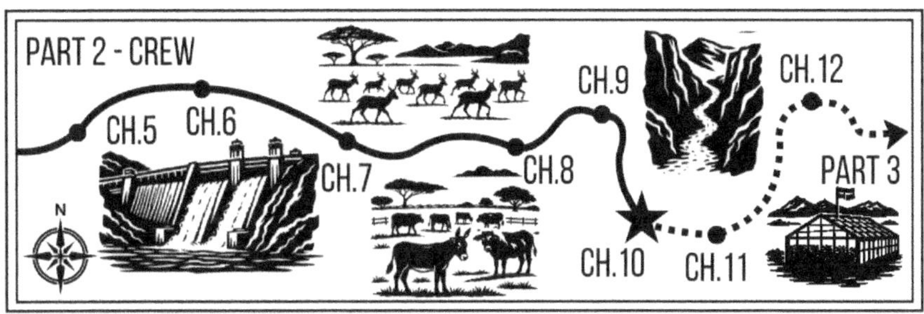

There are some things we know for certain in life: water flows downhill, the sun sets in the west, dogs don't tend to be vegetarians. But most of our explanations should come with varying degrees of confidence. Just how sure are we?

All that nuance takes up a lot of brainpower; brains burn a lot of calories. And, as we covered in Chapter 8, we have a predisposition to conserve energy—which for most of our past was in short supply. The quicker we arrive at an explanation, and the less we question, the more fuel we have left in our tank.

As leaders, we can be more intentional about slowing down and overriding our own natural inclinations. We can encourage others to do the same. But mastering the craft of business requires knowing our crew is likely to follow the path of least resistance.

Fortunately, in the design and operation of our organizations, we get to have some say over which paths people can take and the difficulty of each. And when we don't, we can still predict what people may do based on the context of their situation.

For all the influence that genetic factors, enduring traits, and adopted narratives have over us, they are often overpowered by the last piece of our model: real-time constraints—the "R" in G.E.A.R. It's the topic we'll cover next, and one of the most basic first principles: we can only select from the options that are available.

CHAPTER 11

NARROW TRAILS

REAL-TIME CONSTRAINTS: THE "R" IN G.E.A.R.

"*What do you feed your dog?*" one farmer asks another.

"*Collard greens,*" he responds.

"*Hmmm, my dog won't eat collard greens,*" the first farmer muses.

And the second farmer responds, "*Mine wouldn't either for the first three days.*"

Every joke has a bit of truth, and in this case, it reminds us of something fundamental: no matter how strong our preferences may be, we can only choose from what's available. It's the power of real-time constraints, a useful tool on the expedition of business, but also something we tend to forget.

In 1977, Lee Ross of Stanford University published a paper, "The Intuitive Psychologist and His Shortcomings: Distortions in the Attribution Process." A short summary of the long-titled report goes like this:

We are quick to explain someone's behavior and hypothesize why they did what they did. Or, in the language of the prior chapter, we don't waste any time adopting a narrative that can fill the information gap. But—and perhaps not too surprisingly—research shows we aren't very accurate with our assumptions. What is more illuminating is that we err in a predictable direction.

Most of us systematically overweight personality, character, and preference in our explanations, while underweighting real-time constraints and context. In other words, if we see a dog gobble down a pile of collard greens, we'd likely assume the dog really loves them—or perhaps they were steeped in bacon fat. All the while, we overlook the details of the situation: the dog is hungry—very hungry—and eating collard greens beats an empty stomach.

Ross offers some explanations as to why we consistently make the same mistake.

Information asymmetry: We see our own constraints but not those of others.

When I once slammed on the brakes to avoid running a red light, I knew I had two screaming kids in the back seat. The driver behind me just assumed I was a bad driver, too absorbed in their podcast to think any more about it.

Salience bias: The person acting is more visually prominent than the situation.

A distracted barista fouling up an order and a coffee the "wrong" shade of brown is easy to see. It's more difficult to see her car, the one at her house, the one that wouldn't start that morning, the one that left her scrambling to get to work on time.

Cognitive efficiency: Personality explanation is simpler than situational analysis.

It's easy to label the barista a bad employee and move on. It's more difficult to consider all the possible situational factors. Maybe it's her car issues. Maybe there's new point-of-sale software that's printing order tickets differently. Maybe a new employee rearranged the cups and mislabeled containers—how many more possibilities can you name before you grow tired of the exercise?

There is a multitude of ways that the conditions a person is up against affect the actions they take, and a similar number of ways we can assign blame to the person instead of context. Making this realization is useful knowledge, but the greatest impact comes when we flip the script. When instead of merely observing context and constraints, we craft them ourselves.

So, while the "R" of Real-time Constraints may be the last component of our G.E.A.R. model, it is certainly not the least. And using it to our advantage requires being familiar with the two types of constraints: mechanical and contextual.

A modern home has lots of electrical outlets that look like "A" in the image that follows, some like "B," and even a few like "C." Different outlets for different plugs, different plugs for different appliances.

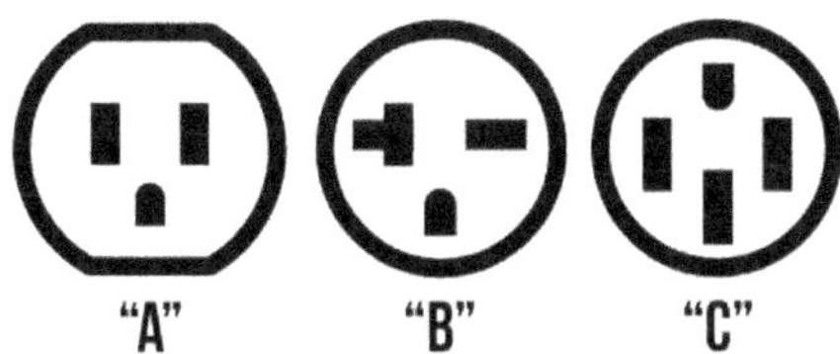

It wasn't always this way. In the early days of electrification, there was no clear standard. If you wanted to plug your 120-volt, 15-amp hair dryer into your 240-volt, 30-amp dryer outlet (basically four times the power), then well, have at it—Godspeed, my friend.

Thankfully, after who-knows-how-many house fires, electrocutions, and similar unpleasantries, we wised up. Now, it is nearly impossible to make that mistake, and the different plug types are examples of **mechanical constraints**. No matter how badly you might want to supercharge your hair dryer, the differences in outlet formats stand in your way.

In business, this is like software that locks down your computer until your timesheet is complete, or a form you can't submit until all required fields are completed.

It is the most brute-force, and perhaps the most reliable, way of getting the alignment we want. It is looking at all the options someone could choose and making all but the intended one unavailable. Unfortunately, eliminating every bad choice isn't always possible.

More common, but still very effective, is taking steps to raise the resistance one experiences when they veer off course. Like water or electricity, people tend to follow the path of least resistance. And part of the craft of business is making it easier for our teams to do the right thing than it is for them to do the wrong thing.

In the workplace, this may look like having pre-built templates for routine tasks, allowing employees to snap a photo of receipts versus elaborate expense reports, and standard file structures that are easier to copy than the work of inventing new ones. None of these eliminate bad options; they just make them more difficult to pursue.

There are thousands of different ways a business can influence its team by dialing up or down the resistance of completing certain tasks. And in Part 4, we'll consider many of them. More specifically, how to provide the reference points, navigation tools, and reconnaissance systems that help our crew find their way on the expedition of business.

It's the idea of the "employee experience journey." When a member of our team sets out to complete a task, what is their experience—the tools and platforms they interact with, the information they may need, and how easy or difficult it is to access?

It is along this journey that we find the constraints—and temptations—that may derail someone from doing their job as we intended. By identifying the pitfalls, eliminating them or adjusting the resistance, businesses can increase the chances that their staff picks the right path.

There is value in guardrails that put our teams hiking along narrow trails, but at some point, the path isn't as well-defined. Then we need the more nuanced category of **contextual constraints**.

—◆O◆—

A business owner faces the annual challenge of getting employees to complete a survey before their insurance renewal. Every year, email reminders are sent out; every year, it is mentioned during weekly meetings; every year, the owner resorts to pleading and threats to get 100% participation; and every year, somebody *"forgot"* or *"didn't have the time."*

This year, a big chart is displayed during their weekly "all-hands" meeting. The chart displays who has and who has not completed the survey. This year, everyone did so with weeks to spare.

The difference? A contextual constraint was introduced.

Many people are prone to ignore the important but not urgent. They lose things in their inbox or forget the reminders given during meetings. Far fewer are okay with having their name broadcast in a negative light.

This isn't about embarrassing someone; it's making a reasonable ask of a team of adults. And then making who has and who hasn't done the work public knowledge. It's acknowledging that our desire for competence and relatedness—part of our Tent of Comfort and the genetics of "G" in G.E.A.R.—is real. And when either is under threat, we will likely respond. A business leader who is a master of their craft understands how to leverage this tendency—and all the other undercurrents that pull on people—to help the team succeed.

The same business leader would understand that there are constraints and contexts they can influence, but there are also ones they cannot.

Multiple times in my career, I went through the following sequence. The performance of an employee starts to decline. I inquire and get an *"I'm sorry, I'll do better."* Maybe this repeats once more, but eventually further action is needed. I meet with the person again; they know…that I know…that they know…things are not going that great.

So, I have two options. I can follow my natural bias to explain everything via their personality, preference, or malice. Or I can dig more into the context and constraints they're facing.

"Are you okay?" "How are things outside of work?" "What's going on?" These are questions that we need to build up the trust to ask, but questions that often reveal what is truly to blame.

Once, I found that someone was driving Uber at night to help support his mother. The lack of sleep was killing his performance at work.

Another time an employee had recently been mugged and was dealing with the aftermath of that trauma.

There were many other conversations, but they all had the same theme. They were good employees, committed to their work and the company; nothing fundamental about them had changed—their situation had.

By having previously built the trust that was needed, we could get to the heart of what was going on; then we could craft a solution. By adjusting the "R" of our G.E.A.R. model, we could get closer to the alignment that—it turns out—both of us were looking for.

Some contexts are external to one's job, but contexts closer to the work are equally impactful.

Is someone being a *"difficult"* employee, or are they getting conflicting advice from two different superiors?

Are they *"unmotivated,"* or are they in a position with no clear benchmarks and limited feedback on their progress?

An employee may be *"irritable,"* but have they been doing the work of two people—trying to cover for a friend?

Often what we're yet to see reveals that our previous assumptions were wrong.

Once again, it's easy to assign blame to an individual when conditions are the problem. And while it's easy—and to some degree justifiable—to expect people to *"show up and do their job,"* part of the expedition of business is understanding the constraints that stand between our crew and a job well done.

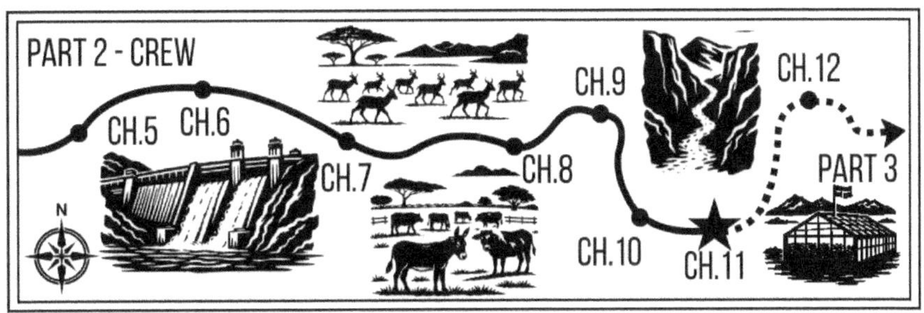

As leaders, we are designers of the organizations for which we are responsible. The craft of business centers around designs that are user-focused. And in our case, the users are the people we lead.

The better we can "put ourselves in the shoes" of those individuals, the more success we will find. Part of that exercise is understanding how external conditions and constraints impact individuals, and part is understanding the forces that work within each of them.

The G.E.A.R. model attempts to consider four undercurrents that drive human behavior, but it is not perfect. There will always be an element of uncertainty with people and how they respond to circumstances. But it is the ability to reduce that uncertainty that gives frameworks and models like G.E.A.R. their value.

The default when it comes to dealing with people is mimicry—assuming everyone is just like us and staying at Level 1 decisions on The Mountain of Why. The G.E.A.R. model gets us closer to the summit and making Level 5 decisions regarding people. It helps us to consider first principles about people and the foundations of their behavior—their genetic wiring and ingrained personalities, the stories they tell themselves and the realities of their situation. From there—a foundation that rarely changes—we can build our Pyramids of Decisions.

When we build them well, the work changes: teams stop feeling like cats to be herded and start feeling like Clydesdales—powerful, aligned, and waiting for someone to point them in the right direction.

At times, it seems as if the business is running itself. The dream of many leaders—a crew in perpetual motion, all moving toward the intended destination.

CHAPTER 12

HARNESSING ENERGY

It's 1812 in Philadelphia. Crowds gather daily at a house on the outskirts of the city. Each pays $5 admission—nearly a week's wages—to witness something extraordinary. Some people leave convinced they've seen the future; others leave confused but intrigued. Arguments erupt in taverns across the city. And the Pennsylvania legislature takes notice—officials conduct an inspection that will determine whether the state should fund this breakthrough.

Charles Redheffer was the source of the excitement, with his claim of building the impossible—a perpetual motion machine, one that could run forever without additional input. If true, the accomplishment would indeed be *"set it and forget it"* and as lucrative as spinning straw into gold.

Many business leaders have a similar vision—an organization that carries on producing and providing with no intervention necessary. Others may enjoy being part of the fray, playing their role and doing the work. But with few exceptions, we all would prefer a business where our input is more discretionary than mandatory.

Unfortunately, it was all a ruse. The belts that Charles Redheffer's machine supposedly turned were actually turning the machine itself. Turning the belts was an old man in the attic. He was discovered eating a slice of bread with one hand and turning the crank of the "impossible machine" with the other. The jig was up, and lunch was over.

Perpetual motion machines were then, and remain now, impossible. It's first-principles physics at work—mechanical energy is always lost to friction, and nothing can be 100% efficient. The park swing may sway for a long time once you give it a shove, or that golf ball may go hundreds of yards when you give it a whack, but eventually, friction, resistance, and gravity win out.

If we approach businesses in a mechanical fashion, the same unfortunate principles leave us giving the belts yet another crank or the swing another push. We spend years with frustration that's like hearing your car engine struggle on a cold morning. The second and third turns of the key produce results no different. You're so close to getting the organization running under its own power, but not quite yet. There's more coaxing to be done.

The problem begins when we set out to build a *"well-oiled machine,"* an organization that *"runs like clockwork"*—believing that we only need *"more horsepower"* and to *"fine-tune the operation,"* because then, once we *"grease the rails"* and *"streamline the process,"* we'll finally be *"firing on all cylinders."*

But again—the metaphors are wrong.

Cars eventually run out of gas, park swings stop unless we pump our legs, and businesses built like machines will struggle to run under their own power. The scientists are right, and Redheffer was wrong—one can't build a perpetual motion **machine**.

That doesn't mean the dream of a perpetual motion **business** is dead. But a new metaphor is needed, one that communicates a new and non-mechanical approach to business—an approach, ironically, driven by our G.E.A.R. model, and a way of seeing business less like a machine and more like an ecosystem.

Mechanical systems are forever in need of new input, while other types of systems can continue on in perpetuity.

The most common business size in the United States is one. It's the default size for a new business, and most continue that way for the duration.

Who can blame them? Building and managing a team is complicated and challenging work. Organizational charts, job descriptions, hiring, onboarding, compensation discussions, communication issues: they all go away in a company of one.

It's the difference between traveling solo and chaperoning a dozen high school students on a spring break trip abroad. Many feelings that we enjoy: autonomy, speed, progress, and not having to explain our thoughts—all are at risk when we add others to our party.

It raises the questions: Why do we even have a team? What is the purpose of having a crew come along with us on the expedition of business?

The conventional answers to this question are both familiar and easy to find. Type "*Why do companies have employees?*" into the web, and you'll get something like the following—my results from searching the same question:

"Businesses have employees for several fundamental reasons:

Getting work done *- Most businesses need more labor, skills, and time than one person can provide.*

Specialization *- Different roles require different expertise.*

Continuous operations *- Employees enable businesses to operate beyond the capacity of the owner. Longer hours, multiple shifts, and customers across different time zones: all made possible by employees.*

Growth and leverage *- Employees are how businesses scale. Employment is a trade: businesses get the time, skills, and effort they need to operate and grow, while employees get compensation, stability, and often benefits they couldn't easily obtain on their own.*

Focused leadership *- Having employees lets owners and executives focus on strategy, growth, and high-level decisions rather than being consumed by day-to-day operations."*

These aren't irrelevant, and any business not leveraging them has much room for improvement. Unfortunately, that improvement only gets one to the baseline, the default of business thinking and strategy.

It's the mechanical approach of deconstructing a business into its parts, pieces, and their benefits: production, leverage, redundancy, and precision. Then assembling them in the "optimal" way. And like all machines, it produces an output greater than we could alone, a business capable of more than a solitary individual.

But we can do better.

We can move away from being beholden to the never-ending refueling, repairing, and inevitable breakdowns. And doing so requires a deeper examination of the question: *"Who are the people within our organization—and what lies within them?"*

Are they gears, drives, and sprockets? And thus—like our stubborn car on a cold morning—are they a machine with a persistent demand for our direction and external energy?

Or is a team more dynamic—individuals with agency, drive, and ambition?

If so, they are more akin to seeds carried by the wind that land upon fertile ground, nurtured and shaped by their surroundings until they grow large enough to shape their environment themselves—and thus the beginning of an upward cycle of producing and growing until an ecosystem of abundance is created.

The latter is what most business leaders are in search of—yet it is rarely found.

The mechanical analogies of old can't create the wonders of self-perpetuation. That requires a team that is not merely a source of leverage, but a crew that becomes the ever-driving force within an organization.

We began Part 2 by arguing for working with, and not against, the natural way of things. Like gravity, wind, and the sun, the people of our organizations can be a renewable source of energy under the right conditions.

A few years ago, my wife and I took a trip to Iceland. As the name implies, this was not a tropical vacation. Though not as glacial as it sounds, Iceland is cold. And for part of the year, the sun only makes a brief and shallow arc above the horizon.

Given such, we were surprised to find ourselves eating at a restaurant that was all things tomato: tomato soup, tomato pie, tomato juice, and even tomato ice cream. And all local tomatoes, grown onsite, only a few hours' drive from the Arctic Circle.

Plane delivery is too expensive and ship delivery is too slow, so Friðheimar Farm stepped in to fill Icelanders' demand for fresh tomatoes.

More greenhouse than farm, the facility looks like a futuristic colony on Mars. The orange glow of grow lamps illuminates the translucent structure and shines on unnaturally long vines growing from tubes of soil-like material. A computerized system waters and fertilizes the plants. Carbon dioxide is pumped in to speed up growth, and hydronic heaters keep the temperature just right even on the coldest Icelandic nights. It's a near miracle of engineering: one made financially feasible by Iceland's bounty of geothermal heat and power.

In contrast, I grew up in North Carolina. Summer gardens were the norm, and tomatoes seemed to be a prerequisite—and it's easy to see why. Tomatoes are native to a similar climate—western South America—and thus they were "right at home" in the backyard.

Just a handful of plants would have my family with more tomatoes than we knew what to do with by late summer. Tomato sandwiches, succotash, salsa, tomato sauce, canning, freezing, and a roadside table with a "free" sign were common solutions.

In Iceland, the question is: *"Are we going to have enough tomatoes?"* Back home, the question was: *"What are we going to do with all these tomatoes?"*

It's the difference between the products of a machine and the abundance of nature at work—and a lesson for business leaders.

Fittingly—in the right climate—tomatoes are perennial plants, the type that returns year after year: budding, flowering, and fruiting when the conditions are right. One could even say that they are perpetual. But they are not the machine that Charles Redheffer was obsessed with, and it's that freedom from being a machine that allows the abundance they produce.

It's the result that business leaders are looking for: moving on from cranking, fueling, and pleading with the machines of our businesses, and arriving at a perpetual source of energy, growth, and productivity at the heart of our organizations.

The unlock is the same in business as it is in North Carolina or Iceland. People and tomato plants—though obviously different in complexity—are both living organisms, and each needs an environment where they can thrive.

My operations director—the one who was ready to quit—had all the potential in the world but found himself in the wrong conditions. What was missing wasn't money or recognition; it was relatedness and certainty—part of our Tent of Comfort and two of the five desires we all have to some degree. His role had him working in isolation, and without clear metrics, he had no way of knowing if he was succeeding. Some may have managed okay in similar circumstances, but he was wilting.

Through conversations with him, I knew his passions and favorite activities involved being part of a team. He was currently without one. He was young and felt insecure in the professional world. Understandably, a lack of certainty was harder on him than it may be on someone more experienced.

The fix didn't require more compensation or a new title. He started getting involved in more projects involving a team. Together we built a dashboard that tracked the metrics he was responsible for—numbers by which he could benchmark his performance. It all improved his environment. The better the conditions, the faster he grew.

His case is easy to highlight because the change was drastic—from quitting to thriving—but there's better performance to be had from everyone with the right changes.

A salesperson's performance starts to dip. She is high on the openness scale and growing bored with the same routines, same pitch, and same clients. She's given the first crack at new product launches and untested markets. The change energizes her, and the solutions she uncovers become standard practice for peers who preferred more repetition in their days.

An accountant is sharp but rarely speaks up in meetings. Thinking on the spot isn't his strong suit, and he is low on the assertiveness scale. His manager starts sending agendas 48 hours in advance. Now, he has time to collect his thoughts beforehand and becomes a valuable contributor to discussions.

My office administrator was once frustrated by the lack of progress she was making on projects. I pointed out the "do not disturb" button on her phone—and that while ideally, she would field every call, I was okay with her using her discretion as to when she needed time to focus. It was a small effort but had a big impact up and down our G.E.A.R. model.

As to the "G" of genetics, she now had more autonomy over her time, better certainty over expectations, and improved relatedness—knowing that I was on her side with this issue. The change also provided her with more opportunities to focus on projects, which kept her more engaged and feeling more competent. The latter was very welcome since she had the "E" (enduring trait) of industriousness and was energized by completing tasks.

Her "A" (adopted narrative) about not answering calls and the consequences thereof was shifted from *"I'll get in trouble"* to *"It's expected that*

I need time to focus on other work." And the "R" (real-time constraint) of a ringing phone interrupting her thinking occurred far less.

None of these required dramatic interventions—only minor adjustments to the climate. They were changes that raised each person's energy level, improved the morale of the team, and compounded into an organization that built and kept momentum.

In business, the climate and the terrain in which our crew operates is what we architect as leaders. From the decisions we make to the leadership we provide, part of the craft of business is using tools like our G.E.A.R. model—as well as the systems and structures we will cover in Part 4—to create an environment where our teams can naturally grow, flourish, and produce.

❖

How a business leader views their team dictates the success of an organization. When we move beyond the idea of people as mechanical components—ones intended only to play their part in a machine created by others—the business changes from the inside out.

When we see people as living organisms in need of the right conditions to thrive, our teams can become the lifeblood of an organization. People no longer just complete tasks; they create ways to improve processes; they solve not only their problems but help others with theirs.

Their work is no longer a drain but energizes them. They enter "flow" states instead of grinding through. One person's breakthrough inspires the team, and success builds momentum that compounds.

The business may not become a true perpetual motion machine. But it can become what most business leaders want: an organization that is more self-managing. And one that makes the efforts and inputs of its leaders more discretionary than mandatory.

It's why we involve other people, the crew we need on the expedition of business—to do the work we can't, to discover the solutions that we overlook, and to ease the load when the burden gets heavy.

It's why we work to get everyone aligned, their G.E.A.R.s turning in the intended direction. It's why we architect the conditions our people need to thrive. And it's why we unlock the perpetual source of energy we can harness to propel our business forward.

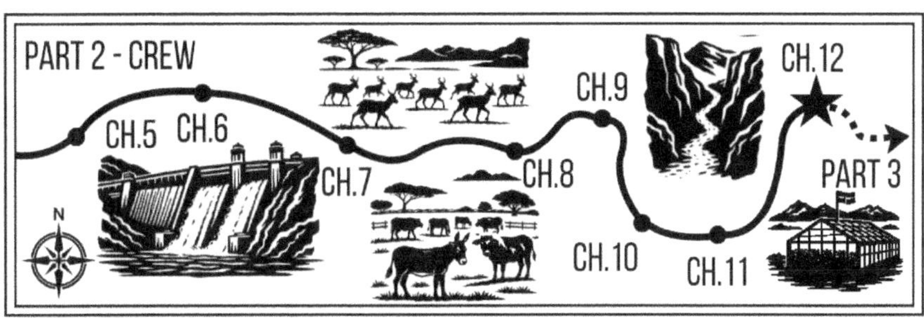

As we said at the end of Part 1, reinforced in Chapter 7, and repeat here yet again because of its importance: the craft of business is one where people are the medium. And like any craft, the further we climb up The Mountain of Why—from mimicry, past frameworks, and to the first principles that govern the quality of our work—the better our decisions become.

The G.E.A.R. model is a tool for that climb. It is a way to manage the complexity of the genetic wiring, enduring traits, adopted narratives, and real-time constraints that drive the people on our crew, and an opportunity to build our Pyramids of Decisions upon solid foundations rather than questionable assumptions.

When we get it right, when we manage to make decisions that are neither awash in complexity nor simplified until important nuance is lost, something shifts. Our organization stops feeling like a machine in constant need of fuel. We begin to tap into its potential and the energy that has been looking to be put to work. Alignment becomes possible—not by forcing people into line, but because what the organization needs and what its people are driven to pursue finally point the same direction.

The business moves closer to the perpetual source of momentum that most leaders are searching for. We stop looking for better parts or trying to put the old ones in a different order. We stop seeing people as parts altogether and see them for what they are: individuals with agency, ready to learn, grow, and perform under the right conditions.

But understanding our crew and what drives them is only half the craft. Knowledge alone doesn't create the environment in which people thrive. Someone must make that happen. Someone must take these principles and turn them into decisions. Someone must use those decisions to architect an organization where potential becomes performance. That someone is a leader.

And unlike the potter who is separate from the clay, or the carpenter who is apart from the wood, a business leader shares the same human nature as the people they lead. What we ask of our crew, leadership asks of us—and then some.

Do we provide the clarity and order that keeps our organization on course? Do we display the warmth to be trusted and the strength to be followed? And are we willing to bear the cost that real leadership demands?

Part 3 is about answering those questions; it's the next leg of our journey, and it starts now.

PART 3

LEADER

CHAPTER 13

BUSINESS LEADERSHIP DEFINED

Most craftsmen enjoy the luxury of being independent from the medium in which they work. A master potter is certainly not a piece of clay, nor is a master watchmaker a series of springs and gears. The greatest of authors has control of a fictional world that is set apart from the day-to-day life of the writer.

The leader of a business has no such luxury. They and the people they lead share the same human nature, the same world of possibilities, and the same reality of constraints.

A piece of leather doesn't care what kind of example the tanner sets. Paint goes onto a canvas the same way no matter who holds the brush. When people are the medium we work with, it's a different story. The relationship is reflexive. The leader has influence over the behavior of their followers, and the behavior of their followers has influence over the actions the leader must take.

It's a relationship that can create an upward spiral. A good leader produces more engaged followers; more engaged followers generate business growth and organizational momentum. And managing and guiding both are new challenges that force a leader to grow and become even better. Yet, when it goes poorly, a downward spiral—one of chaos and disorder—can quickly emerge.

It's no wonder then that every year businesses spend billions on leadership development, leadership training, emerging leader programs, and books and courses by the thousands. As a result, we get swept up in the river of opinions as to what leadership is, and it's hard to keep our heads above water.

"Leadership is influence — nothing more, nothing less."—*John C. Maxwell*

"Leadership is the art of getting someone else to do something you want done because he wants to do it."— Dwight *Eisenhower*

"As we look ahead ... leaders will be those who empower others."—*Bill Gates*

"Leadership is not about being in charge. It is about taking care of those in your charge."—*Simon Sinek*

"[Great] Leaders display a powerful mixture of personal humility and indomitable will."—*Jim Collins*

Well, there you go—*"Leadership is this, but it's also that, and never forget the other, but don't use too much of the same."*

Between all that we hear about leadership, accounts of famous historical leaders, news coverage of modern-day leaders, and our own direct experience of leadership—well, soon it becomes reminiscent of the blind men and the elephant.

One man feels the side of the animal and says, *"An elephant is like a wall."* Another grasps the tusk and says, *"No, it's like a spear."* One more holds the trunk: *"It's like a snake."* The next feels the leg: *"It's like a tree."* The one after him touches the ear: *"It's like a fan."* And the last grabs the tail: *"It's like a rope."*

We often land in the same spot with leadership: we're lost until we have a view of the whole.

When we try and cobble together all the different ways leadership is described, we can easily miss the whole for all the parts.

An elephant is an elephant. Maybe one is a little bigger than another, has a few more wrinkles, or eats a few less peanuts, but it is hard to mistake an elephant for anything else. Leadership is far less a matter of fact—and that's okay. We don't all have to manifest leadership in the same way. But until we have a solid understanding of what leadership is about—a clear view of the elephant—we have no foundation of first principles on which to build our own version.

The definition of leadership that we craft and the type of leader we become on the expedition of business are different for all of us. But the journey often begins from a similar place. Our ascent of The Mountain of Why back in Chapter 2 ended at the summit—Level 5 decisions of first principles. On the way there we climbed past the ideas of using frameworks—both generic and tailored to our business. And then we passed heuristics built on the anecdotal evidence from our past experiences and those of others. But we started off in the same place we all start our leadership journey: Level 1, mimicry, and taking after those leaders who have had an impact on us.

—◇—

I played basketball in high school, and before my junior year, we got a new head coach. At that point, to say our team was bad would be putting it generously. Even as a 15-year-old, it was evident our program was rudderless and destined for the failures that the scoreboard often made obvious. Our new coach had a record of success, of building winning teams, of results far better than what we had recently achieved.

It didn't take long to realize things were now different.

Summer workouts were no longer optional. Practices were now two and three hours long—versus the prior 90 minutes. Kids hamming it up in the classroom were quickly booted off the team, and there was a near maniacal obsession with the execution of offensive plays and defensive schemes.

Put simply: things were intense, very intense—and I hated it.

It was the equivalent of a movie scene where a young soldier suddenly finds themself in army boot camp, being berated at every turn by a drill sergeant who surely slept on a bare piece of plywood and bathed in icy streams. If there's an equivalent of going AWOL in sports, I was trying to find it—until our first game.

This is the part of the story where I'm supposed to say how improved we were, and that our better performance made all the blood, sweat, and tears worth it. But that's not what happened.

At halftime, we were way behind. If anything, we were playing worse than the year before. Our new coach entered the locker room, and for the next three or four minutes, we bore witness to a human volcano.

For some reason—perhaps in a nod to the plywood bed of his drill sergeant doppelgänger—he tortured himself by wearing thick knitted sweaters to games. While he unloaded on us about the innumerable mistakes we had made in the first half, I watched in near disbelief as with every shouted word, his neck—bright red and dripping with sweat—expanded and stretched the collar of that night's sweater wider and wider. His neck eventually reached such a size that any visible jawline was gone, and what sat above his shoulders was a bulging mountaintop of fury and anger.

Again, it was intense.

Then something surprising happened. The hurricane of criticism abated. The red washed from his face, his jawline reemerged, and his sweater collar shrank back to normal. The next words from his mouth were, "*Okay, here's how we get better in the second half.*" What followed was the most instructional and motivational ten minutes of coaching I had ever received. I no longer hated it.

Two years later, the team was winning more, I was a better player, and the volcano was long dormant. As I left the court for the last time, I got a hug from him and an "*I love you man.*" I responded in kind, but I was in disbelief at the transformation our relationship had undergone.

We all have had a similar experience. Maybe it played out in real life, or perhaps in a story or film. Maybe it was a family member, neighbor, or coach—teacher, boss, politician, or a historical figure. But somewhere along the line, we all have had memorable encounters with leaders and felt the benefits of effective, even if imperfect, leadership.

Think for a second: Who do you think of as a leader? How does that example shape your views on leadership? If those leaders were stern and direct, do you find yourself being the same? Perhaps they were more nurturing, patient, and inspiring—is that now your leadership style? When someone is out of line, do you follow their lead as to whether accountability is swift and public or more measured and private?

Chances are we can chart a course from the leaders we are today, back to the leadership we've experienced. Again, that's where most of us start our leadership journey, the base of The Mountain of Why. And how we craft our Pyramids of Decisions becomes hard to separate from those leaders who have influenced us.

Doing as they did is a reasonable approach, but far from the best.

I am not my high school basketball coach, nor am I Abraham Lincoln or Joan of Arc. The style and method of leadership that worked for them may very well not work for me. Part of the challenge is that business leadership is a unique type of leadership, different from the challenges faced by leaders that we may be tempted to mimic.

How exactly they differ comes down to two of the most fundamental questions in business. What are the decisions to be made? And who is responsible for making them?

As we'll soon see, some leadership scenarios are filled with possibilities and rich with nuance and decisions to be made, while others are more of a controlled environment—where there are fewer variables. In other words, one can find a leader in situations of both high and low **complexity**.

Equally diverse are the expectations we have of those being led. Are followers allowed—or even required—to operate with a high degree of independence? Or are they made to *"fall in line"* and do as they're told? The answer dictates the level of **agency** followers are intended to have—a short way of saying their ability to make decisions and act independently.

It is those two variables—situational complexity and agency of follow-ers—that create dimensions on which different leadership examples can be charted. Having a complete view of that chart gives us a better aim for our leadership, and a more usable definition of business leadership.

Every few weeks my youngest daughter gets to act as "circle time leader" at preschool. It's a role composed of haphazardly banging a plastic baton against a board of letters while her classmates sing their "ABCs." She is without a doubt the "leader," but it's a role of low complexity and low agency—one of the four quadrants that leadership roles can fall into.

Fortunately, there is not a tendency for business leaders to mimic "lead-ers" in this quadrant. Parade leaders, jury foremen, or those *"willing and able to serve"* by sitting in an exit-row seat: despite the noise they add to the leadership conversation, it's clear their role is mostly ceremoni-al—leading compliant followers through an exercise of low complexity.

My high school basketball coach, and other coaches like him, may find their leadership style more often mimicked—I certainly have to an extent.

Some of my copying went well: motivating my team by the challenge of the work itself, spreading the idea that "winners" do the little things well, and having my team's back if one of them was on the receiving end of a "hard foul" by a client.

Some of my copying was a disaster: being too stern and direct—bringing a well-meaning employee who challenged my authority to tears, defaulting to putting in extra hours when I was unsure what else to do, and keeping a stiff upper lip too often—letting employees see the person behind the leader too infrequently.

Sometimes we learn the hard way, and that's how I came to understand that following his lead completely in business was a mistake.

He operated in the quadrant of low complexity and high agency. Sports are designed to be less complex than the real world. The playing area is a defined space and the rules are made clear. Games have set conditions for when they are to end and how a winner is determined. The business leader does not share the luxury of such defined conditions. But they do share the need for their followers to act with a high degree of agency. In sports and in business, players and employees are asked to consider the current situation and to make their own decisions as to what actions will benefit the team.

However, just because a leader shares the scenario of high complexity does not mean they are an example worth following.

———◦———

Around the same time my basketball coach made his fiery entrance into my life, the world as a whole had recently witnessed another spectacle of spewing hot gases and energy unimaginable. For almost 18 months in 1996 and 1997, the Hale-Bopp Comet passed close enough to Earth that it became a familiar addition to the night sky.

Unfortunately, what was considered nothing more than *"cool"* by most observers was deadly serious to Marshall Applewhite, one of the most notorious "leaders" of the 1990s. Some 20 years prior, Applewhite had founded the Heaven's Gate cult, using his persuasion and leadership abilities to grow the group to more than 200 members.

If part of a leader's job is to rally their followers around certain beliefs, Applewhite excelled. He did so despite having some—to put it mildly—unorthodox beliefs. The core tenet of Heaven's Gate was that followers could become immortal extraterrestrial beings by rejecting their human nature and living a monastery-like existence.

The discovery of the Hale-Bopp comet in 1995 marked the beginning of the end for Applewhite and his devout followers. In their minds, the comet was providing cover for a UFO that was following closely behind—one that was finally arriving to take their souls to another *"level of existence above human."*

On March 26, 1997, the bodies of 39 active cult members, including Applewhite, were discovered. Under his leadership, the group had planned their suicide to coincide with the comet making its closest pass to Earth.

Jim Jones, Charles Manson, David Koresh, and most recently Applewhite: these are names synonymous with cults and leadership gone awry. When one sets out to define "leadership" and what it means to be a leader, these names—understandably—do not come to mind.

However, one can't have it both ways. If the definition of leadership includes "influence," "persuasion," "rallying people to action," "getting results," and—even if in their misguided views—"taking care of your team," then cases like Applewhite can't be dismissed. They highlight how definitions of leadership are often incomplete, and how even a leader that is "successful" in a world of high complexity is not someone we care to mimic on the expedition of business.

But we don't have to look to the extremes of cult leaders to understand why. It's often hiding in plain sight in the business world itself.

The executive who builds a culture of loyal compliance, where disagreement is quietly punished and "alignment" is code for "do as I say." The founder whose vision is so tightly held that every decision, no matter how small, must pass through them.

These aren't fringe cases. If we look at enough companies, we'll find leaders who check every box of the popular definitions: they influence, they persuade, they rally people to action, and they get results. But like Applewhite, they do so by suppressing the agency of their followers rather than cultivating it.

And for a while, it works. But underneath the surface, trouble is brewing. The individuals being led stop thinking for themselves; they've learned it isn't welcome. Those who need freer rein to do their best work leave. Those who stay grow comfortable being told what to do—their potential wasted. The leader becomes a bottleneck they themselves can never escape, mistaking exhaustion for indispensability.

It all holds together until it doesn't. The economy slows, a key individual leaves, or the leader simply burns out, and the organization—having never developed the capacity to think for itself—collapses under the weight. Not unlike many cults, it seems to work right up until the moment it falls apart.

Thankfully, there are far healthier examples in the world of leadership. Leaders who navigated highly complex situations while not only allowing, but actually depending on, a high degree of agency from their followers—leaders whose concern for human life (and spacecraft) was genuine.

⸺◇⸺

You have likely seen the movie and may remember the scene—actor Ed Harris sporting a crew cut, stern expression, and white vest with insignia, stands before a crowded room of engineers and scientists.

On the chalkboard behind him is one large circle representing Earth and a smaller circle to the upper right representing the moon. Between the circles is an "X," the current location of three astronauts aboard the damaged Apollo 13 spacecraft. Not far from the first "X," Ed Harris draws another one—the location at which the astronauts will run out of power, oxygen, and anything else they'd need to return safely.

Harris deems this *"unacceptable."* He then draws a dashed line from the second "X" to the designated landing site on Earth. The mission simplified: find a way to get those three astronauts from there to here and—famously—*"Failure is not an option."*

The scene is rich with Hollywood drama, and undoubtedly some liberties were taken with exact words and events. But the situation in which Ed Harris's real-life character, Gene Kranz, found himself on the evening of April 13, 1970, needed no exaggeration. Kranz was the flight director of the Apollo 13 mission—a role he defined simply: *"In my line of work there is neither ambiguity [nor] a higher authority. It is go or no go. And I am accountable for the mission."*

After an explosion ripped through part of the spacecraft, Kranz was now accountable for returning three astronauts safely to Earth. Astronauts who were 200,000 miles away, short on water, food, heat, and power, and with reduced control of their engines and steering. It would take his entire team, all the resources at his disposal, and a master class in leadership to bring home their troubled space expedition.

Thankfully, Kranz's leadership wasn't theatrical speeches. It was fast decision-making in the face of incomplete information. It was clear delegation, resource management, and creating space for strategic thinking.

In the end, Kranz and his team successfully navigated the astronauts back safely. It was an extraordinary feat and an example of leadership that—though of higher intensity—is more aligned with the leadership we aspire to in business.

Leveraging a team, utilizing expertise and experience, providing clarity, order, and resources to accomplish a goal well beyond the capabilities of any one individual: watching Kranz during the Apollo 13 crisis would give one more than just the tail or the tusk of the leadership elephant. His results were remarkable.

Unfortunately—and in a dark way—so were Applewhite's. It creates the pressure to distinguish between the two, as we know they are not the same.

They shared circumstances of high complexity. Applewhite was trying to make sense of life and to answer "*Why are we here?*" for his followers, while Kranz had the immense technical challenges of space travel and faced the near-infinite combination of possible failures among only a handful of possible solutions.

However, they differ dramatically in the agency they wanted from their followers. While Applewhite, like other cult leaders, depended on the loyal obedience of his followers, Kranz needed his team to make decisions only they could make.

These two factors, situational complexity and the agency of followers, help dampen the noise around leadership. They also help define exactly what it means to be a business leader.

Business leadership is specifically about leading individuals of high agency in a situation of high complexity.

The business leader who demands blind obedience fails because they bottleneck decisions and waste the capabilities of their team. Eliminating the challenge of having followers with agency comes at the cost of an organization's greatest assets: the talents and capabilities of their people.

The business leader who avoids complexity condemns themselves to irrelevance. Business isn't basketball, and it's certainly not "circle time." No worthwhile problem involving market opportunities, innovation, leading a team, or any other frontier where businesses compete can be reduced to the simple. Both high complexity and high agency are required, and that combination is what makes business leadership its own distinct craft.

It is not necessarily a mistake to mimic some traits of a leader from any of our quadrants. But the further one gets from the high complexity, high agency world of business leadership, the more likely it is that the success of others will not translate.

As leaders, the question often hangs over us: "*What is leadership?*" We tend to start with a Level 1 decision of mimicry. As time goes on, we get a few lessons under our belt—like not to parrot your high school sports coach. Next, we move on to Level 2 decisions, heuristics of what normally works.

Books, training, and courses gave me a better grip on communication, motivation, and pacing myself and the team. And they can get us to Level 3: frameworks. Blending different ones together may move us to Level 4 of synthesized strategies. However, if we're aiming for the top of the mountain, Level 5 of first principles, then our journey can't begin without the end in mind.

And the aim of business leadership is specifically about leading individuals of high agency in a situation of high complexity. No other type of leadership will bring us to the destination we seek on the expedition of business.

Understanding the four possible complexity-agency quadrants is the type of insight that helps us master the craft of business. When we see the nuance that exists in leadership, we can begin to build better Pyramids of Decisions for our organization, but also for how we approach leadership.

Any of those pyramids must have our ultimate objective at their peak. But unfortunately, in the world of business advice, "effective leadership" seems to be an ever-changing goal. As leaders, the list of what we are to be, display, and provide seems to be never-ending. It's exactly in these moments that clarity requires staking our flag in the first principles that we hold to be true.

In the next chapter, we craft those from a core idea: that leadership is a means, not an end. And by distilling the performance of Gene Kranz and other leaders of high-agency individuals, we find there are two things business leaders must provide to leverage their team and manage the complexity: clarity and order.

CHAPTER 14

WHAT LEADERS PROVIDE

Every army has its general, every ship its captain, and every orchestra its conductor. Any government has a chief executive—a president, governor, or mayor. Sports teams may have dozens of coordinators and assistants, but there is only one head coach.

Leaders and leadership seem universal, woven into the fabric of society. As such, it's easy to assume that leadership just is, that any group of people comes by default with someone to lead them. And they will do so, either to the heights of success or to the depths of failure.

In some business circles, an infatuation has emerged; leadership is treated as a subjective art form. Judged by business media, academics, and consultants, it's rare that someone is just "a leader." Instead, we hear of visionary leaders, charismatic leaders, servant leaders, purpose-driven leaders, empathetic leaders, and disruptive leaders.

This is not necessarily a bad thing. Leadership is deeply ingrained in society; most of our celebrated historical figures were leaders, and leaders do have an outsized impact on the performance of the organizations they lead. So, it's understandable that many people want to understand leadership better and become leaders themselves. However, let us not lose the purpose of business leadership in the mystique:

Business leadership is a means, not an end. It is a strategic choice in the service of business goals.

We can have a business without leadership. I don't recommend it, but some current and many more failed businesses have unknowingly given it a try. The decision to instill, foster, or hire effective leadership is a choice. It's an option, albeit a good one, to support the goals of an organization.

Peter Drucker once said, "*Leadership is defined by results, not attributes.*" Unfortunately, business leaders are drowning in a sea of attributes. Like the list of quotes on "what leadership is" that opened the prior chapter, there's a seemingly unending catalog of traits we're told we need to exemplify as leaders:

Confidence, decisiveness, integrity, charisma, vision, courage, resilience, discipline, accountability, empathy, adaptability, patience, humility, curiosity, self-awareness, authenticity, composure, discernment, resourcefulness, tenacity, magnanimity, equanimity, circumspection, temperance, forbearance, dispassion, and whatever the hell "negative capability" is.

Developing a more useful definition of leadership requires moving away from the overwhelming task of putting these 27 attributes on display and toward Drucker's yardstick of "*results.*" However, as discussed in Part 1, "*results*" can be deceiving.

Richard Fuld was once known as the "Gorilla of Wall Street." Having a reputation for being tough and commanding, he consistently produced stellar returns for 14 years. And by the summer of 2007, he had his firm more profitable than ever. A little over a year later, the firm, Lehman Brothers, would be bankrupt and a poster child for the Global Financial Crisis. Fuld's results came with a boatload of risk, leverage, and short-term thinking. So, at what point was Fuld a great leader? And at what point was he a terrible one?

I once had a job selling commercial heating and air conditioning equipment. In the years prior to my arrival, the company was a money-making machine. Unfortunately, they soon lost the contract to sell their most profitable line of equipment.

The years that followed were a steady decline as the company shrank to the size of the owner and a handful of support staff. Was my boss a great leader during the profitable years, and then a terrible leader during the down years? Or were they mostly the same all the way through?

Elizabeth Holmes (Theranos), Adam Neumann (WeWork), Sam Bankman-Fried (FTX), Jeff Skilling (Enron): recent business history is full of "incredible" leaders producing "remarkable" results. Often, reality overtakes both their attributes and performance. And we're left with fallen idols and more noise about effective leadership.

To lessen that noise, let's lean on a framework established in Chapter 4: the **Levers of Control**. As we covered then, the most effective actions of leaders have one or more of four outcomes as their aim:

1. Amassing energy.

2. Unifying its direction.

3. Lowering the resistance of the tasks at hand.

4. Maximizing the yield a business receives for its work.

If leadership is a means, and not an end—if leadership is not purely attributes nor results, if leadership is a choice in service of a business's goals, then good leadership represents a strategy. And the goal of that strategy is to move one or more of the four Levers of Control—and thus the business—in a positive direction.

Leadership implies having followers, a group of people over whom a leader has a degree of influence. As discussed in Part 2, that group of followers—our crew—is the main competitive advantage of most businesses. And they are an organization's core source of **energy**, potentially creating a chain reaction that a business leader must work to guide, direct, and **unify**. Thus, effective leadership maximizes the energy of followers and unifies that energy in an intended direction.

Fortunately, we already have a developed framework for how to align people—the leveraging of genetic wiring, enduring traits, adopted narratives, and real-time constraints that compose our G.E.A.R. model from Part 2.

Leadership done well makes use of those same human tendencies, using them to create an environment where followers can prosper. Part of crafting those conditions is understanding what influences people on an individual level; part is understanding the dynamics of their team's immediate surroundings. But effective leadership requires seeing an even larger context. And again, we find ourselves with one trait of humans that is particularly important.

As stated in Chapter 8, for most of human history our survival depended on being part of a group. The healthier and more stable the group we were a part of, the better chance we had of not only surviving but thriving.

Today, material abundance and technology make it easier to operate solo. But our tendency to operate in small groups remains.

On average, a business in the United States has 24 employees, and the vast majority have fewer than 50 people—roughly the size of the bands our most distant ancestors lived in. Within larger companies, workforces are split into divisions, territories, studios, and the like—an effort that returns the group we feel a part of to a size familiar to humans throughout time.

As a result, we and our teams find ourselves in a parallel mindset to those that came much before us. And that is the larger context an effective leader must grasp.

There is an "*Us*"—our small team or crew, operating amongst a larger backdrop. Our surroundings may be the company we are a small part of, the marketplace we operate in, or the world at large, but it is "*Us*" against what is "*out there*"—the external, a world less familiar and of higher uncertainty.

And while effective leaders successfully manage the internal dynamics of individuals and the teams they make up, leaders also stand in that gap—the void between the group they lead and the larger world they must navigate. More specifically:

Leadership provides clarity in the face of external confusion and order in the face of internal chaos.

And in the process, they give their teams more of the conditions they need to thrive—including better certainty as to what comes next.

*It's fundamentally human to feel part of an "Us" amidst
the uncertainty of what's "Out there".
A good leader provides clarity when uncertainty abounds.*

In March 1865, Abraham Lincoln gave his second inaugural address. He was governing a country mired in civil war and dealing with a population deeply divided over slavery, retribution against *"the other side,"* and the uncertain path forward. In his speech, he spoke to the commonality of us all, our shared humanity, and our shared faults.

"With malice toward none, with charity for all, with firmness in the right as God gives us to see the right, let us strive on to finish the work we are in, to bind up the nation's wounds, to care for him who shall have borne the battle and for his widow and his orphan, to do all which may achieve and cherish a just and lasting peace among ourselves and with all nations."

In 1997, Jeff Bezos wrote one of his first shareholder letters. The internet was in its early days, Amazon showed promise but was losing money, and investors were confused about what their "bookstore" was doing:

"This is Day 1 for the Internet.... We will make bold investment decisions in light of long-term market leadership considerations rather than short-term profitability considerations or short-term Wall Street reactions.... [We will have a] relentless focus on customer satisfaction."

Two different times, very different contexts, but both messages were effective leadership on display.

For Lincoln, his message was clear: retribution is not our path; we want healing and peace—at home and abroad. There was no overpromising, just clarity on direction and intent.

For Bezos, he set the path forward: long-term over short-term, market leadership over Wall Street, and customer satisfaction above all. He gave no guarantee that it would work, just clarity in how they were going to play the game.

In both, clarity was provided and confusion was laid to rest. It was made clear how the "Us" of their groups would proceed—both internally and externally.

These are the types of statements and proclamations that find their way into leadership lore. They provide excellent examples of the "end" for which leadership can serve as the "means." But unfortunately, they come with a risk—one that we as leaders should not fall victim to.

Using examples like Lincoln or Bezos raises the idea that leadership done well is dependent on the number of followers and the drama of the moment.

I disagree.

The warehouse manager who, when facing COVID-induced supply chain chaos in 2021, gathered their team and said: "*We can't control the delays. Here's what we CAN control: we'll triple-check every order, communicate proactively with every customer, and protect our reputation for reliability—that's our path through this.*"

A client of mine who puts together an internal annual report to tell the story of the past year and the plan for the year to come—a document they use to reaffirm their ultimate goal, their core purpose as a business, the values they hold dear, and to provide recent examples of team members acting on those values.

These too are examples of leadership done well.

Every leader on the expedition of business has an opportunity to stand before their team and answer the most important questions. Where are we going? Why are we going? When are we going? What do we need to get there? Who do we need to get there? And how are we going to get there?

With that opportunity comes the chance to address the confusion and uncertainty that the future often brings. It is a moment to distill the future down to a clear and concise path forward—to stand in the gap between "*Us*" and what's "*out there*." Regardless of size and scale, doing so is one half of leadership done well, one of the two conditions leaders must provide: clarity in the face of external confusion.

However, having a clear vision of the future is only one wing of the airplane. We're doomed without the second: creating and maintaining order within.

Like most Americans, I spend part of most days driving. It's me behind the wheel of a 3,000-pound machine, rolling down the highway at 70 miles per hour. I do so in the glaring sun, in the rain, at night, and in the fog—alongside drivers of nearly all ages, experience, and dexterity.

The fact that this scenario doesn't end in disaster more often, that the average driver is only involved in three to four crashes in their lifetime, is remarkable. It's also a product of order.

As an American, the driver's side door is on the left side of my car. Once inside, I find the gas pedal on the right and the brake to the left of it. In front of me is the instrument panel. Though it might differ from car to car, I'm sure to find a speedometer and a fuel gauge. If my car is in the shop and I have a loaner—no problem—all of these remain the same, and I'll be on my way in no time.

Once on the road, things are equally familiar: red stop signs at each intersection, double lines when I can't pass, dashed lines when I can, green means go, red means stop, yellow means see if a cop is watching, and speed limit signs to slow me down.

Of course, if I violate these rules, I might spend part of my drive with blue lights in my mirror and facing a fine—or worse.

All of this is order: clarity in expectations, standards, information readily available, agreement among participants, and penalties for those who break the rules. It keeps our roads from being a high-speed demolition derby; it will be a heavy topic of conversation in Part 4, and it makes success on the expedition of business possible.

It is leadership done well that brings order to an organization. An order that, like driving, allows people to do their work in **comfort** with a high degree of **certainty**, feeling **competent** as they meet or exceed expectations, and operating with a degree of **autonomy** given the familiarity of the situation. If we add in work that is challenging and work that leads to a goal shared with others, then we have **engagement** and **relatedness** as well.

Effective leadership, and the order it creates, checks all the boxes of our Tent of Comfort and the "G" of genetics in our G.E.A.R. model outlined in Chapter 8. And by doing so, leadership becomes a successful strategy that moves our teams one step closer to being aligned and driving our organizations forward.

However, creating order is one thing; maintaining it is another.

— ◦ —

As stated in the prior chapter, business leadership is specifically leading high-agency followers in a high-complexity situation. The expectations, standards, and agreements discussed previously help bring more clarity to that complexity, but overdoing it comes at a cost: the loss of our followers' agency.

Leadership that oppresses our crew might bring order for a short time, but soon we'll have a rebellion on our hands—the high-agency individuals we lead revolting against the lack of autonomy and engagement they're pre-wired to crave.

On the other hand, everyone doing as they please delegitimizes the system of order an organization has agreed to. Part of establishing order requires taking on the unpleasant task of playing traffic cop—taking action when an individual violates what the group has agreed to.

In the end, it's a trade-off. Too many rules, too much enforcement, and we stifle our team; too few rules, too little enforcement, and order breaks down. With the prior, stagnation arrives, and we fail at moving the energy Lever of Control. With the latter, chaos ensues and we fail at moving the unity Lever of Control.

Bringing and maintaining order as a leader is about finding the right balance, deciding what truly matters, and then being unwavering in holding people accountable.

As leaders, we are asking our teams to ski down a mountain. There are many paths to the bottom. Everyone skiing separate lines to different endpoints is chaos. Everyone being forced to ski the exact same line is micromanagement.

Our job as leaders is to determine the finish line—the answer to "*Where are we going?*" the vision, the goal, and the **clarity in the face of external confusion**. It is also our job to figure out how many gates to put along the course—the answers to "*How are we going to get there?*" and the **order to keep internal chaos at bay**.

The ask of our teams is then clear: "*Get to the finish line, make sure you go through these gates. If not, you're doing it wrong. But for the rest of the run, do as you see fit. Be the best skier you can; that's what we need.*"

Providing order inside an organization is like setting gates along a ski course. Not so many and not so tight to frustrate our teams, but enough to keep things from turning into chaos.

The exact finish line and the right number of gates are unique to your organization, as is the leadership style that best suits you. In the end, no one has a patent on effective leadership. As Drucker said, *"It's not about attributes."* But it's also not purely about results.

Leadership is about efforts to provide clarity and order. How exactly you provide those two is your decision. Both are essential on the expedition of business, and making those decisions with sound principles is part of your craft.

The clarity and order framework of leadership may create some tension with positive experiences of leadership in your past: mentoring a junior employee, ensuring a team had what they needed to complete an objective, serving as a role model, or any other example that doesn't map directly to providing clarity or order.

It's important to make a distinction. Positive action taken by a leader doesn't by default make it an act of leadership. Coaching, mentoring, and being a good role model: these are undoubtedly beneficial to an organization, but not necessarily an essential act of leadership. Making that distinction is helpful in getting a better handle on the specific role of a business leader. Otherwise, we sink further into the ever-deeper quicksand of leadership definitions and attributes.

In the end, everyone is entitled to their own definition of leadership, but most agree one's not a leader without followers.

And in business, gaining followers is a product of someone deciding to come aboard the ships we captain. So, it raises the question: Why are leaders chosen?

One could argue that leaders are chosen based on the qualities that define an effective leader, but that's like arguing a new customer buys a product because of user-experience. Until someone knows first-hand how good a product is, they only know the quality of the marketing.

If you're a leader, your product is effective leadership, and in the past two chapters we've come to define just what that is. And so—with our product known—what exactly is the marketing?

The answer is another leadership term in need of demystifying: charisma. And it's why leaders are chosen.

CHAPTER 15

WHY LEADERS ARE CHOSEN

A promising candidate sits patiently in our lobby—dressed professionally, binder in hand, and exchanging pleasantries with the receptionist. They check their watch; they're early but feeling some anticipation—waiting on me, "the boss," the leader, the decision-maker, to come meet them.

Maybe they are already "sold" on our company—impressed by our reputation, feeling good about what they've seen on our website, or maybe they're desperate enough that they'll take any job.

Maybe they're skeptical: "*Who is this company again? What exactly do they want me to do? This chair is uncomfortable. I don't know if this is for me. I'm happy where I am now.*"

The only certainty is that I don't know what they're thinking.

This situation played out dozens of times. Every walk to the lobby came with a sense of pressure. The candidate I was about to meet could be a complete dud or full of potential. Assuming the latter always felt like a must. I needed to be "on" and to make the best impression I could. If that turned out to be unwarranted, we could always say "no" later. But it would be regrettable to lose a great hire just because I didn't give it my all.

So, I double-check I have their name right, refresh my memory of their resume, step into the lobby, put on a genuine smile, extend my hand, and the next several minutes are all about them.

My actions were simple enough, but they play into something more complex—another Pyramid of Decisions. The goal was to have quality candidates want to come aboard. The strategy was to leverage some of our deepest feelings about who we should follow. My performance in the lobby was the execution of several tactics—and it didn't stop after the interview.

———◄O►———

"Everyone is in sales." I heard it first from my grandfather, and many more since. And leading a business emphasized the point. I had to sell to win new business, sell to persuade people on my ideas, and with recruiting talent—I had to sell a potential hire on the idea that I was a leader worth following.

But the selling wouldn't stop after they came aboard. Leaders never stop selling their team on the idea that their company is where they should work. Fortunately, once they are part of the team, the leadership they experience and the clarity and order they enjoy make the task easier. Our crew becomes the equivalent of repeat customers, ones that can be persuaded by the most powerful of customer reviews: their own.

Potential hires don't have direct personal experiences to lean on. They're forced to decide using different information. If the product they are buying is leadership, that information is coming from their interaction with the leader. And if there's one thing they're looking to feel, it's charisma.

The definition is simple enough: "Compelling attractiveness or charm that can inspire devotion in others." Yet, it remains another leadership term that is as often confusing as it is useful.

Oprah has charisma, as did Freddie Mercury and Martin Luther King Jr. Steve Jobs wasn't short on it, nor was JFK. But trying to mimic all of them at once would garner looks of bewilderment. Adopting just one as your charisma archetype might be better, but as discussed in the previous chapter—is that leader safe to mimic?

The best path is to find our own way—once again building decisions upon solid first principles. Thankfully, both the logic and the data are clear. Researchers studying social perception have consistently found that when we evaluate others, especially leaders, we're asking two primal questions:

1. ***Does this person have my best interests in mind?***

2. ***Are they capable of doing anything about it?***

Some researchers call these dimensions "*warmth and competence*," others call them "*communion and agency*." Regardless of the semantics, according to behavioral scientists, warmth and strength are the two traits that account for over 80% of the variance in how we judge others. And the warmth component is irreplaceable.

Without warmth, strength becomes threatening rather than reassuring, while warmth without strength may be welcome—but it isn't reassuring.

Charisma isn't mysterious at all. It's the feeling that someone checks both boxes.

Charisma is displaying warmth first, then strength.

And the impact these two can have on people is often surprising.

<hr>

William Queen is a former federal law enforcement agent. For several years he served as an undercover agent for the ATF (Alcohol, Tobacco, and Firearms), and under the name Billy St. John worked his way into the Mongols—a violent, criminal biker gang.

To do so, he had to play the part of a gang member himself. His look, his supposed history, and his talk: all had to fit that of a typical recruit. There was an ongoing tension around the morality of the crimes his law enforcement assignment forced him to be a part of.

Then things took a surprising turn. His mother passed away, and he took time off from both his ATF and biker gang obligations. The return revealed an uncomfortable truth: our desire to feel a part of a group is often stronger than our rational thought or personal convictions.

In his memoir "Under and Alone," Queen writes:

"I had been back from the funeral for several days. I had met with several ATF agents, and not one had expressed their sympathy to me...I realized that I was just another number to the ATF. I wasn't Bill Queen, a flesh-and-blood man; I was ATF badge number 489."

But when Queen returned to the Mongols, things were different:

"One after another, bikers bear-hugged me, expressing their condolences about my mom, telling me they loved me. I couldn't help myself...They freely and sincerely expressed their love for one another and for me. It was sincere. I knew that they honestly loved Billy St. John. And at that moment I desperately wanted to be Billy St. John."

Queen's experience hints at something we're all looking for, and why leaders are often chosen. The world is big and complex, with infinite possibilities. Some are good, but many are bad. The thought that we might have to go about it all alone is daunting. The people who choose to follow us live in that same world and face the same thought.

So, it's none too surprising that in Chapter 8 we addressed how we're all looking for relatedness, to be part of a group that can help us along. To satisfy that desire, we're back to familiar questions. Does the group have my best interests in mind? Can they do anything about it? The answers are more likely to be "Yes" when the group has a leader with charisma. And Queen's experience is not an outlier.

Tony Soprano is one of the most popular figures in television history. That a character who is responsible for the death of dozens, cheats on his wife, and is involved in nearly every form of criminal activity becomes a lovable fan favorite should be unexpected. But it's not, and it's easier to explain when you consider the two parts of charisma.

Viewers see Tony displaying some of the worst of human behavior, but they also see him looking after his kids, kissing friends on the cheek, and sharing meals with people who could easily be them. The assumption is that they would be in Tony's good graces, not targets but beneficiaries of Tony's temper and disregard for the law—that he would have their best interests in mind.

Perhaps analogies of drug cartels, mobsters, and the previous chapters' references to cults seem extreme for a discussion on business leadership. If so, that may be a product of an unfortunate tendency we have to frame business as a more sanitized, rational, and buttoned-up portion of our lives—as if we leave our human nature behind when we clock into work.

We do try to do so, and with good reason—only a child or an untamed mind acts on every turn of their emotions. But it would be a mistake to forget that people are like the deep portion of a river. The calm on the surface masks the powerful currents that run below.

A leader who is the master of their craft knows how to tap into that power.

Whether we're electing a president, considering joining a gang, or deciding on a new job and a new boss—the emotion of the moment is similar. We're looking to be taken care of, to have an advocate, and to not have to do it all ourselves. The leader who provides us with the feeling that they can deliver such has achieved charisma. And they are a leader who followers are willing to take a chance on.

It may be frustrating to some that we leave such important decisions to emotion, feelings, and gut instinct based on questionable traits. If I'm honest, I too wish we made some decisions more rationally, but that's not how things work on the expedition of business.

As many have said and the research supports—we make decisions based on emotion and rationalize the decision later. That's true of us all at times. It was often true of those who awaited me in the lobby, and it's true of most when they choose a leader. And while some may use a common example to argue that's a mistake, I disagree.

You might be familiar with the old TV game show "Let's Make a Deal." If not, imagine your typical 1970s television program: lots of orange, shag carpet, a yellow tint to the film, and comically bad hairstyles.

The "Big Deal of the Day" was the grand finale of each episode. One lucky contestant would have to choose between three closed doors. Behind one was a new car or a similarly extravagant prize. Behind the other two were "zonks"—maybe a goat wearing a straw hat or 87 lbs. of cheddar cheese.

After selecting their door, the contestant was given some new information. One of the remaining two doors was opened to reveal one of the two "zonks." Then the contestant had a choice to make—stick with their original door or switch to the remaining closed door.

What would you do? What's your gut say? Do you make the switch, or not?

You should switch—that's the statistically correct thing to do, but most of the time the contestant did not. They stuck with their original choice.

I learned the math years ago, and the key insight is simple: when you first pick a door, you have a 33% chance of being right (1 out of 3). But that means there is a 66% chance (2 out of 3) that the prize is behind the two doors you didn't select. When the host eliminates one of the two doors you didn't select, identifying it as a "zonk"—it moves the entire 66% chance of winning to the other door.

Clearly, if my door has a 33% chance of winning, while the other door has a 66% chance, I should switch—but it still *feels* like I should keep my original door.

The fact that I chose my current door gives me a feeling of control. And in my gut, I feel like I'd regret switching and losing much more than standing firm.

Experts, academics, and authors came to name this the "Monty Hall Problem" (Monty Hall being the host of the show). It has become a famous example to argue that feelings and emotions disrupt our decision making. That if we could suppress those forces, the more logical and rational parts of our brain could lead us to better decisions.

For business leaders, the dogma that has emerged around this type of thinking is not without consequences. And while there are times it's the correct approach: game shows, financial budgeting, supply chains, inventory management, A/B testing of product designs and marketing content—these, like the sports example discussed in Chapter 13, are realms of reduced complexity.

To use this tool when a different one is needed is a serious mistake in the craft of business. And there may be no worse time to make that mistake than when trying to "sell" someone on following a leader.

In such a situation, what is actually true or how the other person "should" think about it doesn't matter. It's how they *feel* that will drive the decision. That's not a mistake; in fact, it's often the only logical choice.

⸺◆O◆⸺

For over 10 years, I've carried a handmade money clip. There's a leather pocket to hold my credit card and driver's license, and a metal clip to hold folded bills. I love it.

What would be the cost of losing it?

Reason would say it's worth the cost to buy another one, the value of the cash that it holds, and some compensation for the headache of replacing my credit card and driver's license.

I disagree.

I bought that money clip at a craft market on a trip to Chicago with my wife. It was a nearly perfect June day. The sky was blue, and the air was clear. We walked on Navy Pier and down Michigan Ave, saw "The Bean" and Buckingham Fountain, ate lunch on a rooftop terrace, and met friends for dinner in Lincoln Park. It was also the day I got the call that my grandfather had passed away—someone who meant more to me than words can describe.

The money clip is an anchor to all those memories. So, what's it worth?

I have no idea.

If lost, at what point would I mourn the loss of the money it held more than the clip itself? $500? $5,000? $50,000? My life's savings? I don't know. I can try to visualize the situation, but I'm left with a blank and hollow feeling. I could only answer if it happened. If I experienced the moment, then I'd know my answer—how I *felt* about it.

Give it a shot with something you hold dear. Can you put a price tag on it?

That's just how we make unquantifiable decisions. Who do I vote for? Which TV characters do I like? Which do I despise? Who do I want to work with? And if I find myself sitting in a lobby, waiting for my prospective future boss to arrive, do I *feel* they have charisma or not? Do they have my best interests in mind? Can they do something about it? There is no formula. Right or wrong—our gut tells us what to do, and then we rationalize it later.

I'm belaboring the point because some business leaders dislike this reality. They either wish that those they're trying to impress would make a rational choice, or they feel like intentionally targeting someone's emotions and feelings is unethical or manipulative. I am sympathetic to the latter, but it's only unethical or manipulative if it's rooted in a lie.

The most effective charisma is rooted in truth. I had to truly care about who was sitting in the lobby. I had to truly be able to do something about it. Having the other person feel that truth is part of mastering the craft of business.

Ultimately, when it comes to choosing leaders, "reality" doesn't much matter. It is what followers, both current and prospective, perceive to be "true" that is paramount. If we want them to join us on the expedition of business, then the decisions we make and the actions we take must come from high on The Mountain of Why.

Going through the motions, engaging with new hires and potential followers the same as everyone else or the same as we've always done (mimicry and heuristics) won't scare anyone off—but it's an average approach and destined for average results.

Thinking through how we go about unquantifiable decisions gives us a better framework, but we become most effective as a leader when we get our first principles right. And when it comes to why leaders are chosen, our Level 5 decisions from the summit had best be grounded in the beliefs that people are looking for warmth and strength—that it's the leader with charisma who others perceive as a person worth following.

It's easy to understand charisma intellectually—warmth and competence, caring and capability—but then struggle with the execution.

Some try to fake warmth—deploying practiced smiles and rehearsed empathy, only to be seen through immediately. Others overindex on competence—believing that being good at their job is enough, wondering why their team doesn't follow with enthusiasm. Many leaders already care deeply about their team yet fail to display their concern in ways that register, while others (unsuccessfully) try to hide their lack of capabilities behind bluster and big talk.

In the end, there are more ways to fail at charisma than to succeed. But the questions are straightforward: How do we make warmth and strength true within ourselves? And once true, how do we ensure others can feel both?

While this chapter was all about why leaders are chosen, the next is about who leaders are. Part of that "are" is having true concern and competence, while part of who leaders are is having the ability to communicate both effectively.

CHAPTER 16

WHO LEADERS ARE

"If each of us hires people who are smaller than we are, we shall become a company of dwarfs. But if each of us hires people who are bigger than we are, we shall become a company of giants."

That was David Ogilvy, the "Father of Advertising," in 1983. The idea wasn't uniquely his own, but the articulation was an early link in the chain that's become a popular business maxim today: *"Hire people smarter than you are."*

The appeal is understandable. By vowing to *"hire people smarter than I am,"* a leader can feel confident without being arrogant, authoritative without being controlling, and important without being the smartest. It allows them to appear as a noble and humble individual, one soon to be surrounded by the team of giants they've assembled—it's their view of who leaders are.

Like a big guard dog at our door, powerful friends, or allies with financial resources, it's appealing to surround ourselves with those more capable.

Unfortunately, it's become an example of a story not being *"the shortest distance between a human and the truth,"* but the shortest distance between a human and a misunderstanding. It's a powerful narrative that has run amok. **First this**: leaders are those who hire people smarter than themselves. **Then** the leaders become the less capable—but they are savvy. And because of **that**, their team of giants carries them to success.

The actual story and the original intent go differently—we succeed as leaders when we hire people who are a ***different kind of smart*** than us.

The capacity of those we lead may exceed our own in a variety of ways. But if we expect them to follow us for long, then there is one area in which our capacity must exceed theirs: our competence as a leader.

When it comes to the capacity to lead, the "biggest" is at the front of the line.

The idea that leadership acts as a constraint on the success of an organization is not a new one. Plato argued that the health of the state depends on the ability of those who rule it, and Roman military thought effectively said, "*As the general goes, so goes the army.*"

More recently, Buckingham and Coffman's "First, Break All the Rules" reinforced the adage that people don't leave jobs—they leave bosses. And so, John Maxwell's famous "Law of the Lid" did not introduce a new principle so much as give a modern name to a persistent observation:

Teams can only perform at the level of competence their leaders are able to provide.

We may now know what business leadership **is** (navigating high complexity with high-agency followers), what leaders **provide** (clarity and order), and even why they are **chosen** (warmth and strength), but who **are** they?

In other words, what is the profile of a leader? What are the traits that make us more competent as a leader than the giants we aim to lead?

As we'll see, there is no one answer—and that's a good thing.

An elephant has a small mouth with flat grinding teeth. A T-rex has large jaws and sharp teeth. One eats only plants; the other only eats meat. One is covered in thick skin with sparse hair; the other has scales and maybe a few feathers. But both are giants; each is land-dwelling. And you wouldn't want to have either of them angry with you.

The same is true of any two effective leaders, not the exact traits, but that the profile of either is the sum of what's unique to one plus what's common to both. It's a truth about leadership that makes creating a (i.e. one, singular) profile of a leader impossible.

We may each be asked to lead in similar situations, deliver similar results, and be judged in similar ways—but the being, who we are as a leader or the one we want to become, is as diverse as the businesses we run and the teams we are asked to lead.

A few years ago, I took an extensive executive coaching assessment. Like most, the report that followed outlined my "strengths" and "weaknesses" compared to whatever internal benchmarks the system uses.

This report ranked 25 personal skills—#1 is your best or strongest, while #25 would be your worst. For me, "leadership" was bringing up the rear at #23 (only "teamwork" and "customer focus" ranked lower).

And so, someone who had started, cultivated, and successfully exited a business—someone who had happy employees—someone who received anonymous reviews saying *I can't imagine a better boss*—had "leadership" at the top of their list of "Competencies Needing Development."

I don't share this anecdote to brag or to criticize assessments like these—they are valuable. But I do so to raise three possibilities:

1. I'm delusional.

2. My staff suffered from Stockholm Syndrome (a psychological condition where hostages develop unexpected positive emotional bonds with their captors). Or...

3. Effective leadership is a case of *"one mountain, many paths"*—that there's more than one way to lead an organization to success.

Only you can speak to what is uncommon about the leader you need to be, and so the best published advice on leadership speaks to the other half of the equation: those parts of the profile that are common to effective leaders regardless of circumstance.

At the start of Chapter 14, we covered the "word salads" that are often used by those waxing poetic in their description of leadership. Next we looked at the cost of reducing leadership to traits versus judging leaders by the clarity and order they provide.

However, when we look at effective leaders, there are certain traits that emerge. They stand out because we can chart a clear path from those attributes to the specific demands placed on business leaders (Chapter 13), what leaders must provide (Chapter 14), and why leaders are chosen (Chapter 15).

As a result, a competent leader is an excellent **communicator**, someone with great **empathy**, **strength,** and an **executive mindset**, and above all they are **self-aware**. These are common among effective leaders—five key traits, four pillars built upon one shared foundation that supports them all, and the topics of the sections to come.

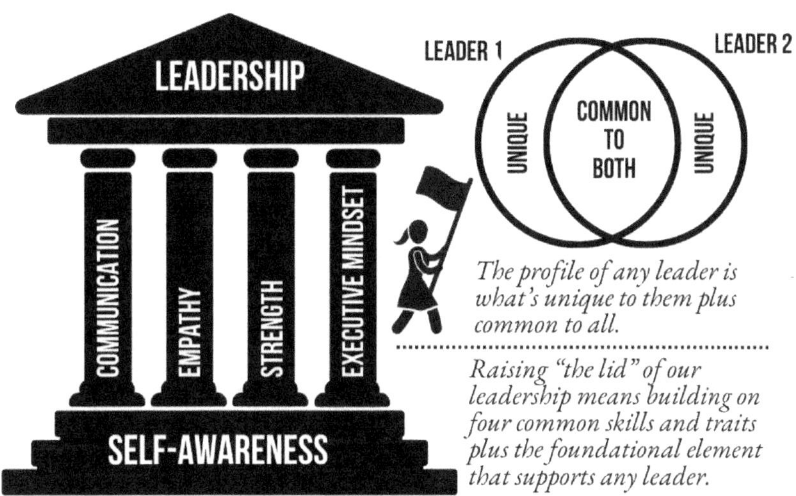

The profile of any leader is what's unique to them plus common to all.

Raising "the lid" of our leadership means building on four common skills and traits plus the foundational element that supports any leader.

These traits set "the lid" of our organizations, and as such, leaders are beholden to improving each on the expedition of business. However, the path of developing them is rarely a straight line, and there are pitfalls along the way. The novice improves quickly in these areas and believes they have reached great heights, only to have experience reveal it was the false summit of "Mount Stupid" as they tumble down the other side. It takes descending into the Valley of Realization for the soon-to-be master to begin their ascent up the Slope of Improvement. But in time, they realize that there is no apex to be reached.

It's true—for these five core traits, we can spend a lifetime improving each and raising our competence as a leader.

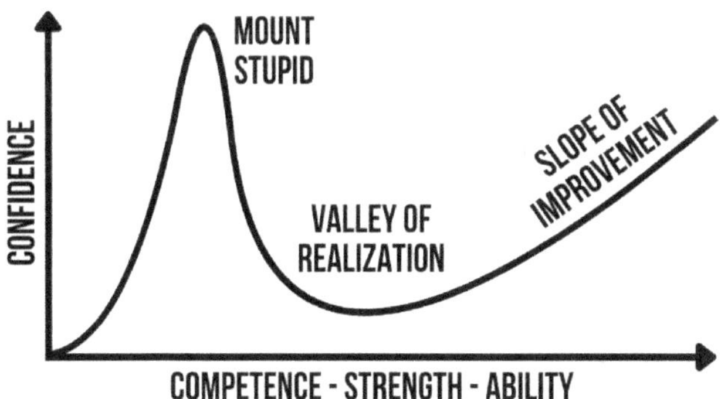

The Dunning-Kruger Effect came from their paper "Unskilled and Unaware of It," how people with low ability tend to overestimate what they are capable of.

Fortunately, there are certain principles that provide footholds on the climb toward mastery. And there's no better place to start than with the trait that bridges the gap between our capacity as leaders and what others assume it to be.

COMMUNICATION

On July 20, 1969, Neil Armstrong and his crew landed in the Sea of Tranquility, completing one of the greatest expeditions of all time. When Armstrong took that first step onto the Moon, nearly one-fifth of the world's population was watching. But of course, nobody saw it.

Armstrong, in his rigid suit and bubble helmet, couldn't see where he was stepping. And every viewer back on Earth saw only a television screen.

That so many can rightly claim *"I was watching..."* speaks to the power of effective communication—the transmission of a situation, event, or thought into the eyes, ears, and understanding of the intended audience.

No one "watching" knew how the moon smelled that night, nor the feeling of the cold "air" above the dusty lunar surface. They were only given a slice of the experience: the visual of Armstrong stepping from the ladder, the audio transmissions to mission control. Both were low-resolution, but it was enough to provide an understanding of what was happening.

It was also a useful model of effective communication: the right amount of information, transmitted in high enough detail, giving an intended audience an understanding that is close to, though not the absolute picture of reality.

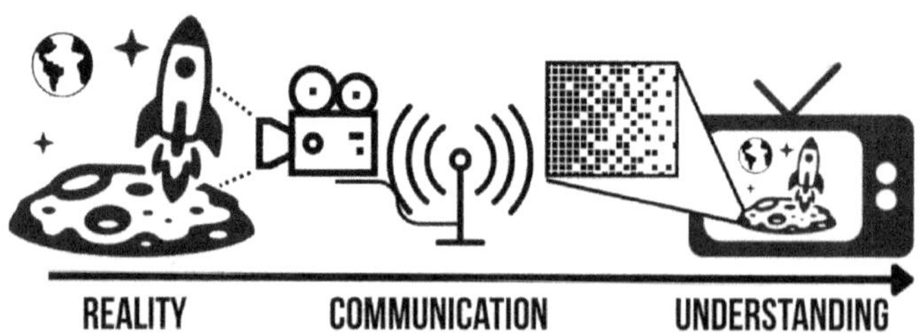

Few have actually seen the moon, but with ample communication we all have a useful idea of what it's like to be there.

My wife sent me a text one day, "*There is something on fire near the house.*" In an age where I could have seen a live video of the situation, I received the equivalent of a cartoon drawn on the back of a napkin.

"*Fire,*" how big? "*Something,*" what exactly? And "*near the house,*" how close?!

I could assume from the medium (text vs. call) and lack of exclamation points that our house wasn't in danger. But it was just that: an assumption. My wife, knowing the truth, understandably didn't feel the need to offer a lot of detail. But therein lies the central problem of communication: the curse of knowledge and the assumption that our audience knows more than we tell them.

In business, this shows up often: in strategy—"*Let's focus on growth,*" in delegation—"*Handle the inventory situation,*" in feedback—"*You need to communicate better,*" and in expectations—"*Take ownership.*"

Each leaves the recipient asking: What exactly? By when? To what standard? With what resources?

The leader possesses context the team doesn't, and their audience is left to fill in the gaps.

The alternative is equally problematic. The email we scroll three times to reach the bottom—only to find the actual request buried at the end, the PowerPoint slide that looks like a page from an encyclopedia, the budget discussion that says new equipment will be "*8,836 dollars and 17 cents plus tax and shipping*" versus "$9k": all are examples of noise over signal.

Too little information and people are watching TV through the "snow," adjusting the rabbit ears, and trying to piece together what little they can see. Too much information and they're clutching their armrests in an IMAX theater, overwhelmed by the unnecessary.

When viewers watched Armstrong take that "*giant leap,*" they really saw a screen, but the screen was a whole made of smaller parts: tiny individual lines of dots, the modern TV equivalent of pixels, the smallest units of information that could be transmitted, all stacked together. When enough of the pixels were correct, everyone could see the "big picture."

It might not have been perfect, but the gaps were small enough that no one was questioning whether their house was on fire.

Effective communication is about bringing things into focus while not wasting time on extra detail.

As leaders, our first job is to get to the moon—to create the reality that we want. That may be about the decisions we make: a new strategy, firing a customer, or pulling the trigger on a new hire. It may be about who we are: someone who cares, someone who is capable, or someone who is frustrated as hell. But none of that matters if we don't do our second job: transmitting the reality to our "viewers"—with clarity but without overwhelm. Doing so is part of the craft of business, and mastery requires understanding all the pixels on the screen.

The pixels streaming back to Earth from the moon were rudimentary—low resolution and black, white, or gray. As leaders, we have more options to fine-tune our messages, but using them all effectively is difficult. It starts with knowing how the "screen" we are "seen" on is composed:

- The **language pixels** of the words we choose, the order we put them in, and how they are grouped together.

- The **verbal pixels** of tone, pace, and volume.

- The **body language pixels** of posture, eye contact, expression, and gestures.

- The **positioning pixels** of standing or seated, of front or back of the room, and of dress and appearance.

They all comprise a snapshot in time of how we're "coming across," but it's only half the battle.

There's also the question of how the signal is transmitted: in-person, email, text, or phone.

There's the question of what additional information streams are needed: slide decks, printed materials, demonstrations.

And there's the question of bringing our audience up to speed—what prologue do they need to make sense of what they're "watching," the background and context that's necessary for understanding.

As leaders, our greatest thinking and our greatest attributes mean little if we can't transmit a clear picture to the audience of our teams. Mastering all the pixels at our disposal may take a lifetime, but that's okay. Often all we need is some grainy footage and choppy audio.

The first step is understanding that our reality is just that: ours. That for our teams, it doesn't matter if we become the Neil Armstrong of leaders. What matters is what they see on their "screen," and that being an effective broadcaster—from our head to another's understanding—is part of the expedition of business.

NASA had an advantage in broadcasting the lunar landing. What they were transmitting was real. The work was not in inventing a story or sustaining an illusion, but in overcoming the friction between what was happening on the Moon and what people on Earth could understand.

This is when communication is at its easiest—when our job is simply to close the gap between reality and someone else's understanding. It becomes more difficult when we need to perform rather than reveal—when we hope our words can distract people from what is real.

Effective communication begins by ensuring that what we are portraying actually exists. That takes work; there are no shortcuts. And if there is one reality leaders must make true, it is this: as leaders, we understand, and we care.

EMPATHY

There's a reason I didn't rush home when "*something [was] on fire near my house.*" It's part of our process for understanding vantage points from Chapter 6 (*Relate to their perspective. Explore what they think is happening and why. Affirm understanding by repeating back. And then, but only then, respond.*), and it's a superpower of effective leaders: **cognitive empathy**.

It was by "putting myself in my wife's shoes" that I correctly filled in the gaps of the low-resolution broadcast of her reality. A leader skilled in cognitive empathy enjoys similar benefits. It's akin to knowing the cards your opponent is holding, sitting in on your competitors' meetings, or hearing the conversation of a couple gossiping in the corner. It's a skill that provides an inside view which leads to better decisions.

Correctly imagining what our customers value—not just what they say they want, accurately theorizing what motivates our top performers versus what motivates our struggling ones, successfully anticipating how our competitors will respond to actions we take: the mechanics are the same—cognitive empathy brings insight.

It's a skill that comes with intention and practice. It worked for me decoding my wife's text. It works for effective leaders. And it works best when paired with the second type of empathy: **emotional empathy**.

Any effective leader must care about their mission and, more importantly, the people who are a part of it. For some leaders, the latter comes easily; for others, it's more of a struggle. But for all leaders, there are a few of our crew who are harder to develop our concern for.

Some people are easy to like, others we are more neutral on, and then there's a third group that seems to always be testing our resolve. Unfortunately, to be an effective leader, we can't pick and choose. If a true measure of character is how we treat those from whom we have nothing to gain, then a true measure of leadership may be the level of concern we have for those we like the least.

There are scenarios where it is hopeless—where our negative feelings toward someone are justifiable and should not be suppressed. In that situation, effective leadership is about making a change that serves the individual, ourselves, and the organization.

But when the problem is more difference in personality than subpar performance, it's the novice leader who spends their time complaining but taking no action. A master of their craft understands that in such situations there are three options.

1. The individual must go.

2. The leader must go. Or...

3. We use the tools at our disposal to muster up the concern that is required of effective leaders—and none may be as powerful as our G.E.A.R. model.

The "G" may be for genetics and our innate wiring, but it also speaks to the fact that we are far more alike than we are different—that when we peel away our more surface-level traits we all have similar desires: love, happiness, accomplishment, to earn a living, to make a better life for our family, to see our kids grow and succeed, to feel like somebody, to be seen, heard, and capable of making a difference.

No matter who might be a thorn in our side, chances are we share common goals.

We pursue those goals in the same world—one that often seems bent on standing in our way. All the disappointments, all the heartbreaks, all the trials and tribulations: they too are common. We may have been stolen from, lied to, cheated on, or excluded—so have they.

It's a messy world. And while it's easy to get sucked into the idea of us—doing our best to lead, versus them—making it difficult, the healthy position to take as a leader is it's all of us—doing our best to fight against the headwinds of both business and life—together.

The "E" is for enduring traits, but the keyword is "enduring." No one chooses to be tall, short, or have blue eyes. And the same can be said for the quirks, tendencies, and personalities that may drive us up a wall.

We all have had moments when "how we are wired" produced consequences we'd like to avoid—and so have they. We may think they don't try to do better, but a leader with empathy knows that they themselves, despite their best efforts, often resort to their old ways. Suppressing what comes naturally, in favor of how we want to show up in the moment, can be a struggle for us all.

The "A" stands for adopted narratives, but "resulting narratives" is often more fitting. How we come to see life and explain the world is inseparable from our experiences with both.

Does one have a growth mindset by their choosing, or because they had parents and teachers who believed in them? Does one have a cynical view about jobs and bosses because they decided to be jaded, or because their trust has been eroded by poor leaders and bad places to work?

It's not about excusing anyone; it's about the wisdom to consider the power of circumstance.

All of it ties together with the "R" of real-time constraints and the lessons of Chapter 11. While we're quick to assume people's character is to blame, it often has more to do with their situation, both present and past—conditions which we weren't always responsible for in our lives, and they often weren't responsible for in theirs.

It's all an exercise in cognitive empathy to build emotional empathy—using our G.E.A.R. model to better understand how we all operate in life, and then putting ourselves in their shoes: our most challenging employees, staff, and co-workers. When we do that well, when we make improving the skill part of our growth, we will find ourselves with more concern for our team—even those who are difficult—and we will be better leaders as a result.

But having someone's best interests in mind is only the first step. The next trait in being an effective leader, in displaying the charisma we want others to feel, is being able to do something about it.

STRENGTH

A technical founder of an early-stage startup believes her success will depend on **intellectual** strength—solving the hard problems no one else can crack.

A sales-driven CEO leading a company through a growth phase believes his effectiveness depends on **relational** strength: closing deals, building partnerships, and attracting talent.

A president leading a turnaround believes their company's survival hinges on **emotional** strength—staying calm when everything is on fire.

All three are right; all three are wrong.

While each leader correctly identified what their situation demands most, their analysis is incomplete. An astute leader can identify the strengths needed to drive results, but a master of their craft knows an insight we keep returning to: how they are viewed by their team is as much a question of perception as reality.

No one chooses to follow a leader they see as weak over one they see as strong. And it raises the question of how we perceive strength: when we believe someone cares for us, how do we judge whether they can do anything about it?

Our rational brains may work like the previous examples—drawing a straight line between a specific need and a certain quality. But again, it comes back to how people *feel*. "*Is someone a strong leader or are they not?*" That's how others frame the question.

And the path to a "*Yes*" often includes six ways in which we both perceive and display strength:

Physical strength - Our embodied capacity. Presence. Energy. Stamina. Do we show up with vitality, or do we look like we're barely holding on?

Intellectual strength - Our ability to make sense of complexity. To learn. To understand what's happening and why. Can we adapt to and navigate the situation we're in?

Emotional strength - Our composure under pressure. Our ability to regulate ourselves when things go sideways. Will we stay steady when everyone else is panicking?

Relational strength - Our access to people. Our ability to build trust and influence. Can we draw on others and mobilize support when we need it?

Volitional strength - Our persistence. Our follow-through. Do we finish what we start, or do our commitments dissolve when things get hard?

Moral strength - Our integrity. Our willingness to constrain ourselves by principle even when it costs us. Will we do the right thing when no one is watching?

Different situations demand the right balance of each.

Suffering setbacks, losing a key client, or seeing a long-time employee retire may draw most heavily on our **volitional** strength—our ability to stay "up" when our team gets "down."

Giving a keynote address, speaking to a large crowd of influential partners, potential employees, or prospective clients goes best when we bring our **physical** strength.

And few are exercised as consistently as **moral** strength: keeping to our standards when competitors abandon theirs, giving honest feedback to a client and living with the consequences, having the humility to tell our team "*I don't know*" or "*This may not work*" when embarking on a path of uncertainty.

Different leaders in different contexts find themselves leaning on one strength most often, but leadership rarely allows us to neglect the others entirely—no matter how tall or robust a dam, water finds its way through the cracks.

But these six strengths are not boxes to be checked; they are capacities we are always working to improve. The profile of an effective leader is not excellence in one, but adequacy in all—and continual effort to strengthen what is weakest.

Yet leadership demands more of one aspect of our strengths than any other. It's part of our intellectual strength. And when it's weak, our other strengths are often wasted.

EXECUTIVE MINDSET

I have a friend who grows orchids—a flower whose beauty is rivaled only by the attention they demand and their intolerance for poor conditions. Yet, he's good at it. Picking the right plants, using the right soil, keeping temperature and humidity where they need to be: even if we've never grown an orchid, we can relate to the work that is to be done—at least we think we can.

What's easy to miss is what an executive mindset sees: the different levels of growing an orchid—not just at the scale of planting, watering, and tending, but at all the levels that impact the outcome.

Zoom in, and orchids aren't just plants; they're roots, stems, and leaves. Zoom in further, and they're the cells that reproduce and turn sunlight into energy—one plant seen at multiple scales. The reverse has us seeing the greenhouse they grow in, the climate outside, our planet as a whole, and the cosmos within which we orbit—again, one plant seen at multiple scales.

Business is the same.

An employee sits at their desk—answering emails and making calls. Zoom in and we find our G.E.A.R. model, the inner workings that drive our actions. Zoom out, and there are roles and responsibilities. If we go further, there are processes and systems. Next would be the environment in which the work happens: the tools, the incentives, and the culture that shapes what matters and the goals pursued. All of this sits inside a market, which is inside an economy—locals making up the national, nationals making up the global.

We have one employee, but multiple scales of view.

Businesses and orchids exist on many different scales. Knowing how far to zoom in or out, and on which level to take action, are keys to mastery.

An executive mindset is the ability to operate across different scales—to orchestrate the parts and pieces of each, then to act at the right level to produce the desired outcome. Many capable leaders flounder because they continue to think at the scale that made them successful, long after their role requires a different one.

In our brains, "executive function" belongs to an area called the prefrontal cortex. It doesn't help us see, move, or remember—those tasks belong to other systems. Instead, it integrates signals, resolves conflicts, sets priorities, and decides where attention should go next. It does not do the work; it ensures the right work gets done, in the right order, by the right parts of the system. Effective leaders do the same.

They stop trying to be the best engineer, salesperson, or operator in the room. Instead, they become the coordinating intelligence of their business. Their value is no longer in personal output, but in alignment, sequencing, and leverage.

At their best, effective leaders get all the scales of their organization operating in harmony. But it's no easy task—every dimension worth considering has scales of its own, and having an executive mindset means constantly zooming in and out across all of them.

Customer fit—we move from whether one client is happy to whether we're serving the right market entirely. Market opportunity—we move from a single deal to an industry-wide shift. Competitive positioning—from how we win this proposal to whether our business model survives the decade.

There's no shortage of dimensions a leader might consider, each with scales of its own. But there are three dimensions that are critical for any effective leader to traverse in their decision making: **time**, **altitude**, and **risk**.

Time

Novice leaders stay stuck in the present; better ones see into the near future; the best integrate across time. They understand how past decisions constrain current options, and how today's choices will shape tomorrow's landscape. They tolerate short-term discomfort in service of long-term optionality. And they recognize when future promises must give way to present realities.

The executive mindset knows when to act and when to wait—that time is a river that brings new information. The novice feels pressure and reacts immediately. The executive asks: What will we know tomorrow that we don't know today? What is the risk in waiting? And what is the delay between the action we take today and the result it produces later?

Time is a dimension, and an executive mindset requires considering it at the correct scale. What happened in the past? What's happening now? And what's likely to happen in the future? But also are we looking across hours, days, months, or years?

The novice sees an open position and thinks *"We need someone now."* The leader with an executive mindset asks different questions: Will we still need this role in a year, or will it evolve into something else? Will the person we hire today grow with us, or will they become a bottleneck themselves? And what decisions did we make six months ago that created this urgency in the first place?

They're not just deciding about a hire; they're deciding how to build their business over time. They do so partly by understanding the dimension of time and the scales in play, but also by knowing at what level action needs to be taken—the right scale along the dimension of altitude.

<u>Altitude</u>

Most leaders begin their careers in the "weeds"—doing the work of the day-to-day. Their world is the blades of grass in front of them. As managers, they start to see the whole yard: the fence lines, perhaps some bare patches, or where things are overgrown. But the best leaders can zoom in and out—down to the roots and up to see the rainstorms coming next week.

Much like our orchid example, zooming out along the elevation dimension moves us from a leaf, to a tree, to the forest they're within.

When we change altitudes, we can better see where action should be taken. A task-level problem (a specific customer complaint) looks different from a process-level problem (why do we keep getting the same complaint?). That issue looks different from a policy-level problem (what principles should guide how we handle all complaints?) which looks different from an organizational problem (should we even be in this business?).

The leader stuck at ground level is in every email thread, approving every expense, and tweaking every detail. They solve the task in front of them but guarantee they'll face it again tomorrow. The leader stuck at altitude speaks in vision and values but has no idea how work actually gets done. They set principles that sound good but can't be executed.

With an executive mindset, we recognize whether a recurring problem needs a process fix, a policy change, or a principle clarified. We can zoom out to see patterns that others cannot. And most importantly, we make decisions that have a lasting impact.

But no decision guarantees the results we intend. Some are more certain; some are less. And all need consideration with an executive mindset—selecting the right scale along our third dimension.

<u>Risk</u>

Every decision carries risks, but not the same kind. The novice leader sees risk as high or low. The more experienced leader makes multiple stops along the dimension of risk—each revealing something different about the decision at hand.

Certainty in our decisions runs from *"We know exactly what will happen"* to *"We're completely guessing."*

Do we renovate the office? We can estimate the cost, the timeline, and the disruption.

What about entering a new market? Now we're making educated guesses about customer response, competitive reaction, or regulatory differences.

One comes with more risk than the other, but being clear on why that is true matters. And what makes it true are three aspects of risk related to most decisions: **control**, **reversibility**, and **stakes**.

Our level of **control** determines whether we're driving or just along for the ride. Launching a new product line is lower risk—we control pricing, features, timing, and positioning. Relying on a single supplier for critical components is higher risk—their delays become ours, as do their quality problems; we control neither.

Reversibility asks whether we can undo this if we're wrong. Testing a marketing channel, hiring a contractor, or piloting a new process: they're lower risk because hitting the brakes or shifting into reverse is easily doable.

Selling the company, exiting a market entirely, or firing a senior executive: the boats have been burned—there's no retreating, so we best be sure. But decisions of low control and low reversibility aren't necessarily risky—it depends on our third variable: the **stakes**.

Some plans are likely to fail, but have capped downsides—the stakes are low. Others are almost certain, but an outlier result would be catastrophic—the stakes are high. Is either a decision we should make? That depends on the stakes in the other direction—the potential reward.

These three aspects of risk interact. A decision might be irreversible but have low stakes. Another might be high stakes, but within our control. The leader with an executive mindset doesn't reduce risk to an average or a median. They can handle the complexity and navigate risk more strategically. And both help them make better decisions.

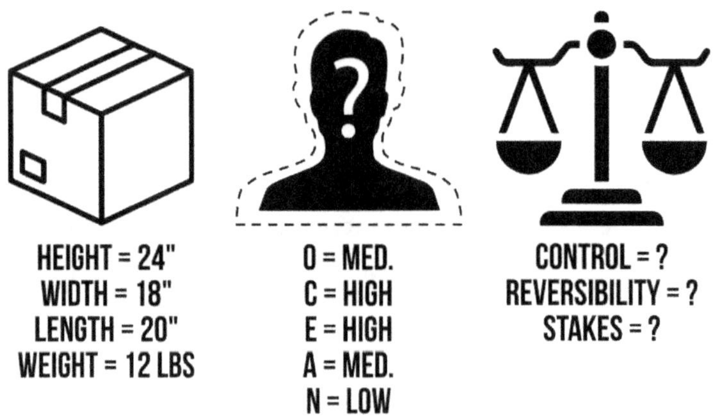

Like the dimensions that define a package, or personality dimensions that tell us how people are "Made Different" (Chapter 9), better understanding risk comes down to examining the control we have over the outcome, the reversibility of our decision, and the stakes of being wrong (or right).

When understanding risk is paired with leaders integrating across time and choosing the right altitude, a distinct benefit to an organization emerges. Mastery across dimensions and scales produces clarity. It's often mistaken for instinct, but it is really intellectual strength.

It's the ability to look at the dozen urgent demands vying for attention and distinguish between what's truly important and what just feels that way. The urgent versus important matrix isn't a separate framework; it's what happens when we consider multiple dimensions and scales simultaneously. What brought us to now and what happens in time? At what levels are we impacting our teams and the organization? And how likely are we to be right, and what happens if we're wrong? Those are the valuable questions a leader with intellectual strength asks.

This is the hallmark of an executive mindset—not having all the answers but consistently asking the right questions along the right dimensions at the right scales. It's being able to see the Levers of Control from 30,000 feet, but then zooming in and knowing what actions, on what dimension, at what scale will help us amass energy, build unity, lower resistance, and improve our yield. And then zooming back out again to see how those actions interact across different dimensions.

In a way, it's a matter of perspective: not so close that we miss the big picture, not so far away that we can't see the detail we need, and not so fixed at one point in time that we can't foresee the rewards or consequences to come. But having the right perspective isn't exclusive to an executive mindset. To be an effective leader, there's one view of one situation we can't be without, and it's a view we only gain through one essential trait.

SELF-AWARENESS

The other four traits are destinations we work toward. Communication, empathy, strength, and executive mindset can all be made better with deliberate effort. But none of them improve without one thing: seeing the need.

Without self-awareness, we can't improve our communication because we don't know how we're coming across. We think we're being clear when we're confusing. We think we're being concise when we're overwhelming people with detail. We default to our natural communication style and assume misunderstandings are the other party's fault. In each case, we miss the problem that we're best able to fix: us.

Without self-awareness, we can't develop genuine empathy. We assume others think like we do, want what we want, and struggle with what we struggle with. We can't use the G.E.A.R. model on difficult team members if we haven't used it on ourselves first. When we see more of ourselves, we see more of others.

Without self-awareness, we can't assess our strength. We overestimate in areas where we have natural confidence and underestimate where we feel insecure. We don't recognize that what made us strong as individual contributors might be making us weak as leaders. And we don't design the systems and processes that could buttress our weaknesses.

Without self-awareness, we can't develop an executive mindset. We rush decisions if we're naturally tenacious and wait too long if we're naturally reflective. We stay stuck at the altitude that feels comfortable. We misjudge risk as we mistake our past individual experiences for being universal.

Self-awareness is what shows us the gap: the distance between where we are and where we need to be. And it's that difference, that discomfort, that drives improvement. Without it, we continue as we are. Meanwhile, our team improves only until they hit the "lid" of our leadership—our business plateaus, and so do they. But not for long; soon they go looking for more room to grow, to become a giant somewhere else.

—◦—

We can indeed recruit giants to surround ourselves with, but only if we can stay ahead of them in our competence as leaders. To do so requires raising "the lid" of our leadership and thus the capacity of our organization. It is not an easy task, but it starts with having the foundation of self-awareness and seeing the gap between who we are as leaders and who we could become.

The journey to close that gap involves ascending and descending the peak of Mount Stupid, and making our way through the Valley of Realization. It is only from there that we can bolster the pillars that determine our competence as a leader. There may be some additional pillars that are unique to your organization and the work you are tasked with, but all business leaders share the four of communication, empathy, strength, and executive mindset.

Together these traits and capabilities tell us who leaders are, and the profile of someone worth following. And while the demands of business dictate the needs, it is we who develop our capacity to meet them. Our intentions, the efforts to learn, the practice we put in, and our self-reflection: they are all part of our craft.

And perhaps that is at the heart of who leaders are; they never stop improving—for their own benefit, but also for their organizations and the teams they lead.

The climb to mastery isn't an easy one, but that's the challenge we seek as leaders. Knowing where to focus our efforts allows progress to come faster and for our "lid" to rise higher—as do our chances of success on the expedition of business.

There is a parallel between leading an organization and our own journey to become a better leader. Plenty of expeditions fail when one contingent of the crew races ahead and breaks the unity of the whole. As leaders, we have our own harmony to maintain—the cohesion of the teams we lead, but also the traits and characteristics that comprise the leader we are.

Neither is static—our crews can be shaped by adding new people, removing others, or developing the skills and talents of those involved, while building our competence as a leader is a similar approach. Where do we need more of something? Where should we have less? What should we keep doing, but in a slightly different way?

It's an iterative process: trying, failing, learning, improving—bolstering weak spots, but also not devoting too much attention to any one capability.

Similar to Chapter 1 and our vision of the perfect business, knowing which step to take next requires a vision of business leadership done well. What is unique about business leaders? What must they provide? Why are they chosen? And who are they? Having an answer to these questions helps us direct our aim and focus our efforts. And in time, we can raise the lid of our capacity as leaders and the success of our organizations—but only if we don't overlook the final obstacle between us and a clear view of business leadership: what leadership costs.

CHAPTER 17

THE COST OF LEADERSHIP

One Saturday, a new employee sent me an email. He was *"sick,"* and it would be *"at least Wednesday"* before he could return to work. I was skeptical—to say the least. This was the same guy who couldn't seem to stop answering ***my*** phone, the same guy who had a résumé showing five years of experience but displayed the skills of an intern, and the same guy who had accidentally sent me a half-finished email a few weeks prior. Addressed to a long-time employee, it was a cobbled-together manifesto about all the problems with the company and how he would do things differently—not something you want to CC your boss on.

It wasn't long after that I got a different message, a text, a question of how he should submit his two-week notice—he fired himself before I could. I told him that his text would suffice and to clear out his desk by the next morning.

It was easy to say *"goodbye."* Asking other members of the team to take over his projects, asking them to work late when they have a spouse and kids waiting at home—not as easy.

Waking up to emails that an employee won't be in today, not because they're *"sick,"* but because a family member suddenly passed away—not as easy.

Watching a large invoice go from 60 days to 120 days to 180 days overdue, key employees starting a conversation with *"I wasn't looking, but a recruiter reached out,"* having a large client be acquired by a competitor—one that offers our services in-house: not as easy.

Ransomware attacks, server crashes, and power outages—economic downturns, pandemics, and pressure to take a stand on social issues: not as easy.

We know leadership can fail because of bad decisions or the wrong motivations, but it also fails when we underestimate the emotional cost our plans require. And often, that cost is high.

If Chapter 8 is correct, if we seek **certainty**, **competence**, **autonomy**, **relatedness**, and **engagement** to set up our Tent of Comfort, then leadership may be the worst place to look.

Almost by definition, we as leaders are "out in front"—doing our best in a world of complexity, one that provides enough **uncertainty** on its own. Add in the unpredictability of employees, customers, and the economy, and our situation becomes that much more uncomfortable.

Being "out in front" also means there are few benchmarks by which we can measure our performance. And while falling short of a goal understandably gives rise to a feeling of *(in)*competence, reaching our goal often has us wondering if we could have done more.

Feeling competent becomes a balancing act—walking a tightrope between obvious failure and wondering if the bar was set too low. It's a downside to the little **autonomy** leaders do enjoy. And while it's easy to mistake "being in charge" for having freedom to do as we choose, the reality of leadership tells a different story.

Delegating tasks that we enjoy—a necessity to free up the time for tasks that only we can do, biting our tongue to keep important but difficult clients satisfied, having to slow down to communicate clearly, to listen to concerns, and to resolve conflicts: all remind us how infrequently we can do as we please.

As for **relatedness**, there's a reason we know the phrase *"lonely at the top."* And while we're constantly reminded that we are indeed part of a team, there's an element of leadership that always has us more personally and socially detached than we may like from those in our charge.

Leadership is a position rarely lacking in **engagement**, but is it always the kind we want? There are moments when we find "flow," where the challenge of the job and our abilities perfectly align. But again, it is a precarious balance, and we can quickly find ourselves back in the tedious and routine or on the opposite end—a position of overwhelm and scrambling to find answers.

It's easy to make the case that we'd have to be crazy to want to be a leader.

And while some of us surely are, we know there are more defensible reasons for being one: the challenge, accomplishment, and financial rewards—having a greater impact on others, our communities, and the world at large—the freedom to do things our way, to move at our own pace, to bear more risk but for greater benefit—to push ourselves, to learn, and to grow—to feel proud of the work we do and who we've become along the way.

They are many of the same reasons explorers lead expeditions to parts unknown. They are the reasons why we work to master the craft of leadership—despite the discomfort the journey often brings.

So, we're not crazy to be leaders, but we would be crazy not to understand what it costs. Any well-run business starts the year with a budget. No expedition begins without the supplies they'll need along the way. And nearly two thousand years ago the apostolic writer Luke warned us of starting ventures without a full understanding of what they require:

"Suppose one of you wants to build a tower. Won't you first sit down and estimate the cost to see if you have enough money to complete it? For if you lay the foundation and are not able to finish it, everyone who sees it will ridicule you, saying, 'This person began to build and wasn't able to finish.'"

We see how things could be better: the changes we'd like to make and the goals we'd like to achieve—both personally and as an organization. But we often fail to realize why many opportunities remain possibilities: it's because of the cost.

The financial cost, the cost of time, the opportunity cost—but most leaders are good at foreseeing these. What's less foreseen is how our minds will fail us—that many of the decisions which build our Pyramids of Decisions come with a cost. They may be emotional costs, the costs of discomfort, and they may need to be paid by our team, but often they are the cost of leadership.

And it is underestimated time after time on the expedition of business. We see the next peak; it's where we want to go, but are we considering the valley we must pass through along the way?

We see the high points of delegating more. The logic is sound: build capacity and free up leadership bandwidth—but what does it cost?

Investing hours explaining processes for tasks that would take minutes if we simply did them ourselves, giving others a chance at success—but knowing we could do it better, letting go of the controls—allowing someone else to make mistakes, knowing that we'll have to play clean-up: it's all part of the price to be paid.

We recognize that some client relationships no longer serve us. We know that strategically we should part ways. But are we prepared for the emotional toll of those conversations: the potential hurt feelings, the short-term revenue impact, the quiet whispers that might circulate about our loyalty?

Growth demands that we invest in new opportunities, enter different markets, develop new platforms, and launch initiatives that stretch our current capabilities—but growth may not be free. Are we willing to pay the cost of temporary profitability reductions, a little less cushion in the quarters to come, and the discomfort of moving beyond what we know works?

We know we need to have some difficult conversations with our team: the employee whose performance is sliding, the team member whose attitude is negatively impacting the group. The responsible path is clear: address the issue directly. But are we prepared for the emotional fallout: the potential tears, the defensive responses, or the tension that might ripple through the team?

These and situations like them are the cost of leadership, the intangible ones that don't show up in a budget projection. They are the emotional requirements of plans too often designed around numbers, facts, and rational logic—but with little consideration of how they play out with real people in real life.

Similar are the costs we must pay to become a better leader, as there is a price for executing the plans we have for ourselves.

Self-awareness sounds noble—identifying our strengths, confronting our blind spots. But are we truly ready for vulnerability—the emotional work of acknowledging where we fall short, the effort required to become a better communicator and develop other strengths? Can we do so knowing that our friends, family, and other interests are competing for the same time and energy—can we pay that cost?

We might see the value in being more empathetic, but are we willing to take the time to pause and understand others' points of view? Or does the cost have us assuming *"they just don't get it"* and moving on?

We know we need to care for our team, but can we carry the weight of their struggles and failures? Or will we pretend we can separate work from the messiness of personal lives and save the cost?

If we have a natural inclination to get too involved, can we keep from doing more than we should—to not overinvest in any one individual just because they tug on our heartstrings? There's a cost to showing restraint.

And when the right thing to do isn't clear, can we live with that uncertainty? Can we be patient enough to wait? Are we willing to devote the time to let our executive mindset do its job—to sort through and deal with the complexity as we should, while the opportunity to generalize or assume is always there? Or is the cost too great—will we give in to our impulse to act and move on?

None of this diminishes the rewards that leadership can bring, and having to navigate the challenges is typical in the craft of business. But if we don't count the cost, our emotions will push us off course long before we reach the destination we seek.

That's a scenario none of us wants for ourselves, and one that spells disaster for the organizations we lead.

There is undoubtedly a cost to leadership, but equally true is that there's a cost to bad leadership: expeditions left wandering in the wilderness, companies floundering and falling short of potential, frustrated employees—both underperforming and underpaid, wasted time and human potential, disappointed clients and dissatisfied customers, and the world left without a business that could have made it a better place.

Organizations have a tremendous impact on their employees and those they serve, and no one has a bigger impact on an organization than its leader. The impact comes from our unique position and unique responsibilities.

Only the leader can set the destination a crew is to seek. It's the leader who provides the clarity teams need to move forward. It's the leader who realizes the potential of their people. It's the leader who provides the structure and order that unifies the energy that results.

It's the leader who ultimately decides on the best path forward and how to lower the resistance of the journey to be made and the work to be done.

And it's the leader who ensures the results and yield of everyone's efforts are maximized—to the benefit of the individuals and to the organization as a whole.

Without good leadership, it all falls apart. But there is no good leadership without good leaders. And good leaders know the cost of leadership. It's a cost they are willing to pay—not because they're crazy, but because the reward is worth it.

We began Part 3 with a question: What makes leadership in business different from leadership anywhere else? The answer—leading high-agency followers in a world of high complexity—set the stage for what followed.

What leaders must provide—clarity and order, why they are chosen—charisma, who they are—those with five essential traits, four pillars built on a foundation of self-awareness: all were products of the necessity of navigating complexity without suppressing the agency of the crew we depend on.

And it's that same complexity and agency that creates the cost of leadership. Oversimplifying complexity, ignoring nuance, treating every situation the same: that's the easy way, and there's little cost to be paid. Going the way of "command and control" and making every decision ourselves: that's also a climb that's not as steep. Both are easier paths to follow, but the potential reward is less.

To reach the destination we seek, we must take a different route. It means climbing higher on The Mountain of Why, and reaching the first principles of the summit is expensive. Doing so requires us to think when mimicry would be easier, to sit with discomfort when a shortcut is available, and to trust our decisions even when the outcome is uncertain.

It's why so many leaders plateau at the lower elevations—not because they lack intelligence, but because the emotional price of the next level is more than they expected to pay. Yet that is the cost of good Pyramids of Decisions—the thought, the work, and the likely discomfort that goes into every decision that comprises them.

The same is true of the Levers of Control. We know what moves a business forward: more energy, greater unity, lower resistance, and higher yield. But pulling those levers differently than the competition requires a leader willing to bear the cost: the difficult conversations, the uncertainty, and the patience that real leadership demands. Understanding the levers is intellectual work. Operating them requires emotional work. And it's the latter that separates the novice from the master in the craft of business.

Part 1 was about the destination and the direction of each step forward. Part 2 was about the people that get us there and what directs their steps. Part 3 has been about the leader who orchestrates it all.

Part 4 is next, and it's about the expedition itself: the challenges we face, the crews we select, the tales we tell, and the systems, structures, and routines that keep everyone moving forward. It is the operational core of the expedition of business, where everything we've covered so far is put to work, and where the lessons of past expeditions are put on display.

PART 4

EXPEDITION

CHAPTER 18

RULE #1: DON'T DIE ALONG THE WAY

On the east coast of England, there's a small town most have never heard of: Hartlepool. With a population under 100,000 and few attractions, it's a rather unremarkable place. Its one claim to fame is the legend of the Hartlepool Monkey.

The story goes that during the Napoleonic Wars, some 200 years ago, a French ship sank off the coast of Hartlepool. The lone survivor was the ship's mascot, pet, and chief source of entertainment: a monkey—dressed in a miniature version of an official French sailor uniform.

The monkey, soaking wet and exhausted, found his way to shore. The English residents of Hartlepool, having never seen a monkey nor a Frenchman, could not make sense of the strange "language" he was speaking. Convinced by his uniform and their distaste for the French, they did what any patriot would do: they took him prisoner.

It's easy to laugh at this story today, but it wasn't long ago that what was beyond the next ridgeline, or what "strange" people lived on the other side of the sea, was indeed a mystery. In a time of internet searches, Google Earth, and travel television, there are few "parts unknown" left to explore.

Does it mean that the age of expeditions is over? Certainly not.

While the common person will never explore the last depths of the sea or the "final frontier" of space, we're all left with the chance to continue the journeys many started before us: the journeys of thought, of art, of science, and for the business leader—the ever-expanding horizons of economies and the marketplace.

Business may not carry the same romanticism as Magellan attempting to sail around the world, Shackleton trying to reach the South Pole, or Lewis and Clark searching for a land route to the Pacific, but there are commonalities.

Expeditions exist at the margins, pushing into territories yet to be mapped, and are rich with uncertainty. Business is no different. We may not mistake a waterlogged primate for an enemy soldier, but there are plenty of scenarios equally befuddling. We too are left to make sense of those situations and to push on.

To be truly successful, both must do something different or better than any that came before. Following the footprints of those who went before may keep us safe, but it ensures that we are always behind.

Finding a new way forward takes a team and a good leader. Business and expeditions each require coordination among people of varying skills, experience, and authority—all aligned and pursuing a clear goal, overcoming challenges as they go. It is how both find success.

But it is difficult to put all those pieces together, and as a result, there's the truest commonality: the default for both is failure. Most expeditions turn back before reaching their destination, and most businesses fail or flounder long before being remarkable.

It's a fact which reveals the most durable strategy for either:

Rule #1: Don't die along the way.

Obeying the rule means staying in the game long enough to find success, not to be forced to turn back (or worse) before our plans come to fruition. It's obvious but often overlooked:

One of the most reliable ways to win is simply avoiding the ways we lose.

And not losing requires being aware of a central truth—that while there's an endless number of ways an expedition can fail or a business can go belly up, most of the time four root causes are to blame.

1. **Competition** – Others force us into tough decisions.

2. **Human Nature** – We sabotage ourselves.

3. **Limited Resources** – Constraints require that we choose wisely.

4. **Entropy** – Systems, plans, and the order of our organizations decay over time.

In total, they are the Four Horsemen of the business apocalypse, and the topics of the four sections to come.

Anyone who's led a business is all too familiar with these challenges. But too often they are met with frustration, complaints, despair, or even surprise—when what is needed is a plan that gets at the root of the problem.

And the best plans to deal with fundamental problems include fundamental solutions—attacking the challenge at the same base level. It's why back in Chapter 4 we simplified the Levers of Control available to business leaders. When facing the Four Horsemen, the solution is based in the fundamentals—amassing **energy**, building **unity**, reducing **resistance**, and increasing the **yield** of our efforts.

Part of the craft of business is building a plan that favors the basics over complexity. What we've covered so far and the chapters that are to follow provide the insights to do so and to keep these Horsemen at bay. The first step is taking an honest look at what we're up against—and often, *who* we're up against.

COMPETITION

I had a conversation with an architect recently. Their firm was submitting a proposal for a large, prestigious project. Unfortunately, though common, three other firms were doing the same. More unusual were the details of the request from the potential client. As part of the proposal package, they wanted extensive concept drawings of the project included—roughly 30% of the design work, completed by each firm on their own dime, with no guarantee of compensation. By industry standards, it was an aggressive request. The architect would be justified in saying "*No.*" However, would their competition say "*Yes*"?

In business and expeditions, there's often no reward for coming in second. And coming in first can mean being crazy enough to stay in the race.

Charles Lindbergh was the first to make a solo flight across the Atlantic. It's easy to look at a story like his and take away that "*fortune favors the brave*" or "*no guts, no glory,*" but perhaps the more useful lesson is how competition can force us into difficult, if not unwise, decisions.

Before Lindbergh made his successful landing in Paris, there had been other attempts to complete this marquee aviation expedition. The results included four crashed planes, six lives lost, and three more seriously injured. So surely Lindbergh took pause and doubled down on safety, right? Wrong.

Lindbergh's plane had the fuel tanks located forward of the cockpit, completely blocking his view. His 33-hour flight would have to be made using a periscope to see around the tanks. Reducing the weight of the plane was paramount; every unnecessary item was left behind: no radio, no parachute, no gas gauges, no navigation lights. Lindbergh even sat in a lightweight wicker chair instead of a heavy leather pilot's seat. And bordering on the obsessive, he cut his maps down to include only the reference points he would need.

Why such tolerance for risk? Competition.

Had Lindbergh delayed his attempt to engineer safer solutions, we would know the name Clarence Chamberlin instead. He flew from the US to Germany, breaking Lindbergh's distance record, only 15 days later.

Among seven serious competitors racing to be the first across the Atlantic, only one emerged as the winner. For the rest, the loss was catastrophic. As for my architect friend, they and their competition all acquiesced to the client's demands. There will be one winner and three big losers.

There will always be someone out there willing to do the same work for less money, to cut corners, pay higher salaries, and favor the short over the long run. It's what makes coming in first so hard. Accepting that reality is part of the expedition of business.

But it's not all doom and gloom. Competition is also the force that causes us to think differently, to zig when others zag, and to put serious thought into how we avoid crowded opportunities. It's competition that motivates us to climb higher on The Mountain of Why, to reach a higher elevation than our competitors. They have likely set up camp at Levels 1, 2, and 3 of mimicry, heuristics, and generic frameworks. We can pass them by if we reach Level 4 of synthesized strategies tailored to our organizations, and ultimately the summit—Level 5 of the first principles on which we plant our flag.

Electing to choose a different path and avoid the crowd may seem obvious, but the average business spends much of their time chasing the same prize and playing the same game the same way as everyone else. They build their Pyramids of Decisions, decide on their goals, strategies, tactics, and execution, just as their competitors do. The results are predictable, failure remains the default, and they risk violating Rule #1 because they didn't see the Horseman of competition coming.

But their mimicry is our gain. While they are stuck at a lower elevation, we can move higher—crafting a plan to deal with the three remaining Horsemen that await. And one of them we know all too well.

HUMAN NATURE

Imagine you are considering a new hire. It is revealed that the person is more self-seeking than focused on the collective good. They tend to lose interest in tasks and assignments. They are often misunderstood by others, and others are often misunderstood by them. They default to their own beliefs—even in the face of compelling contrary evidence. And they are inclined to get defensive, if not outright rebel, when their authority, competence, or status is questioned. Would you hire them?

There is no other option. We may vary in how strongly we exemplify these traits, but all of us have them.

Part 2 gave us a good explanation of why, but also the tools to battle against the Horseman of human nature. To do so, we must have a plan to use the strengths that our ancestors and life experiences have passed along, but also one to buttress the weaknesses. That often means relying on systems instead of willpower and trusting processes over our memory. Without such reinforcement, businesses are ripe for failure, just as expeditions opposed by the same Horseman often ended in disaster.

Henry Hudson was a brilliant explorer obsessed with finding the Northwest Passage. On his fourth voyage, he explored the massive bay that now bears his name. But after the initial thrill of arriving, the unglamorous work of exploration—carefully mapping the area, maintaining crew morale, and rationing supplies—bored him.

As winter closed in and starvation loomed, Hudson's attention drifted. He spent time in his cabin with maps and journals while practical leadership evaporated. The crew, starving and convinced their captain had lost focus, mutinied. Hudson and eight others were set adrift in a small boat. They were never seen again.

The history of expeditions is littered with similar breakdowns—highly capable explorers succumbing to some of our worst tendencies: boredom, impulse, favoritism, and plain dereliction of duty. If left unchecked, the same tendencies lie waiting to derail any business.

A senior project manager, reliable for years, eventually masters the challenges of the job, loses interest and leaves a giant mess for others to untangle after they leave. We hire someone we *have a good feeling about* only to be disappointed and soon dealing with problems a more time-consuming interview process would have avoided. A company owner spends days designing the perfect company holiday card. They pick just the right graphics, fonts, and colors—all work they enjoy doing, rather than taking on the less appetizing task of preparing next year's strategic plan.

These aren't fictional; I've seen them all happen, and chances are you have seen similar episodes of human nature pulling leaders off course. Left unmanaged, human nature quietly undermines organizations. And enough small failures eventually violate Rule #1.

Our shortcomings wouldn't be such a problem if not for one thing. It's the difficult reality any expedition or business must face, and our third Horseman.

LIMITED RESOURCES

What problem in business can't we solve with unlimited money and unlimited time? Similarly, what expeditions lose much of their challenge if they are able to take along all the food, equipment, personnel, fuel, and water they could ever possibly need?

Of course, we know that's not how the world works. Businesses are forever constrained by money and time. And those two parents give birth to some difficult children: limited talent—we can't hire enough good people, limited marketing—we can't find enough good customers, limited systems—we can't get the consistent results we want.

Yet limited resources can be clarifying. When the crew of Apollo 13 had CO2 levels spike during their troubled and "failed" expedition to the moon, the critical need to make an adapter for air filters with only what they had on board focused everyone's attention. The constraint: "*Make Filter A fit into a hole for Filter B, using nothing but parts C through Z,*" forced innovation that abundance never could.

In business, constraints force prioritization, creativity, and focus. The company with abundant resources often wastes them. The one that must choose carefully often does so wisely. Our competitors face the same resource constraints. And so, the question isn't necessarily whether we have enough; it's whether we're more thoughtful about deploying what we do have.

However, there is one resource problem child that is less obvious: the challenge of limited information.

In an age where we can see aerial photos and street-level views of almost any place on Earth, quickly search nearly the entire canon of published writing, and be aware of "breaking news" all over the world, it would be nice to think the challenge of limited information has been reduced. It hasn't; it has merely moved.

Like a false horizon, with every step forward that fringe of familiarity moves farther into the distance, with both businesses and expeditions in chase. What was once new information quickly turns into common knowledge as it becomes commoditized and accessible to many. Operating at the frontier means having more reliable information systems—ones that automate the data collection we need and eliminate the noise that drowns out the signal. All to combat the three types of missing information: **known unknowns**, **unknown unknowns**, and the **unknowable**.

Unfortunately, for the decisions that matter most, we just never know for sure.

What is the current lead time of materials for a new product launch? How would employees rate their current benefit package? What's our current market share among key demographics? All of them are **known unknowns**.

Who was asking in the early 1990s if their computer infrastructure would be Y2K compliant? In 2010, was anyone asking if their insurance covered ransomware and the demand for Bitcoin payments? Pre-2020, everyone seemed focused on questions related to "just-in-time" inventory, speed, and efficiency—how many were asking about resilience to a global pandemic? Unfortunately, **unknown unknowns** are just that—unknown.

What exactly emerges as a business's main challenge in 3, 5, or 10 years? Why exactly did their competitor fail a few months prior? We can estimate, predict, and assign probabilities, but often we're left with the **unknowable**.

It's all part of what makes both expeditions and business hard.

There are things we can do to close our knowledge gaps. But sometimes success doesn't come from making extrapolations of limited information; it comes from humility. It requires accepting that we don't or can't know as much as we'd like to, and that some situations are beyond our control.

In the end, constraints don't kill businesses—poor decisions do. And the tighter the constraints, the less margin for error we have as leaders before we violate Rule #1.

So, while we make the best decisions we can, we also need contingencies and plans for resilience in the face of uncertainty—because our fourth Horseman can cause even the best-laid plans to devolve into chaos.

ENTROPY

When Lindbergh lifted off for Paris, it's likely his cockpit was in perfect order—flight maps neatly arranged, the lens on his "periscope" crystal clear, and his pilot suit fitting perfectly for the cameras to see him off. It's equally likely that Hudson's crew started out with organized trunks of gear and backpacks of supplies. Their plans were equally tidy—the destination clear and agreement on how to proceed. From these high levels of organization, there was only one direction to go: toward disorder—entropy at work.

How many planning or strategy sessions have you been a part of where clarity was the end result of the day—only to feel like it was all a dream a few months later? The mental effort that was spent to arrange a plan is slowly wasted as the noise of the day-to-day moves you from a mountaintop view back to the shadows and limited visibility of the valley.

We give firm and clear directions to an employee on Day 1. Day 2 goes as expected. Day 3 is not quite as good—and a few weeks later we're having the same conversation all over again.

A marketing campaign kicks off with enthusiasm and initial success, only to be derailed later by less and less consistent follow-up with leads and the drift of messaging.

While the disruption of competition, human nature, and limited resources are often abundantly clear, our Horseman of entropy is slyer and more patient. It doesn't bring down organizations overnight—it simply ensures that if leaders ignore the slow slide toward disorder long enough, Rule #1 will be broken.

It may be the most fundamental of the Four Horsemen: the undeniable tendency for systems and structures left unattended to decay. It's another problem that can be mitigated—partly by pausing to re-center ourselves and our teams, partly by designs that make the right way easier than the wrong way. But, like our other three Horsemen, it can never be fully eliminated.

——◆◇◆——

Zooming out and seeing the four fundamental forces that work against us in business can be illuminating. It can also be depressing—realizing that the headwinds we fight in business never really stop.

But our success doesn't depend on whether business feels hard—to a degree, it always will.

Competition never stops pressing in; information is never fully complete; people will remain both perfectly and imperfectly human, with entropy always at work. These forces are not problems to be solved once and set aside; they are the permanent operating conditions of any business that intends to last.

Others may promise to solve all our problems—the program, consultant, or latest technology that's the "complete solution": all are a mirage.

The headwinds are real, and if we pretend they're not, we will soon violate Rule #1. But the challenges are not ours alone. Our Four Horsemen don't discriminate; every business is in their sights. And thankfully for us, most don't even see the root of what ails them.

Mastery of the craft of business is not about eliminating the Four Horsemen; it is about accepting their reality, designing strategies to minimize their impact, and getting on with the work of building something that holds together despite the challenges they bring.

To that end, we are fortunate to have the records of past expeditions and the tactics that were common to them. It is a welcome opportunity to use survivor bias to our benefit. We often don't know what caused some expeditions to fail—no one is left to tell the tale. And while correlation does not equal causation, it stands to reason that when certain tactics appear time and time again in successful expeditions, business leaders fighting against the same fundamental forces should take note.

In the chapters that follow, we'll look at several tactics that have a history of leading to success. They are the tools, systems, and ideas that we need on the expedition of business. They are the insights we need when we're at the Levers of Control. And they are the efforts we can make to obey Rule #1, do battle with the Horsemen that oppose us, and reach our intended destination.

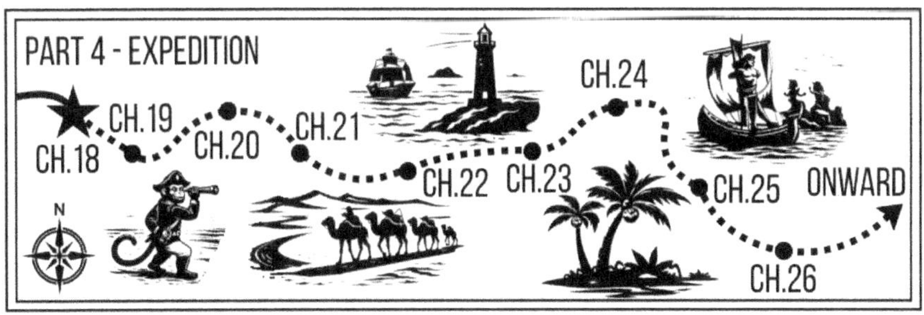

Business is a fight against the same Four Horsemen at every turn. Competition, human nature, limited resources, and entropy will always be waiting.

Our job is not to eliminate them; it is to survive them better than our competition—and to not violate Rule #1.

We start our journey to do so with some big advantages: clarity of our aim (the perfect business), a guide to organize goals versus strategies, tactics, or execution (Pyramids of Decisions), a grasp of the Levers of Control, and a tool for understanding our crew—the G.E.A.R. model of genetics, enduring traits, adopted narratives, and real-time constraints.

In total, they allow us to climb to the top of The Mountain of Why—to lead our business from the position of first principles. It is a strategic position which can only be equaled, not surpassed in our battle against the Four Horsemen and our race against the competition.

But arriving there takes more than the necessary tools; it also takes knowing how to use them effectively. As we said at the outset, part of that learning comes from our own practice and experience, while part comes from hearing the experiences of others. We alone are responsible for the former, but the chapters to come will provide plenty of the latter.

We start with one of the most fundamental questions of any expedition. How do we select the people that make up our crew—the team we depend on?

CHAPTER 19

COALITIONS AND CARAVANS

For most of the first millennium, an untold number of adventurers made the expedition to travel the infamous Silk Road, a dangerous series of routes stretching from China to the Mediterranean. Completing the journey would mean crossing the Gobi Desert, climbing up and over the *"roof of the world"* in the Pamir Mountains, and doing so under the constant threat of bandits, sandstorms, and some of the most extreme weather on Earth.

At the outset, the leaders of these expeditions faced the same challenge as business leaders: building a crew for the journey ahead. Assembling the team we need requires good answers to certain questions.

Who do we bring along, and who do we leave at home? How do we keep the entry gate to our organization wide enough to get all the people and talent we need, while narrow enough to keep the team cohesive and manageable?

We may not be facing bandits and sandstorms, but bringing on bad hires is equally "fun."

The novice leader may hire based on skills and experience alone, or they may default to their *"gut"* and who they *"like."* But for anyone who's inevitably learned better, we know there is something more to consider.

And there is no shortage of opinions as to what that "something more" is.

We're told to *"start with why"*—that anyone who's a part of our crew needs to find meaning in the same "why" that we do, to define our "core values" and use them as a litmus test for whoever comes on board, or to hire for a *"cultural fit."* And then once that produces a monoculture, hire for a *"culture add."* And if all else fails, simply hire someone we *"would want in a foxhole"* with us.

The appeal is understandable. I would love to hire a team that always believes what I believe, thinks how I think, and finds meaning in what I see as important. Through the lens of our G.E.A.R. model, it removes the variable of Adopted Narratives. I don't have to deduce what someone believes about the world; they think like I do, and it makes them more predictable—alignment comes easier.

Unfortunately, it's all a mirage—impractical advice that can be tempting when you're wandering the desert looking for that "something else."

The VP of pre-construction at a mid-sized general contractor has been trying to hire an additional estimator for months. Job postings, recruiters, referral bonuses, LinkedIn: they've tried it all. So far, no one's been a perfect "fit."

The dogmatic view says not to settle, to keep the bar high. It's a convenient position for someone who doesn't have the pressure of their current estimators becoming disgruntled, the bottleneck delaying project starts, and impatient clients.

We've all likely found ourselves in similar situations—torn between the dream of managing a team where everyone *"is one of us"* and easing the immediate pain of being short-staffed and worried about burnout.

What's the answer?

Navigating that question and getting the width of our entry gate right is part of the craft of business. It's also been part of leading successful expeditions for a long time. And history shows us that achieving a utopia of uniform motivation and values isn't required for success.

Undoubtedly, the journey of the Silk Road was made by some uniformed armies or commissioned envoys of a single origin, but just as often the expedition parties were a caravan of all types. Persian traders in search of goods from afar, Buddhist monks seeking and spreading enlightenment, and Islamic scholars in search of knowledge: despite their different beliefs, *"whys,"* and values, they were able to work together to reach their shared destination. And they weren't the exception.

Lewis and Clark may have been two army officers, but their coalition included French-Canadian interpreters, an enslaved man, and an indigenous Shoshone woman—all of whom played important roles in their journey. Darwin's famous voyage on the HMS Beagle included a crew of gentlemen scientists, ambitious rivals, an artist, a missionary, sailors, and naval officers.

All involved had their own agendas, yet they completed some of history's most consequential journeys.

In the history of expeditions, these cobbled-together teams are as much the rule as the exception. They weren't ideal situations, and we can almost always do better in a modern-day company, but they were akin to the reality of most business ventures. When people are a scarce commodity, our Horseman of limited resources is to blame, and we must find a way to work with who's available.

For years, my team included an A+ project manager. He was a workhorse; projects got done on time, and the staff respected him. Did he show up at many company get-togethers? Ever speak or show much interest in our *"mission"* or *"values"*? Not really. That wasn't him; he liked the work, he wanted to do a good job, be compensated fairly, and that was enough.

It wasn't ideal. If I was a Persian trader, he was a Buddhist monk. But I was sure glad to have him in our caravan.

—◆—

Business leaders face the constant challenge of adjusting the Levers of Control. Getting the balance right is part of our craft, and like most things, there are tradeoffs.

Widening the gate, letting more people in, may increase the **energy** we have inside the organization—but it comes at the cost of our ability to **unify** it all in the same direction. And bad hires increase the **resistance** of the work and lower the **yield**, as poor performers make everyone's job more difficult and potential profit goes to unproductive employees.

To make better decisions around building our crews, we can learn from fellow craftsmen who traveled the Silk Road. They were artists skilled in a particular technique and medium. If caravans help explain **who** we include on our journeys, mosaics help explain **how** we select those individuals.

Putting together a crew for our expeditions is a matter of finding good pieces, shaping as necessary, and putting them in the right spot.

Modern artists benefit from access to just about any materials their hearts could desire. They do indeed enjoy a limitless pool of resources. However, their Silk Road predecessors are more relatable to business leaders. Stones, gems, animal bones, shells: whatever they could get their hands on, those were the parts and pieces that craftsmen of the Silk Road trimmed, massaged, and doctored to fit through the entry gates of their artwork.

Crafting the mosaic of our organizations requires a similar approach. It takes answering the same questions about people that the mosaic artist asked about each tile.

What are the characteristics I should consider? How strict are the criteria? To what extent can each piece be modified? And most importantly, just where in the picture is the next tile going?

The questions are hard enough for artists. For leaders operating in a world of greater complexity, finding the answers is an expedition all its own. Before we can build our caravan wisely, there are three rivers to cross on the journey to mastery. And we will ford each of them in the sections to come.

The first river asks us to rethink how we evaluate the people standing at the entrance to our organizations—not just whether they "*fit*" but which dimensions matter. And of those, which can we shape over time? This river lays out the full spectrum of what we're really judging: that there is not one entry gate to our organizations, but nine which new hires need to pass through—from teachable knowledge to immovable traits. And our crossing of this river challenges us about why we so often make one gate impossibly narrow while leaving others too broad to be useful.

The second river takes us upstream to the headwaters of decisions. Before we can know how much alignment we need from someone, we must understand what alignment means. There's a reason creating alignment after the fact is so difficult; it's easier done when we focus on the Pools of Beliefs from which our Pyramids of Decisions emerge. How one decides on goals, strategies, tactics, and execution isn't random; it's predictable if we know where to look.

The third river then makes it all practical. It divides our caravan into three groups: Leaders, Crew, and Hired Hands. And it argues that the overlap of beliefs we require should be proportional to the authority someone has within our organizations.

Together, the three rivers give us a framework for building a team that can be assembled from the people who are actually available, while still unified enough to reach our intended destination.

RIVER ONE: PROGRESSION OF FIT

Any business leader who has filled an open role knows doing so is always a judgment call. We can and should have a systematic approach to hiring, but in the end there's no formula for answering some questions.

Just how much additional experience is needed to offset a lack of familiarity with certain software platforms? Is $5,000 more a year a fair premium to pay when there are no other promising candidates in the pipeline? Are short stints at their last three jobs enough of a red flag to turn down someone who checks every other box?

We know our decisions and the people in question lie on a spectrum. On one end there is anyone with a pulse and the basic credentials, on the other is a candidate who meets every listed requirement and three we forgot to include. Those extremes are obvious; all the other possibilities are somewhere in the middle. Determining exactly where is easier with the right tools.

If the artist of a Silk Road caravan comes across a shiny stone, they ask: *"Can I use this in my latest mosaic?"* Subconsciously, their mind is making several qualifications: the size of the stone, the color, the shape, the appearance. Next, they consider where it could go. Does it work as a background piece? Could it square up a corner around the edge?

If it doesn't seem to fit anywhere, then there's a different thought. Instead of tossing it away, could they change it a little? Trim it down to size, adjust the shape, or polish it up for a brighter shine: there are lots of things they could do to make it work.

But then there are some they can't. There's no changing the fact that it's a stone, and the color is fixed as well.

Picking a candidate for an open role is the same exercise; while some qualities are what they are, other facets we can adjust. But the question is the same all along: should they be part of our mosaic, part of our caravan?

The image below maps out the nine core aspects of a candidate we examine when thinking about role, company, and yes, even cultural fit. As one moves down the list, the opportunity to "modify" the potential candidate decreases. The categories move from **Company-Specific Knowledge**, which is modified through onboarding and training, to **Fundamental Needs**, which without a time machine or genetic editing is impossible to change.

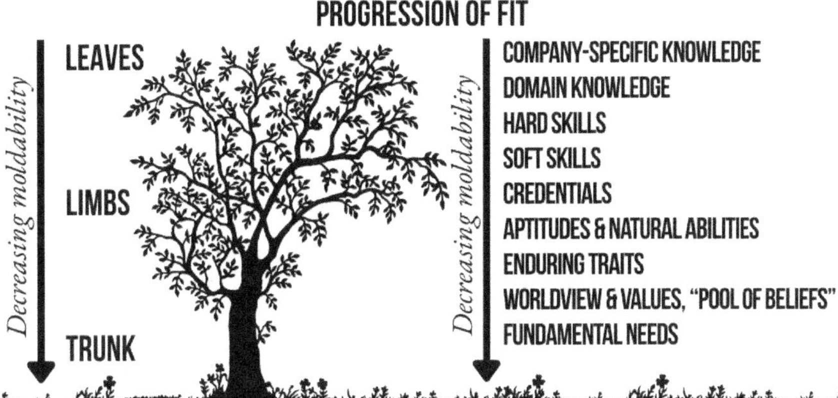

While we can shape the leaves of a tree anyway we wish, we lose flexibility when it comes to the limbs, and the trunk remains mostly fixed. People are similar, there are things we can, and should, adjust, while other aspects we accept as they are.

Each of the nine represents a separate entry gate to our organization. And we set the width of each. If they're all too wide, anyone can wander in; too narrow, and no one will be able to pass through them all. Part of the craft of business is considering and getting the right balance of each:

Company-Specific Knowledge is information unique to an organization. It includes processes, systems, relationships, history, and institutional knowledge that can only be learned on the job.

Domain Knowledge is industry-specific expertise: understanding of market dynamics, technical applications, regulatory environment, and specialized knowledge relevant to the field.

Hard Skills are learned technical proficiencies: software platforms, analytical methods, and demonstrable competencies acquired through training or experience.

Soft Skills include interpersonal and adaptive capabilities. Communication style, collaboration ability, emotional intelligence, adaptability, and behavioral competencies: all can be developed in individuals, but doing so requires significant time and effort.

Credentials are formal qualifications: licenses, certifications, degrees, and other official documentation of capability or authorization to perform specific work. It's debatable how easily these can be added—some are no more than an online test, while others require years of schooling.

Aptitudes and Natural Abilities are our inherent capabilities: problem-solving capacity, pattern recognition, spatial reasoning, learning speed, and cognitive and physical horsepower.

Enduring Traits are our core personality characteristics, the "E" of our G.E.A.R. model, the O.C.E.A.N. dimensions (Openness, Conscientiousness, Extraversion, Agreeableness, Neuroticism), and facets of each. They shape how someone naturally approaches work, people, and challenges.

Worldview and Values are part of our foundational beliefs about what matters, how the world works, and what gives work meaning. They are the adopted narratives and the "A" of our G.E.A.R. model. Shaped by upbringing and life experiences, they include both loosely and deeply held opinions.

Fundamental Needs are our most basic requirements, the "G" of genetic wiring in our G.E.A.R. model, and the five poles holding up our Tent of Comfort (Competence, Certainty, Autonomy, Relatedness, Engagement). They are the needs that must be satisfied before anyone can thrive in our organizations.

If part of our recruiting and interviewing process doesn't give us real insight into each of the nine, then we're navigating without a compass. It's tempting to deduce, reason, and "gut feel" our way based on references, resumes, and how well they interview. But doing so leaves us at the level of mimicry and heuristics on The Mountain of Why. Making better decisions means climbing higher and paying the cost of putting in more work and more time.

Let's not forget an important first principle: we love to make emotional decisions and rationalize them later. When we have a more structured process for evaluating our crew members, it saves us from the Horseman of human nature.

But having information on each of the nine entry gates is useless without benchmarks. At each stop along the way, one has the decision of just how wide the gate should be. The bigger the pool of candidates, the more we can tighten things up. But when candidates are in short supply, keeping too many gates narrow means we end up doing a lot of considering but little—and perhaps too little—hiring.

Let's say you're our aforementioned VP of Pre-Construction and are considering Sarah to fill the open estimator role. A quick look at the nine entry gates helps bring the overall picture into focus:

Company-Specific Knowledge? Zero. But that's fine; everyone starts here.

Domain Knowledge? She's got construction experience but not in your specific sector. That's teachable in a few months though, and she can still get to work right away.

Hard Skills? She knows the software but not your process—a couple of weeks of learning and she'll be familiar enough.

Soft Skills? This is where you pause. She seems... abrasive? Or is she just direct? You're not sure. Can you help her with this? Just who does she have to deal with regularly? Can they handle it? This gate could be a problem.

Credentials? She has some third-party certifications, but the role doesn't require any formal licensure.

Aptitudes? Quick learner, you can tell from the interview—that will help with the prior challenges.

Enduring Traits? Ah, now things make sense. Low agreeableness, high conscientiousness: that explains the abrasiveness, but also why she's focused and organized. It's a trade-off that might be required with any good candidate.

Worldview? She seemed to just have a blank stare about our company mission, but did seem to perk up when talking about our values. She has kids and a family, and she seems to be most interested in good work and fair pay.

Fundamental Needs? She's human, right? Other people are happy in the role; you're delivering on these. There is structure, clarity, and opportunity to succeed; the role requires a lot of interaction with others, and it's easy to feel as part of the team. And she won't be micromanaged.

So, do you extend an offer? Or do her soft skills and personality hold you back?

She really didn't seem that "*all-in*" on the mission and values. Do you bring her on—ease the pain and worry of late starts and current staff wearing thin? Or stick to your guns on "culture"?

Part of the craft of business is thinking through judgment calls just like this. One could write an entire book on balancing these trade-offs—where to be lenient, where to be strict. But business leaders get most of the benefit from having a framework to organize their thoughts and the information available—a structure that can save us from purely gut-feel and emotional decisions.

Unfortunately, that is easier said than done. And one of the best ways to "win" in hiring is to avoid how we often "lose."

We have a powerful attraction to candidates who think, believe, and "fit" the organization like we do—and an equally strong repulsion for those that don't. It's why **Worldview and Values** is the most contentious of the entry gates.

It's also why a common mistake is making this gate too narrow, and as a result, the others too wide. It is easy to become so focused on finding someone who "fits in" that we overlook red flags in competence, experience, or aptitude. We hire the person we'd want to grab a beer with, brushing aside legitimate questions as to whether they can do the job.

To do it right, we can leverage the same truth that helped our caravan friends on the Silk Road: building a coalition requires a degree of alignment, but it doesn't have to be perfect.

Determining how much is needed is a challenging question. And while River Three will bring some answers, we can't get there until we cross River Two—moving from the water's edge of talking about alignment to the distant shore of defining what it actually means.

RIVER TWO: HEADWATERS OF DECISIONS

My A+ project manager was a good example of someone we wouldn't want to exclude from our organizations by making the gate of **Worldview and Values** too narrow. He was also a great example of someone I would have never promoted into leadership, nor put in a position where his decisions would shape the environment for other members of the crew.

To understand why, we need to look upstream—to where decisions come from.

We can qualify decisions with The Mountain of Why framework and understand their place and importance with our Pyramids of Decisions, but those tools are mostly backward-looking. They help us explain and categorize decisions after the fact. What they don't explain is the *source* of the decisions we make.

Through the lens of our G.E.A.R. model, both the decisions we make and the actions we take are a product of four undercurrents. When we're deciding how wide to make the gate of **Worldview and Values**, it's the "A" of Adopted Narratives that matters most.

Because before we choose a goal, the associated strategy, or the tactics and execution that support it all, we already carry beliefs about what's true, what matters, and what's right. We can inform those beliefs with data, expert opinions, and experience, but what we believe at a fundamental level directs our next step.

Those beliefs collect into something like a reservoir: a **Pool of Beliefs**.

Individuals have one; organizations have one too—whether they've defined them or not. And when the Pools overlap enough, we call it *alignment*. When they don't, conflict isn't an occasional hiccup; it's the norm.

I recently spoke with a business owner who fired their business development director. One believed that *"people don't buy from you just because they like you."* The other believed, *"That's the only reason people buy from you."*

Who was right isn't the point. Their Pools didn't overlap on a belief that directly shaped the strategy, so every downstream decision became friction. They didn't disagree on tactics. They disagreed about the world. It was never going to work.

That example also highlights something important: only our convictions that are relevant belong in the Pool of Beliefs.

You're welcome to believe aliens exist, that red wine is good for you, or that college football is better than the NFL. Those opinions might make me like you more (or less), but they don't shape the decisions you'll make at work.

Other beliefs are so universally agreed upon that they don't add anything: gravity exists, the earth is round, customers prefer low prices to high ones—fast service more than slow service. There's no reason to dilute the pool with obvious realities we can safely assume won't derail our efforts.

And just as importantly, not all beliefs are held with the same conviction. Some are loose preferences we can be flexible on, while others are where we dig in our heels. The latter hold up entire sections of how we think and how we decide. If they're violated, we're not just being asked to change our minds; we're being asked to change who we are.

So, it's beliefs that shape our work decisions which belong in our Pools of Beliefs.

And such beliefs become more impactful on our organizations when their holder has more autonomy in their job. If an employee is working on the factory floor, pulling packages for delivery, or doing scripted cold calls, then fewer of their beliefs are relevant. If one is setting policy, making strategic decisions, or managing others, then more overlap in their Pool of Beliefs is necessary.

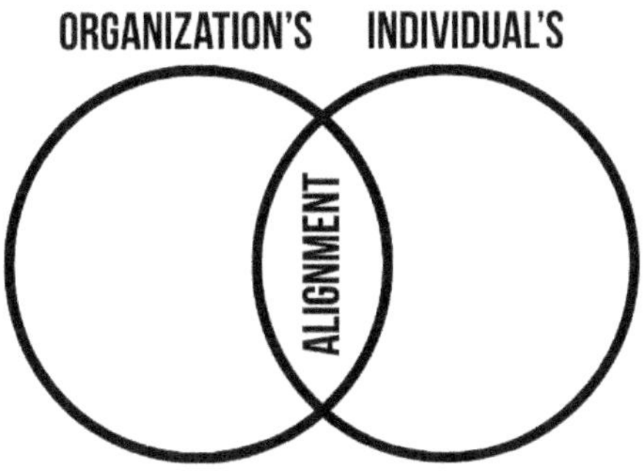

Pool of Beliefs Pool of Beliefs

The required overlap between an individual's Pool of Beliefs and those of the organizations we lead is a necessity of scale.

If we as leaders could be everywhere, doing everything, and making every decision, then no overlap would be required—every decision and action would flow from the same pool: ours.

Similarly, if we could hire people **exactly** like us, then there would be no need to predict the decision-making of others—again, everything would flow from the same pool.

But as we know, both are impossible. Beyond a certain size, the scale of our organization is too big for us to do it all alone. Science hasn't yet made cloning ourselves possible. And so, we're left to rely on others, and we are beholden to the decisions they make.

Such decisions have a better chance of aligning with what we would have done, and what our organizations need, when someone shares more of the relevant beliefs. When everyone's decisions flow from similar headwaters, the actions that occur downstream are more aligned.

What beliefs are relevant, and how Pools need to overlap is different for every role. Someone who's managing sales requires a different overlap than someone who's setting HR policy. But our Pools of Beliefs often trace back to a small set of higher-level questions.

They are questions that sit at 30,000 feet, above strategy, above tactics, above execution. They are more "meta" level questions that define who a business really is.

They are also the kinds of questions most organizations never ask, ask but half-answer, or assume they agree on—and then wonder why the actions and decisions that flow downstream feel inconsistent.

In total, there are seven of these meta-level questions that shape most decisions in an organization:

1. What is a business for? Returns? Livelihoods? Solving meaningful problems? Building something that outlasts us? The answer sets the moral center of gravity for the organization.

2. What is success? Revenue? Profit? Reputation? Longevity? Impact? Lifestyle? Different answers build different companies. People may have more than one answer, but there's an order of priority.

3. What is failure? Financial collapse? Reputational damage? Violating an ethical line? Mortgaging the future for short-term gain? What we define as failure determines what risks we will take and the paths we avoid.

4. What are employees? A transaction? A partnership? A mutual commitment? A family? Whatever our answer is, it determines what people grow to expect, what leaders feel entitled to, and what betrayal looks like—in either direction.

5. What is competition? A war? A market reality? Friendly rivals who sharpen each other? The answer changes how we price, how we hire, how we collaborate, and whether we see "*win-win*" as naïve or strategic.

6. What are customers? Always right? A means to revenue? Relationships to nurture? The answer determines whether we fire problem clients, bend to unreasonable demands, or redefine what "good service" actually means.

7. What time horizon are we operating on? Quarterly? Annual? Five years? Generational? The answer governs everything from training investment to product quality to whether we take the tempting shortcut.

These are not questions with universally correct answers. Our answers might make competitors scoff—and that's probably a good thing. A business needs to differentiate, to go their own way, but if we believe the same things as our rivals then inevitably our strategy and value proposi-tions will be indistinguishable.

But the point isn't to be intentionally contrarian or universally accepted. The point is to be coherent—among leaders, among the members of our crew that we trust to make good decisions, and particularly within ourselves. The goal of answering these questions is to be clear about what we believe. Because it's those beliefs—if stable and firm—that form the foundation from which we can build our Pyramids of Decisions and shape our first principles of Level 5 decisions atop The Mountain of Why.

Once an organization is clear on its Pool of Beliefs, then decisions get easier. Delegating authority can be done with more confidence, and the gate of **Worldview and Values** becomes easier to set—not because it becomes "wide" or "narrow," but because it becomes specific.

And that brings us to a question we haven't resolved:

Once an organization knows its Pool of Beliefs, how much overlap do we actually need from a person? Do we need them aligned the same way regardless of role? Or does the required overlap change with the individual?

The answer flows from our next and final river to cross, and it's the final step in determining who to make a part of our caravans.

RIVER THREE: LEADERS, CREW, AND HIRED HANDS

Alignment isn't binary. It's a matter of degree. And more importantly, on the expedition of business, it's a matter of consequence. The greater the impact of someone's decisions, the greater the cost of misalignment.

This is where many leaders get into trouble. Some talk about "culture fit" as if every role carries the same weight, as if the beliefs of a janitor matter as much as those of a VP of Operations. They both may be valuable to an organization, but the impact of one's decisions is clearly larger.

The required overlap between an individual's Pool of Beliefs and that of the organization is proportional to the latitude they have to decide, influence, and interpret uncertainty. And it divides people in our caravans into three broad categories: **Leaders, Crew,** and **Hired Hands**.

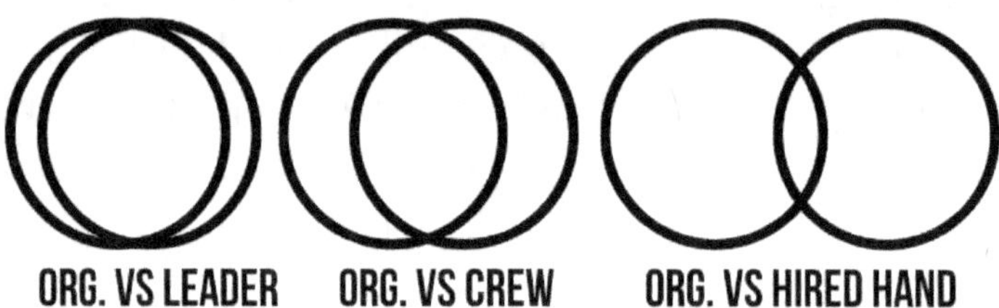

Leaders require the highest degree of overlap. Their decisions don't merely flow from the Pool of Beliefs; they actively shape it.

Leaders define success. They determine acceptable tradeoffs. They set strategy, resolve conflicts between competing priorities, and decide what the organization will and will not tolerate. When ambiguity appears, leaders don't just follow rules. They interpret meaning.

This is why misalignment at the leadership level is so destructive. When leaders answer the meta-level questions differently, the organization doesn't drift—it fractures. Teams start to receive conflicting signals, strategy becomes incoherent, and decisions that should reinforce one another cancel out instead.

This is also why promoting top performers into leadership without examining the entry gate of **Worldview and Values** is a costly mistake that organizations often make. Competence without alignment destabilizes the environment for everyone.

Crew members occupy the middle ground. They aren't defining the organization's beliefs, but they are expected to act with good judgment when the path isn't clear.

Crew members work through uncertainty; they adapt tactics, and they coordinate across functions. They make decisions that don't rise to the level of strategy but still meaningfully affect outcomes.

Because of this, crew members require substantial, but not complete, overlap with the organization's Pool of Beliefs. They don't need to share every conviction, ***but they must align on the beliefs that shape the decisions they're empowered to make***. Otherwise, consistency across the organization suffers.

This is where the delegation of decision-making lives or dies. When belief overlap is sufficient, leaders can grant autonomy without constant supervision being required. When it's lacking, leaders are forced to either micromanage or accept risks they can't fully understand.

Crew members are what allow coherence to scale. They make it possible for the organization to act as a coordinated body, because the decisions of individuals flow from a shared source.

Hired hands require the least overlap, but that doesn't make them less valuable.

It's just that their work is bounded. The decisions they make are constrained by process, policy, and clear expectations. They execute within frameworks defined by others. Their value lies in reliability, consistency, and craftsmanship—not interpretation.

For hired hands, their Pools of Beliefs only need to overlap on foundational ethics and basic expectations: honesty matters, accountability matters, and similar. But agreement on deeper meta-level questions isn't required, because those questions don't meaningfully surface in their daily work.

A hired hand with strong execution can be invaluable, as long as they aren't placed in roles where their beliefs silently shape decisions they were never meant to make.

These distinctions aren't about respect, prestige, or the value of the individual. They're about risk containment, organizational harmony, and being pragmatic in building the crew we need.

⸺◈⸺

When organizations pretend every role requires the same depth of alignment, they make the gate of **Worldview and Values** too narrow and starve themselves. When they pretend beliefs don't matter at all, they grant autonomy where it doesn't belong and invite chaos.

As we move down the ranks of an organization, influence decreases and execution increases. Fewer decisions are made by the individual, and more are inherited from the structure above them.

Leaders operate where belief-driven judgment dominates. Crew operate where interpretation and adaptation matter. Hired hands operate where clarity and consistency are paramount.

This is why belief overlap must match decision authority. Autonomy without alignment isn't empowerment; it's bad leadership and a recipe for disaster.

Sarah, the prospective estimator, doesn't need to wrestle with the seven meta-level questions. She isn't setting strategy or redefining success. She executes within an existing framework. That makes it reasonable, even wise, to bring her into the caravan—as a hired hand.

My A+ project manager thrived for years for the same reason. His Pool of Beliefs overlapped where it needed to for execution, even if it never did for leadership—and that worked for both of us.

The craft of business isn't about finding people who believe everything we believe. It's about understanding which beliefs drive which decisions, knowing who is responsible for those decisions, and setting our entry gates accordingly.

If we get this wrong by underplaying the beliefs of individuals, we'll find ourselves leading multiple expeditions—all supposedly headed toward the same destination but guided by fundamentally different answers to the questions that matter most. Overemphasize the need for certain beliefs, and we'll be shorthanded—lacking the talent and energy we need on the expedition of business.

If we get the balance right, we can assemble a coalition of different travelers—each contributing their strengths and operating within a framework they understand. Our teams become caravans unified enough to overcome the resistance between where we are and where we're trying to go. It worked for those traveling the Silk Road; it can work for us as well.

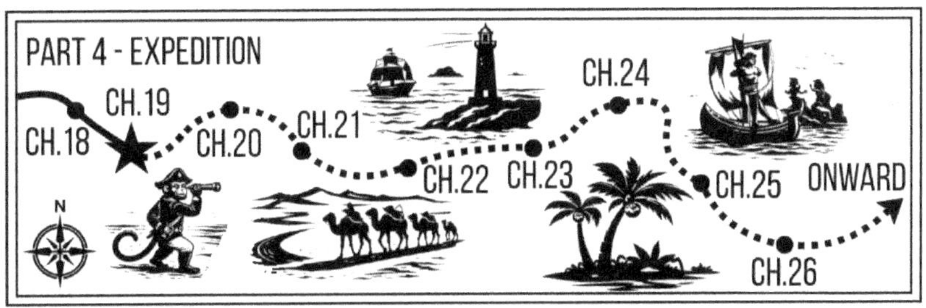

We know we all want different things. We know we all have different beliefs. And while it's nice to imagine that in a world as large as ours we can assemble a team that aligns on all fronts, when we go to do so, our options are more limited than we would hope.

The pool of candidates to add to our caravans is often too limited for dogma or strict adherence to the ideal. But that doesn't mean we have to sacrifice talent or performance; it just means we must be more insightful and nuanced in how we select our crew.

Doing so means dealing with the complexity. But along the way, we develop some of our greatest assets: the tools and processes for building our teams and the Pools of Beliefs which help define our organizations.

And while there's value in knowing who's right to bring aboard, it matters little unless they want to come along. So, while this chapter may have helped answer which candidates we say "Yes" to, the next chapter looks at why people (both staff and customers) say "Yes" to us and our businesses—and there is one tool that is essential for managing all the nuance involved.

CHAPTER 20

TELL THE TALE

When exactly do expeditions begin? Is it the moment the dock lines are untied at port, when the first step is taken from camp, or right as the reins are pulled and the wagons begin to roll?

What about a business? When does it begin? Is it the first time the office lights are flipped on? Is it when the first dollar enters the cash register? Or maybe it's when someone signs on the dotted line?

Those events are easy to see, but the wheels are set in motion long before—expeditions and businesses both begin when someone sees an opportunity.

A cartographer traces a river on a map and knows it must begin somewhere. A founder notices a problem no one is solving well. An explorer hears an account of a distant land yet to be explored. An entrepreneur walks through a neighborhood and sees what's there but also what's missing.

Or, in my case—an employee leaves a company full of broken processes, poor leadership, and bad customer service, knowing that better is possible.

The origins differ, but the visions are the same: potential becoming reality.

Before any expedition sets off and before any business opens its doors, someone somewhere saw the gap between what is and what could be. And while those visions are innumerable, it is the small minority that are translated into a decision and an action to go forward.

For the few who do so, their vision is the destination they seek. The journey to come starts with the decision to proceed, but that is only the first of many. Each step along the way becomes a new decision—one after another until the destination is reached.

In the previous chapter, we considered who to bring along on the expedition of business, and how those decisions are made. However, before anyone can join a crew, two very necessary prerequisites must be met. First, the candidate in question must say "*Yes*" to coming along. Second, we or some other leader must say "*Yes*" to starting the venture they seek to be a part of.

How any of us arrive at "*Yes*" is a hard question to answer. It's complicated work deciding which efforts are worthy of our time. There is the potential reward but also the risk, the opportunity to do something meaningful but the chance it's all a waste. Having a clear path forward helps, but the higher the certainty, the lower the sense of adventure.

There is the temptation to break our decision-making into parts, a pro-con list of going or staying, but considering factors individually risks losing the power of the whole. To cut through the jungle of possibilities, we need a powerful tool. Fortunately, there's one available, the same one that humans have been using to make sense of and communicate complexity for millennia: a story.

⸻ ◆ ⸻

Let's say I asked you to deliver a package to a small town in Arizona. Would you do it?

The answer is probably "*No.*"

Arizona is likely far away, you've got other things to do, and isn't this what UPS is for?

But what if I offered you $100? ... $1,000? ... $10,000? ... $100,000? ... $1 million?

At some point—north of $100 and south of $1 million—I would at least have you asking for more details.

What if I then told you the town was Supai, Arizona? Named *"the most remote community"* in the lower 48 states, Supai sits on the valley floor of the Grand Canyon, and it is only accessible by foot, mule, or helicopter. Does your price go up or down?

It's logical if it goes up, my "ask" just got a lot bigger. Or did it?

Maybe the price goes down. What was once an everyday package drop-off just got a lot more interesting—and became much more of an adventure.

What if I then told you the package contained essential electrical and navigational components—needed to repair the town's only helicopter landing pad?

Recently damaged by a flash flood, the pad is effectively the town's main port, and it's the only way a town full of elderly residents and children can receive emergency medical supplies.

It's unlikely the price will go up; it likely goes down—or maybe it goes away altogether?

But can I offer a clear plan—answer the question of just how the journey gets completed?

If I have a plan that makes sense to you, then the odds of you heading to Supai rise. If not, if the voyage seems like a disaster in the making, then the odds understandably fall.

It's hard to know exactly the compensation or the details that would have us setting off for northwest Arizona. What we do know is that we'd likely make our decision based on emotion—letting the components of our G.E.A.R. model dictate what choice brings us the greatest feeling of comfort. And then, we would rationalize our choice—explain to ourselves and to others why we're going or staying home.

In the end, that explanation would contain one or more of the three forms of human motivation—the reasons any of us say "Yes."

1. Extrinsic motivation for any compensation, karma, or notoriety we expect to receive.

2. Intrinsic motivation for the sense of capability and growth that comes from doing hard things. And...

3. Altruistic motivation for what we can do to benefit others and the world at large.

And the tool that we would use to tie all the pieces together, to help both ourselves and others understand our decision—the who, what, where, when, why, and how—is a story.

Any leader putting together a team faces a similar challenge: how to get people, including themselves, to say "*Yes*" to coming along—to their version of Supai.

The part of the challenge leaders are most familiar with is the extrinsic part of the deal: the salary, the fringe benefits, the PTO, even the job titles to be bestowed. But they are all limited resources. Our ever-present Horseman means we can't keep upping the offer.

To push more people into being a "*Yes*," to get someone on the team that may have said "*No*" to a competitor despite the same or better compensation, and to keep them with us for the long run, we need the other motivational levers at our disposal—and nothing pulls those levers better than a story.

But no story can be compelling if the parts and pieces of the narrative are not first clear to the author. As a writer, I had to know about Supai, understand the difficulty in getting there, and craft a reason for going. More importantly, I had to know what you would see as a formidable challenge and as a meaningful goal.

Leaders are the authors of the narrative of their organizations. They are the keepers of the prologue of the past, the framers of the present, and the directors of future acts. And knowing these parts of our plots and how to make them compelling to our teams is part of the expedition of business—and how we get more people to say "Yes" to coming along.

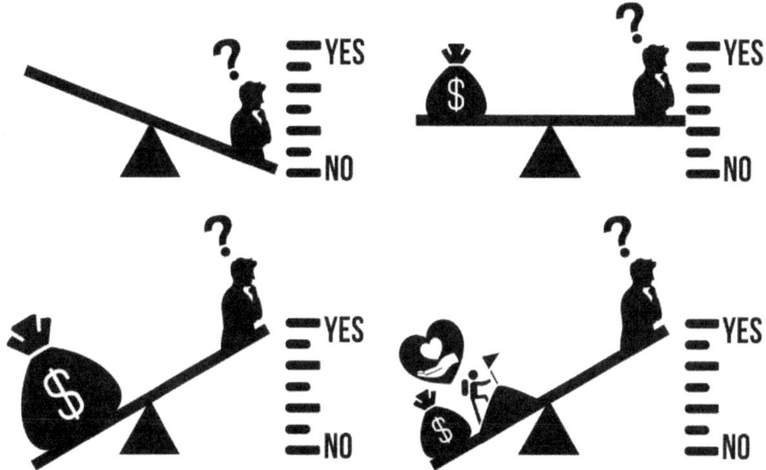

No one says "Yes" to no rewards and no incentives.
Reasonable pay and salary might get a few to come along.
Many businesses think the answer is more money, but adding
intrinsic and altruistic motivation to the standard extrinsic
motivation of money can tip the scales in everyone's favor.

A mentor of Stephen King once told him: "*When you write a story, you're telling yourself the story....When you rewrite [the story], your main job is taking out all the things that are **not** the story.*"

It's no different in business. Providing a good story brings clarity to a team on what is meaningful and gives them an additional source of motivation. And writing that story reveals to us what is actually part of the plot and what is merely background noise.

The reward to be had by crafting a compelling story is significant, but so is the work to do so. The journey from beginning to end is a plot all its own, three acts that are essential to any expedition—the same three acts that are essential to crafting a good story.

The first is about seeing the terrain—understanding the landscape of story itself, why it matters, and the pitfalls that await those who treat storytelling as a checklist rather than a craft.

The second is "setting the course"—the work of actually building the story of our organizations: defining the goal we pursue, the challenges that await, our plans for resolving those challenges, and the character who has what it takes.

And the third is about traveling together—making the story real, keeping it fresh in the minds of our crew, and ensuring it guides our expeditions well after the first draft is written.

It's a long journey—but the destination is worth it.

ACT I: SEEING THE TERRAIN

We know people love stories. As we covered in Chapter 10, they're our "internal maps" for making sense of the world—the "A" of Adopted Narratives in our G.E.A.R. model. And our favorite story? That's the one we tell about ourselves.

Who we are, how we came to be, what we've overcome, where we're headed, what stands in our way, and how we believe we can get there: those elements compose the narratives that run in our mind about our favorite character. And part of that plot is why we go on the expeditions and do the work that we say "*Yes*" to.

There is no getting away from the story of us. We might not dream of being a celebrated hero, but rarely do we want to be a villain. We may acknowledge that others have faced more difficulty in life, but that hardly makes our own challenges insignificant. And while we may seek a more comfortable life—a little more money, a higher status, or some more leisure time—we also want to make an impact for the good that extends beyond ourselves.

We want the story of our life to be significant—but also the story of the organizations we lead. Who we are, what we're out to do, our reason, our purpose: these are the elements we want our teams to know, and they make up the story we want them to be a part of.

The desire creates tension between competing narratives: those of the leader, the crew member, and the organization as a whole. Each wants their story to be compelling and with themselves playing a force for good. If the story of an organization doesn't allow that opportunity, then people are quick to make a villain out of anything that stands in their way. And that is why the story of a business falls short if it doesn't fit the plot of the stories that we and the members of our team are trying to tell about ourselves.

Businesses fail at this more than they succeed, because writing *A* story for an organization isn't hard. If they mix a little background, a goal, and something about how they get there, any business can muster up some form of this:

We're ThreeDucks Technology, a mid-sized software company founded in 2015. Our mission is to provide innovative cloud-based solutions that empower businesses to achieve digital transformation and operational excellence. In today's rapidly evolving technological landscape, companies struggle to keep pace with change and maximize their potential. Through our cutting-edge platform and dedicated support team, we partner with our clients to drive growth, increase efficiency, and unlock new opportunities for success.

This story isn't "wrong," but who's the hero here? It's not the employees; it's not even the customers. The hero is "*innovative cloud-based solutions*" and a "*cutting-edge platform*"—abstractions that no one can see themselves in. The challenge and path to success aren't any more engaging. And the good they are doing in the world leaves much to be desired—"*growth,*" "*efficiency,*" and "*unlocked opportunities.*"

It's hard to imagine this being compelling to anyone, that anyone sees themselves as the hero. And I doubt any leader learned anything about their business by writing it.

In the competition of narratives, stories free of people finish a distant third. Those about other people take home the silver. Because nothing beats a story about us, our challenges, and our past or future achievements.

Now consider this one:

Every day, millions of hardworking people show up to their jobs ready to do their best. They're nurses, schoolteachers, and firefighters. They're our neighbors, friends, and family members. They're also our customers. And none of them sits down at their desk or powers on their tablet hoping their software will crash or that their file system is down. But too often, that's the frustrating reality.

Technology changes at an overwhelming pace, hackers are always up to something new, and companies face the reality of limited IT budgets. At ThreeDucks, our work may focus on technology, but our results focus on people. By ensuring that any solution starts with empathy for our users and ends with a deliverable they can both understand and afford, we let them focus on the important work they do.

Our customers are okay with not having all the bells and whistles. They don't expect the latest and greatest—as long as we deliver one thing: solutions that work, each and every day.

Responding with "*I fight against computer hackers,*" is a much better answer at a party than "*I work at a mid-sized software company.*" And if each of our stories about ourselves includes being a good person, would you rather show concern for nurses and teachers, empathize with the limited resources we all face, or be "*cutting edge*" and "*efficient*"?

Writing *A* story isn't hard; writing a ***good*** story is more of a challenge.

But again, the climb is worth the summit. The intrinsic and altruistic motivation levers a good story pulls are a significant change in recruiting, keeping, and motivating a team. As leaders, playing author helps us have a better grasp on the work we're trying to do—clarifying what's actually part of the story.

Notice what had to be true for the leaders at ThreeDucks to write the second version. They couldn't just wordsmith the first story into something better. They had to answer harder questions:

Who are our customers, really? Yes, "*businesses that need cloud solutions*" is true, but "*nurses, teachers, and firefighters*" and those like them are who they are actually trying to help—real people with real jobs who deserve better than frustrating technology.

What problem are we actually solving? Not "*digital transformation*" but the gap between how fast technology changes and how much time and money real organizations have to keep up. That's a problem they can see, measure, and rally around.

What makes us different from competitors? Not "*cutting-edge*" and "*innovative*"—every software company can claim that. ThreeDucks chose empathy over features, reliability over novelty, and affordability over maximum capability. Those are actual trade-offs, not marketing copy.

What do we believe about our work? That technology should serve people, not the other way around. That having "*all the bells and whistles*" isn't the point if the system crashes when you need it most. That a solution people can understand and afford beats one they can't—even if it's technically superior.

These aren't mission statement exercises. These are strategic decisions that became clear when the pressure was on to tell a compelling story. In a bullet-pointed strategic plan, it's easy to hide behind vague platitudes. Good stories require specifics: real people, real problems, real choices, real consequences. And articulating all of that makes us better leaders—and our organization clearer on the path forward.

Fortunately, we already know more about good stories than we think. However, trying to put one together the same way we might assemble a new IKEA desk often sabotages our efforts. In the world of business advice, it's too common that we are told to break the whole we are trying to accomplish into individual parts and pieces. It's the belief that the gain to be had by simplifying the steps outweighs the loss in value that occurs when those steps are taken in isolation.

Putting together the stories of our organization carries the same risk: handle it one piece at a time and we're bound to be disappointed. The power of a story comes from the gestalt of the whole. Just as we can't reduce a painting by Van Gogh into individual brush strokes, we can't develop our stories one piece at a time. If we do, we end up with a confusing mess rather than a work of art.

"Guiding Principles," "Cultural Pillars," "Mission Statements," "Our Why": there is a long list of exercises businesses are encouraged to go through to map out their story. But few tactics demonstrate the downside of turning story building into Lego sets like "Core Values."

<hr>

Patience, Loyalty, Resilience, Observant, Adaptive.

These words read like those that you might find emblazoned on the lobby wall of a large corporation. Some say they are there to remind us of the "North Star" of an organization, the beacons that employees and leaders can turn toward when the path isn't clear. Others believe they are the yardstick by which new candidates are vetted, and by which the non-quantifiable performance of current employees should be measured.

The more cynical see them as a bunch of bullshit—nothing but obvious virtues like "honesty," "responsibility," and "hard-working," wordsmithed into "candor," "ownership," and "grit." That they're a flashier package put on traits that no one is disputing as being good—that's the cynical take.

It raises the question: just what are leaders trying to do with concepts like core values? Because why does something so popular in the world of business advice fall flat with employees so often?

We may find the answer in those five words: **Patience, Loyalty, Resilience, Observant, Adaptive**. Because they aren't words I pulled out of thin air. They came from a story—a damn good one. One that demonstrates core values are the tail, not the dog. That they are the characteristics which speak to what already is, and the words that we use to explain why an otherwise generic character is actually a compelling protagonist—the force for good.

When applied correctly to a business, core values should do something similar. They should define the story and help bring cohesion that must exist between the who and the what, when, where, why and how. They are also at their best when they follow a chief rule of story writing: don't tell your reader what you can show them.

We err with character traits and "core values" when we treat them as ingredients in a recipe. They should be the impression that is made by what already is, and the fruit by which you know the tree.

What do you know about Roald Amundsen?

Chances are, if you're like me before writing this—not much. And so, I could tell you this:

In 1903, a Norwegian explorer named Roald Amundsen set sail with his crew to navigate the Northwest Passage, a sea route through the Arctic to connect the Atlantic and Pacific oceans.

But doing so would leave you uninterested and bankrupt of what Will Storr, in his book "The Science of Storytelling," calls the four essential parts of most good stories: a likable and relatable **character**, in pursuit of a meaningful **goal**, in the face of a substantial **challenge**, and with a plausible but not guaranteed path to **resolution**.

So, I will tell you this instead:

In early 1903, a 31-year-old Norwegian prepared to attempt what had killed all those who had tried before. To most people it seemed like lunacy, but to Roald Amundsen it was a journey more than 20 years in the making. At the age of 8, he had read of Sir John Franklin's expedition to navigate the Northwest Passage, and how all of the 129-man crew perished in the ice. At the age of 17, he stood in the crowd as Fridtjof Nansen returned home from a successful crossing of Greenland. His voyage had extended trade routes, fueled national pride, and advanced science's understanding of the Arctic. Amundsen thought he could do the same. He knew where, but not yet when or how.

*Unfortunately, Amundsen's mother wanted him to be a doctor. He enrolled to honor her wishes (**loyalty**). And while he was heartbroken by her death three years later, it provided the reprieve he needed to pursue his childhood dream. He soon joined a Belgian Antarctic expedition—a near-fatal mistake. On a journey where many men went mad from the 24-hour darkness of an Antarctic winter, he avoided the same fate and fought off the effects of scurvy (**resilience**). Mostly the trip taught him what NOT to do.*

*In response, he did something radical: he lived with Netsilik Inuit, learned about dog sleds and igloos, and studied survival techniques indigenous people had perfected in the Arctic over millennia (**observant**). That experience set the stage for his attempt at the Northwest Passage. Every notable expedition before him tried brute force, large ships, and massive crews. It never worked. Amundsen's plan was different: one small boat, seven men, learn from the locals, take as much time as needed, work with the environment instead of against it (**patience, adaptive**).*

In June 1903, Amundsen, his crew of six, and their tiny vessel, the Gjøa, set sail—he would return a hero.

The story of Amundsen had those five core values interjected to make the point, but they only labeled what we already knew. Each one was demonstrated before it was named, shown before it was told. That's the difference between core values as aspirations versus core values that represent the character that already exists.

And it's that marriage of true character with an interesting goal in the face of substantial challenges that holds our attention. And then, when we're presented with plausible paths to a resolution, our engagement level rises, and we say "yes" to coming along for the ride.

Few of our organizations have a tale as dramatic as Amundsen's to draw from. But every organization has their past, a set of challenges they have endured, and choices that reveal something about their character. The raw material is waiting; it just needs crafting into a compelling story.

ACT II: SETTING THE COURSE

Most writers will tell you that the hardest part of putting together a story is staring at a blank page, ready to begin. At that point, the possibilities are endless. Nothing has been set; nothing is defined. One could write about the past, present, or future—set the scene in a world we're familiar with or a galaxy far away. It's on par with starting a business from scratch—anything is possible. And the infinite number of options can be paralyzing.

Fortunately, the story of your business already has a first draft. It has a past—something brought it to now. It has characters key to the plot: founders, owners, leaders, people who played an important role in the past or will do so in the future. It also has a defined place in the world: your core business, the industry you are in, your geographic presence, and the types of customers you serve. You might need to make some changes, but these parts of the story usually survive until publication.

The first step is getting started—actually writing it all out. The second step is not falling into the trap of *"this isn't for us"*—believing "story" is reserved for larger, more "glamorous" organizations.

The world of business is full of media outlets, writers, and gurus that love to glamorize the most famous of organizations: SpaceX on their *"mission to Mars,"* Apple's putting a *"dent in the universe,"* Patagonia being *"in business to save our home planet."*

They make most businesses seem "boring" in comparison. But that's the view from the outside. On the inside, any business is full of people who want to be part of a bigger story. Something akin to the "*Us*" versus what's "*Out there*" that helps explain why leaders are chosen (Chapter 15). And so, we err when we believe that it takes a blockbuster movie to engage our teams—the bar isn't that high.

An employee either sees their company as a virtuous character they want to be associated with, or not. They view the goal as meaningful and compelling, or not. The challenges seem real and formidable, or not. And they believe in the ideas and strategies meant to overcome those challenges, or not.

We don't have to be a famous corporation. The world needs smaller, well-run businesses just as much. And most employees want to be part of those stories—our stories. They just need them to be defined and compelling. But that doesn't happen until leaders put in the work to make the story clear to themselves.

And clarity comes when all the pieces work together.

A **Challenge** only makes sense given the right **Goal**. Certain **Resolutions** are only believable coming from the right **Character**. And all of the pieces influence each other, while needing to find harmony between them.

It can be tough to know where to start, but most often our story crafting starts with the **Goal**: just where are we trying to go—and why?

GOAL

No expedition can begin, and no story can be told, without a destination in mind. Choosing and framing that goal is one of the most important decisions an organization makes. Less obvious is the need to understand the cost of pursuing that goal.

When Amundsen set out to cross the Northwest Passage, that came with an opportunity cost—the cost of any other goal he might otherwise pursue during the buildup to the expedition and the three-year journey itself.

Business leaders face a similar cost. Each wants to find their own balance of extrinsic, intrinsic, and altruistic reward, but going up on one likely means going down on another. If the goal is to become the quality leader, that may require premium pricing that limits how many people can be served—or a hit to profitability. If the goal is to scale and grow fast, that may mean more repeat and fewer challenging projects. And having a company that *"gives back"* might mean a less robust P&L in the short run.

The decision is difficult enough for a single leader. If there are multiple people in charge, the task is even tougher—but the importance is that much greater. Often the right answer is to pick a goal that gets everyone what they want along the way.

I once worked with a leadership team of three. The first leader was focused on revenue levels, the second on industry reputation, and the third on work-life balance. There is no way to make all three the top priority. However, once we worked through what each of these meant, why they wanted them, and what each looked like in practice, we were able to pick a final destination that worked for everyone. The goal became building a self-sustaining business, one not dependent on any of the three.

The road there required growing the company and thus increasing revenue—satisfying the first leader. Growth would only be possible by doing quality work and increasing the size of their projects. Doing so would boost their industry reputation—satisfying the second leader. And, of course, building a self-sustaining organization would deliver the work-life balance the third leader directly sought.

It wasn't the goal any of them had in mind at the outset, but it was the destination that they could all agree on. Instead of *"One mountain, many paths,"* it was a case of *"One path, many mountains"*—a peak for each stakeholder.

Agreement among leaders is the first step, but not the last. Employees may adore their leaders, but it's unlikely any of them wake up every day determined to provide their boss with more free time or the beach house they've always wanted.

The story and the framing of the goal must speak to everyone.

It helps to recognize common patterns. Expedition goals have long fallen into familiar categories: *"The First"* (Amundsen navigating the Northwest Passage), *"The Conquest"* (summiting Everest), *"The Discovery"* (Lewis and Clark mapping the unknown), or *"The Return"* (getting everyone home safely).

Business goals follow similar archetypes: *"Market Leader"* (dominate a category), *"Problem Solver"* (make something accessible or affordable), *"Craft Excellence"* (set the quality standard), *"Community Builder"* (provide good livelihoods and serve your region), or *"Legacy Creator"* (build something that outlasts you).

Which of these speaks to you?

Making these choices isn't wordsmithing—it's strategy. Just like our friends at ThreeDucks, choosing a goal for an organization forces leadership alignment on the actual destination, requires navigating real trade-offs, and distinguishes between private motivations and public narrative.

In the end, the public-facing version of my client's goal spoke of growth, serving the needs of their community, opportunities for their staff, and improving the lives of their families—same destination, different emphasis.

No one's goal was wrong, and neither the internal consensus nor the public-facing statement was misleading. It was all a product of picking a goal—and phrasing—that worked for everyone.

But a story was only possible once it was clear what stood in the way of that goal.

CHALLENGE

We're all too familiar with the difficulties we face every day: impending deadlines, personnel issues, IT outages; the list is endless. But the challenges in the story of an organization tend to exist at a higher level. The more meta and structural headwinds—they are the real forces we fight against, the villains that contrast us as the hero, and the challenges that we want our teams to see clearly.

ThreeDucks faced more problems than hackers, the rapid change of technology, and the limited IT budgets of their clients. But they chose those three to be the right balance between a compelling story, informing their employees, and not diluting their message. The other challenges they faced could be addressed by strategies and tactics outlined elsewhere; they did not belong in the story of the organization.

But as leaders we need to make sure that the challenges of the organization aren't overshadowed by the struggles of individuals.

It's human nature to pay outsized attention to the difficulties we are closest to. As Dale Carnegie made famous: "*A person's toothache means more to them than a famine affecting millions.*" In business, the right portrayal of the challenges an organization faces can give our teams a better perspective. But only if we address the ones that are more in their face.

In my business, a common role was CAD designer. Having this job meant you spent the bulk of your day at a workstation producing designs for projects. The deadlines were often tight, and the most common obstacle was getting the information that was needed from our clients.

So, it was understandable if those in the role saw our customers as a challenge in their ***individual*** story.

As a leader, I had to control the narrative and frame the bigger picture. Yes, clients were often slow to respond, but they were no villains. While our designers were important, they played one role in our firm, and our firm was one of eight or nine our clients had to interact with. Complexity was the real villain in the story of our company—a point I made often and loudly. Once it was made clear, attitudes shifted.

Clients moved from being seen as headwinds and hindrances to being viewed as our partners. And ***together*** we were fighting against the complexity, bureaucracy, and never-ending struggle of supply chains and labor shortages—the "*forces of evil*" that kept the projects our communities needed from becoming a reality. It was all a product of setting the challenge right in everyone's story.

Complexity is not your typical villain, but it is one of the common challenge archetypes. Just as the obstacles that expeditions must overcome often rhyme, so do those faced by a business. Any organization almost certainly does battle with one or more of the following—some are our Four Horsemen while others are less common.

The Bad Actors - Every industry has competitors willing to cut corners, sacrifice reputation, bend rules, or race to the bottom on price. Whether you frame them as villains in your story is a choice. Some businesses thrive on *"we're fighting the unethical players."*

The Resource Gap - You can't match the bigger players' budgets, reach, or economies of scale. The challenge is succeeding despite the imbalance—often by being nimble, focused, or excellent where they're merely adequate.

The Trust Problem - Your industry's reputation precedes you. Like the stereotypical used car salesman, customers assume you'll rip them off before you ever shake hands. You're fighting perception before you can prove reality.

The Complexity Barrier - What you do is hard to explain, hard to price, or hard for customers to evaluate. There is a challenge to doing the work, but also in helping people understand why it matters and what they're actually buying.

The Access Problem - People who need what you offer can't find it, can't afford it, or don't know it exists. The challenge is bridging the gap between those who need help and the organization which can provide it—yours.

The Legacy System - *"This is how it's always been done"* is the enemy of progress. Whether it's outdated technology, entrenched processes, or cultural resistance, you're fighting inertia itself.

The Pace Problem - Change is happening either too fast (customers can't keep up), or it's happening too slow (innovation is stalled). Your challenge is helping people adapt or forcing necessary evolution.

Getting the stories of our organizations right means including the higher-level challenges we are up against.

But including a challenge in the story of our organization only generates despair unless we have a plan to overcome it.

RESOLUTION

Once we know the deep-rooted challenges that stand in our way, the question becomes: what are the unique ways the characters of our organizations will try to overcome them in the story of our businesses?

Like those explorers who came before Amundsen, or those in the same space as ThreeDucks, many of our competitors face the same challenges that we do. Doing the same things that have failed before or matching our competition step-for-step are neither the ingredients for a compelling story nor likely paths to success.

In the world of business, there are numerous ways to differentiate: cost vs. quality, breadth vs. depth, vertical vs. horizontal integration, novel vs. tried and true.

We don't have to be different in every dimension, but we must be different enough to avoid being a rehashed sequel of some other business. Picking the right way is strategy at its core and part of mastering the craft of business.

It's hard work, and it requires answering some core questions.

- Is it clear how our resolutions to challenges add value for our clients and customers?

- Do our choices work in harmony, or are they creating tension by pulling us in opposite directions?

- Are they truly different from our competitors' or just the same methods wrapped in different language?

- And can we live with the tradeoffs?

Any resolution must also walk a narrow ridge—achieving the balance of being ambitious enough to be compelling, while plausible enough to be believable.

"We'll focus on customer service" has no tension; everyone assumes a business does that.

"We'll choose product excellence over speed in an industry racing to the bottom on price," creates real suspense—because success isn't guaranteed.

As leaders, we need to be clear on where our organization is both the same as and different from the competition. But including every unique facet of our business would be a mistake. It would overwhelm the audience and dilute the messaging on the actions we want our teams to take. As the saying goes, *"When everything is important, nothing is important."*

A business might make the strategic choice to focus on high-income households in the upper Midwest. But how does that change the actions employees take? Other than some sales and marketing folks, it's immaterial. And it certainly doesn't reinforce the character traits of the organization.

However, if they focus on quality over speed, that does need to be part of the story. That speaks to the character of the organization—patient, craft-focused. And more notably, the story then gives their team direction when the next step isn't clear: *"Slow down, go back and fix any mistakes, take the time to get it right."* It's the equivalent of Amundsen's small versus large—Don't ask what we can take, but do ask what we can leave behind.

When we get it right, our stories then serve to engage and inform all at once. But only if the details remain coherent.

Any useful resolution must flow from our Pools of Beliefs—introduced in the previous chapter. If we believe customers are relationships to be tended, we shouldn't choose a transactional resolution. If we believe a business has an obligation to provide livelihood stability to employees, we shouldn't make *"moving fast and breaking things"* part of our strategy. Fractured strategies produce fractured organizations, and that's what we get when our goals or our resolutions don't align with the character of our businesses.

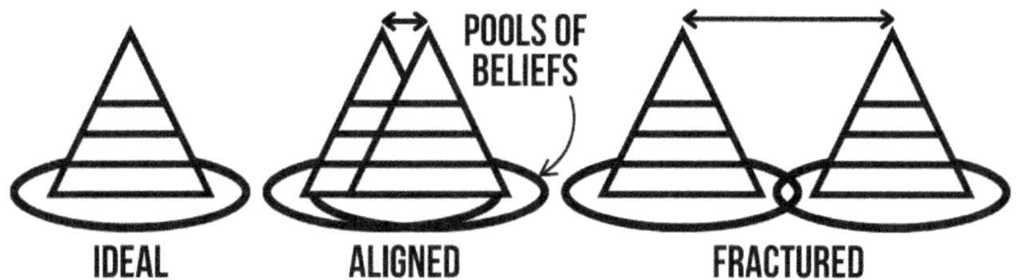

*The choices of goals, strategies, tactics, and execution that make up our
Pyramids of Decisions reflect how we understand the world.
They arise from our pool of beliefs. And when the pools diverge, the plots of
our organizations become harder to follow.*

CHARACTER

Fifteen years before Amundsen and his team left port on their way to
expedition glory, his hero Fridtjof Nansen did the same. And while their
journeys were similar, the methods that led them to success, like the traits
that defined their character, were very different.

If **Patience, Loyalty, Resilience, Observant**, and **Adaptive** are the
words that belonged on the lobby wall of "The Amundsen Corporation" (and represent their crossing of the Northwest Passage we covered
earlier), "Nansen Inc." would select **Bold, Self-Reliant, Driven, Decisive**, and **Committed** as the words to describe the character of their
organization.

Nansen came by these traits honestly. He grew up in the forests and
mountains. While other boys sat in classrooms, Nansen spent weeks
alone in the wilderness. At age 10 he defied his parents and launched
himself off Norway's tallest ski jump. He crashed spectacularly but got
up laughing.

And like Amundsen, the passing of his mother shaped his journey. After
his mother died suddenly when he was 16, something hardened in him.
The boy who loved risk became a man who refused to retreat. At 18, he
broke the world skating record. He won Norway's national cross-country skiing championship 12 times. He could ski 50 miles in a day with
nothing but his dog for company.

In his early twenties, he glimpsed the Greenland ice cap in the distance from his passing ship. Others had tried to cross it. All had failed, but Nansen knew why. They had left themselves an escape route. He wouldn't make that mistake.

He had a plan: start from the east where there was nothing but ice and ocean; once you're ashore, there's only one direction—forward. Success or death: there would be no middle ground.

Amundsen and Nansen sought similar goals, but their pasts and the resolutions to the challenges they faced spoke to their differences in character. Which one speaks more to you?

Patience, Loyalty, Resilience, Observant, and **Adaptive**?

Or

Bold, Self-Reliant, Driven, Decisive, and **Committed**?

There is no right answer, and chances are we see all of them as positive traits. This *is* a case of "*One mountain, many paths.*" And the path you choose, the character you feel fits your organization, is the right one to get you to the summit.

But which comes first? Does the character dictate how we seek resolution to challenges, or do the resolutions we pick speak to our character?

It doesn't matter. What is important is that all the parts of the story work in harmony.

When they do, we get cohesive stories of our businesses—ones that both we and our teams are more likely to find compelling and informative.

Amundsen's patience and observant nature made his resolution of learning from the Inuit and working with the environment believable. If he'd claimed those character traits but then chosen Nansen's resolution of metaphorically burning the boats and pushing through by force, it would have been incoherent. The crew would have lost the plot, and we, as readers of the story, would have been confused as to who he truly was.

The same applies in business. Once again, when character and resolutions don't align, we get organizations with an identity crisis. It confuses employees about the company they are a part of and the actions they are supposed to take.

This is where our Pools of Beliefs become critical once again. Those beliefs about customers, employees, competition, and success: they aren't just philosophical musings. They're the foundation of character.

If we don't get our beliefs squared away, little else of the story matters. The goal, the challenge, the resolution: none of it matters if the main character doesn't know who they are. The identity crisis causes our team to lose interest.

They, as individuals, will always be the protagonist of their own story. And when we fail to display the character of our organization as a worthy ally, we become just another challenge in the plot of their life—one they'll find their own resolution to.

However, if we get it right, we find one of the most powerful forces in our human nature on our side. It's the desire to be part of something bigger than ourselves, to fight against the *"villains"* of the world, to be the protagonist who—through our own unique character—makes the world a better place.

As leaders, we gain clarity on the stories of the organizations we are trying to manifest. We learn to *"take out all that is **not** the story."* We strip out the noise and gain a better understanding of what truly matters. And that helps us make better decisions and make more unified use of the energy we've unlocked in our teams.

But be warned: our Horseman of entropy awaits. Putting together a story is a challenge, but so is keeping it together.

ACT III: TRAVELING TOGETHER

No novel goes to publication after the first draft, and the stories of our businesses are no different. Getting it right is an iterative process; after a first pass, they likely need to be revisited a second, third, and maybe even a fourth time.

Eventually, we will have stories that are cohesive, compelling, and more importantly, a true reflection of our organizations. They are one of the most powerful tools we can have on the expedition of business, and one that brings definition to a popular but nebulous trait of any organization: culture.

Anthropologist Clifford Geertz is credited with saying that *"culture is the stories we tell ourselves about ourselves."* For the king of business buzzwords, one that's often labeled as *"good," "bad,"* or *"toxic,"* and intermingled with stories of kegs in the break room, flip flops versus dress suits, return-to-office against work-from-home, or office politics—Geertz's claim is a refreshing and useful definition.

Too often, *"cultural fit"* becomes whether someone is part of the *"in crowd"*—whether they have similar hobbies, interests, demographics, or availability for a beer after work. We know it is and should be something more. If "culture" is about stories, then one's "fit" should be whether they find the story of an organization compelling and one they want to be a part of.

But for that to happen, three things are required.

First, there actually needs to be a cohesive, thought-out story of the organization—one on par with what we've mapped out in this chapter.

Second, that story must be genuine. People's bullshit detectors are more accurate than we think. Or, as George Orwell said:

"The great enemy of clear language is insincerity. When there is a gap between one's real and one's declared aims, one turns as it were instinctively to long words and exhausted idioms."

It's why the idea of "story," "core values," and "mission statements" has come to induce eye-rolling in so many. The concepts work, and they can be powerful—but only if we put in the work to find what is actually true about our organization and act accordingly.

And third, the story can't sit on a shelf. An untold number of hours have been spent by leadership teams at retreats or locked in conference rooms with some consultant. They iron out the details of what could be a compelling story, an effective strategy, and an engaging culture—only to have it forgotten once a few posters go up and some copy is added to the website.

We can make it more.

We can weave our stories throughout our organizations, recognize people and examples that demonstrate living out the character and acting on the resolutions, celebrate steps taken toward our goals, and remind people often of the real enemy and the challenges they're working against.

This shouldn't be that hard. If it is, the story isn't working.

And too often that's the problem. Not because we don't care, but because we haven't yet gotten it right. We find that other leaders are reading from a different script. Or we lose the plot—we get so busy in the day-to-day details that we forget to zoom out and see the overall arc of the narrative we are trying to live out. Or, as we said earlier, and as Stephen King's mentor told him, we fail at our main job as the author: *"to take out all the things that are not the story"*—and we lose track of what's important.

However, when we succeed at our task, when the story is true, when it's told consistently, when it guides our decisions and clarifies the path, then we've built something powerful. Our story gives us another way to motivate our crews—we are no longer left to rely on extrinsic means and our limited resources alone. Our narrative better defines the cultures of our companies and makes them appealing to a larger number of people. And it moves our Levers of Control—energy up, unity up, resistance down.

Without a good story, we're just another adventurer wandering in the wilderness—bribing our crew to come along. With one, we have a clear plan of where we're going, how to get there, and who to be along the way. We become an expedition worth saying "Yes" to.

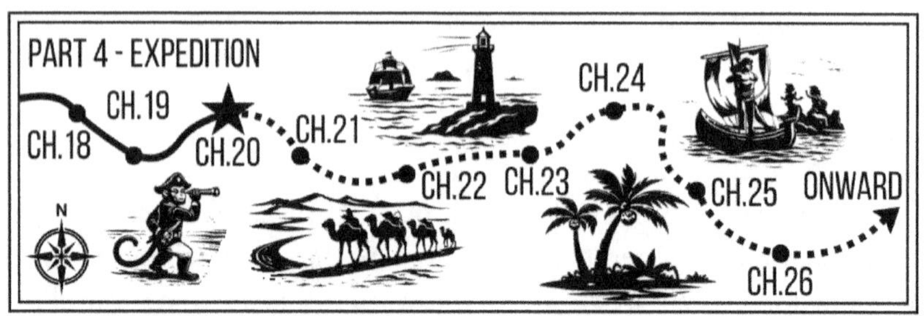

A clear and compelling story may be the greatest asset a business has to attract, engage, and retain their team. If our aim is to climb high on The Mountain of Why by building decisions on first principles, then there's a truth about humans that serves as a solid foundation for good decisions: stories are how we make sense of the world.

And in business, they serve as a high-level view of where the organization has been, the character developed along the way, where it plans to go, and the obstacles that stand in the way. Reaching our intended destinations becomes easier when everyone is part of the same story. But a story alone is not sufficient.

While our stories act like a North Star—providing a general direction to turn when uncertain—and help build the goals and strategies atop our Pyramids of Decisions, the immediate next step we should take is determined by the tactics and the execution that form the base of those Pyramids.

As leaders, we must either decide on those ourselves, or—when size, scale, or economics dictate—we must delegate to others. And it's the latter where things really get challenging on the expedition of business. How do we get others to make good decisions without us being ever-present to guide them?

Just as a compass must be adjusted for the location in which it is used, as business leaders, it's our job to help our teams make sense of the organizations they navigate. That means providing a clear story that clarifies the "big picture," but it also means providing the structures, benchmarks, and catalogs of information they can use to further orient themselves.

The next chapter provides the principles needed to do just that, and it shows how they were used by others tasked with helping crews operating in uncertain waters.

CHAPTER 21

SETTING NORTH

If you look at the state of North Carolina on a map and trace your finger along its eastern edge, you will find a skinny strip of land called the Outer Banks. Primarily consisting of sand dunes, with various bays and sounds to the west and the Atlantic Ocean to the east, the undulating land that is visible is representative of the ocean floor that is not. Rich with sandbars, shoals, and shallows, it's a stretch of sea that has been the demise of over 5,000 vessels—rightly earning the nickname "*The Graveyard of the Atlantic.*"

As you move your finger down the coast, you will find three different points sticking out into the ocean: Cape Hatteras to the north, Cape Fear to the south, and between them, Cape Lookout. Each is a difficult area to captain a ship, and each is home to one of the Outer Banks' seven lighthouses. Today, technology has rendered them little more than tourist attractions. But for nearly 100 years, from the 1870s onward, these lighthouses were an essential part of traversing North Carolina's treacherous shores.

Few of us are sailors, but we all do our share of navigating. We "*navigate conflict,*" "*navigate relationships,*" "*navigate traffic,*" "*navigate uncertainty,*" "*navigate change,*" and if you're old enough, you may have once "*navigated the web.*" The word implies that we have some sense of control—using tools, information, and reference points to find our way to a desired destination.

As leaders, others look to us to navigate our organizations. And indeed, it is our responsibility to chart and make known the intended course—to tell the story of the journey ahead.

However, no leader has the time, energy, or capacity to be with each member of their team every step of the way. As a result, we face one of the chief challenges in leadership and in business: just how do we get our team to make good decisions when we aren't there? Or, said differently, how do we get others to navigate dangerous waters safely when we can't be onboard?

One possibility is to hire better sailors. It's an unsatisfying and often economically unfeasible suggestion, but it's a solution, nonetheless. Another potential path is that we give up and do it all ourselves. And while equally unsatisfying, this is the outcome for many business leaders. The temptation or necessity to get tasks completed is too great. They then step in, and as a result, *"wearing too many hats"* and *"too busy working 'in' the business to work 'on' the business"* are among the most frequent complaints of business leaders.

Common business advice offers the solution of documenting everything: job descriptions, SOPs, best practices, organizational charts, and results or accountability matrices. This can help, but it is often a *"take two aspirin and call me in the morning"* type solution—a prescription without a diagnosis and an effort blind to the root of the problem.

Many companies are then left with "document museums." They are repositories of SOPs people rarely follow, job descriptions referenced during onboarding but then never seen again, and results or accountability matrices which no one is measured against. Like most "employee handbooks," they sit collecting dust as time renders them woefully out of date—and a bit of a joke among staff.

These documents are intended means to an end, but too often, the means are executed without a grasp of the "end" these paper mountains are meant to direct us toward.

The strategy that these tactics support within our Pyramids of Decisions, whether spoken or unspoken, has always been about the goal of "Setting North"—providing the necessary information and reference points so that our teams can orient themselves. Just as any expedition must first adjust their compasses such that true north and magnetic north align, inside our organizations we need to provide the correct bearing points such that our crews, independent of our direct instruction, can find a path to good decisions independently.

Understanding the principles around designing such an environment, a *"navigable waterway"* in the language of sailors, is part of the craft of business. There are past examples to learn from. And perhaps none are better than the work of the men and women who transformed the "Graveyard of the Atlantic" into more navigable waters.

⸻◆⸻

A captain piloting their ship toward Cape Lookout in the 1840s faced a formidable challenge. While the Sun, stars, compasses, clocks, and sextants had reliably guided them across the Atlantic, approaching the shore meant navigating the shallow and ever-changing coastal waters—and a need for new tools.

As the captain sailed closer to land, they would have encountered buoys made from wooden barrels—painted a variety of colors, their true meaning rarely known to anyone but the installer. They would have referenced a privately published, but rarely updated, chart of the area—official government-issued charts were decades away. And in the distance, they would have seen a small, dimly lit lighthouse. It would have been painted with red and white horizontal stripes. It was a color scheme that, in the words of the lighthouse's designer, Winslow Lewis, caused the lighthouse to *"appear at a distance like a ship of war with her sails clewed up, and was often [mis]taken for such."*

Unfortunately, employees in many organizations have a similar experience. While the leader has a complete vision of the terrain to be navigated, employees are left with a less advantageous perspective. While the leader has a bird's-eye view—one made possible by either years of experience or they themselves being the creator of the correct path to port—employees are tossed into the waves and the wind with limited visibility and confusing signals.

Leaders are often blessed with the vision of the path forward.
The perspective of their team is often not as clear.

A sales representative joining a new company finds that the CRM is filled with outdated customer notes from three different systems that were never fully migrated. There's a "pricing guidelines" document somewhere on the shared drive—but nobody can remember if it's the current version. The discount approval matrix says to get sign-off from regional directors, but half those positions don't exist anymore. And when they ask how to handle a customer who wants to negotiate terms, three different managers give three different answers—all delivered with confidence.

So, the rep does what the 1840s captain did: the best they can with the limited information available. They watch what other successful reps do. They make educated guesses. Sometimes, despite their best efforts, they lose a deal or give away too much margin—not because they're incompetent, but because the system they're working in leaves much to be desired. Meanwhile, their boss, with a perfect vision of how things are *"supposed to work,"* grows irritated that their team *"just can't seem to make good decisions."*

For millennia, sailors navigated by the stars above. A necessary component of the expedition of business is providing similar reference points to our crews. As leaders, we have our own constellation to guide us in helping them find the way—seven stars that point the way to a more self-sufficient organization. If we follow them in the design of our organization, our teams will find themselves sailing in more navigable waters.

And our journey begins with our first star.

DEFINE WHAT QUALIFIES AS A "GOOD" DECISION

"What was the right thing to do?"—It's a common question when a member of the crew veers off course on the expedition of business.

Unfortunately, the default answer for many leaders to this question is effectively: *"What would they—the leader—have done in that situation?"*

The "right" decision becomes *"what I would have done,"* and we leave our teams with an often impossible and almost inevitably flawed benchmark. It's an answer that confuses the likely actions of the leader with the correct question to ask:

"Did it serve and meet the needs of the organization?"

I have met some business leaders who are remarkable salespeople. But they often struggle to train new sales staff. When the new staff engages with a prospect, the leaders are quick to intervene and *"do it their way."* It's a reaction to the discomfort they feel when a prospect gets anything but "the best."

But *"their way"* or *"the best"* was never the right metric. If 100 is the necessary score for a sales performance, the leader may indeed be capable of 130, but that does not mean that a sales rep scoring 110 isn't doing a "good" job.

Meanwhile, the same leaders may be thrilled with a new, but mediocre, director of operations—someone who might score 85 versus the 100 that is needed, but still well above the 70 of their boss.

The difference between the abilities of the leader and the employee becomes the thumbs up or thumbs down for an effort. It leaves good employees underappreciated and bad employees with free rein to make a mess of things. It's a consequence of not creating a defined threshold of "good"—and one independent of any individual's capabilities.

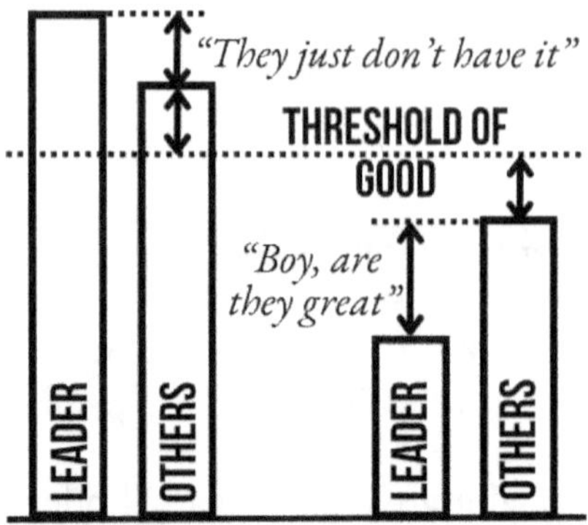

The capability of the leader should never be the measuring stick for the performance of others.

So, what is the right definition of "good"?

If a sailor found their way safely to port in 1845, did they do as "good" a job as a sailor doing the same today?

We know that context plays a role, and that there is always more variance and luck to outcomes than we would prefer. And defining "good" can be a slippery slope—greased by all the possible considerations. They did a good job...

"Considering their experience level."

"Considering the conditions."

"Considering the time they had."

"Considering their resources."

But unfortunately, we don't get to put any asterisks next to results in business—nor ships that found their way to the sea floor. We have to live with the results, and as such, like our definition of "perfection" from Chapter 1, we need a definition of "good" we can live with.

I have found the following definition to be useful:

Did the person use judgment on par with others in similar roles and seek out and utilize the tools and information available to them?

If so, then they've made a good decision.

A new sales rep may not close a deal, but did they research the prospect before the meeting? Review the CRM? Portray warmth, strength, and our unique value propositions?

If the answers are "*Yes*," if they used reasonable judgment and the available tools, then they've made a good decision—and their leader is without grounds for complaint.

However, like those responsible for the waters off the North Carolina coast—who watched ship after ship sink despite captains doing a "good" job—if the results are too often not to our liking, we have work to do. It's then that we need to make the waters we are asking our teams to sail more navigable, which brings us to our second star.

REDUCE THE NUMBER OF DECISIONS TO BE MADE

By 1851, the United States Congress had seen enough—too many ships gone missing and too many complaints from sailors. Efforts by local municipalities to make their stretch of coastline more navigable were inconsistent and often embarrassing. In response, the Lighthouse Board was created, and "The Professionalization Era" of coastline management began.

The Board must have realized that two of our Four Horsemen were at the root of the problem: human nature and limited resources. Whether we're a sales rep or a ship's captain, we each have one brain and 24 hours in our day, and thus, there is a limit on what we can remember and the number of decisions we can make.

Part of the craft of business is adjusting our Levers of Control, and a good way to lower the lever of resistance is by reducing the cognitive load on our team—making sure their limited time and limited brain power are reserved for decisions truly requiring their judgment. As business leaders, we have dozens of tools to help us do just that:

Templates & Pre-Populated Forms – Proposal templates, email templates, meeting agendas with standard sections already filled in.

Checklists – Pre-call prep, quality control, and project kickoff. Less memory is required; follow the list.

Default Options – Standard meeting times, default shipping method, standard payment terms, items we customize only when needed.

Naming Conventions & File Organization – Standard file naming, predictable and intuitive folder structures, no hunting for documents.

Automated Workflows – CRM auto-logs calls, automated follow-up reminders, order routing; these remove entire categories of tasks someone must remember to complete.

Standard Meeting Structures – Every sales meeting follows the same agenda; every kickoff covers the same topics; there should be no reinventing the process or "forgetting" to cover key topics.

Batching & Routine Scheduling – Process all orders at 2 p.m. daily, review invoices every Friday, do similar tasks together—all reduce context switching and save on brain power.

The Lighthouse Board wasted no time in creating tactics to support the strategy of preserving sailors' memory and cognitive energy. One of their first acts was to create a standardized buoy system: red buoys mark the starboard (right) side of channels when returning to port—the familiar *"red on right returning"*—black buoys (changed to green in the 1980s) mark the port (left) side.

This one rule eliminated thousands of judgment calls for ship captains approaching unfamiliar harbors. There was no more guessing what the colorful wooden barrels meant, no more asking locals, and no more consulting fragmentary notes—"red right returning" decided for them.

The board then turned to consistent lighthouse designs. Cape Hatteras with black and white spirals, Bodie Island with horizontal stripes, and Currituck Beach with unpainted red brick: distinctive exteriors complemented unique light patterns to make each unmistakable by sight alone—day or night.

There would be no more squinting at the coastline—wondering, *"Is that the lighthouse or another ship?"* The Board understood that every moment a captain spent figuring out which reference point was which was time not spent navigating safely. They weren't trying to eliminate judgment; they were eliminating **unnecessary** decisions. That way captains could focus their mental energy on the decisions that were more contingent on time, place, and context: reading the weather, handling changing conditions, and determining when it was safe to enter port.

However, the new systems put in place would only work if they were adequately operated, maintained, and upgraded. With hundreds of miles of coastline to service, the Lighthouse Board became a complex organization and needed to turn their own operation into navigable waters. A necessary step was our next star.

MAKE OWNERSHIP CLEAR – WHOSE DECISION IS IT?

If my business career were a person, when the time came, the tombstone on my grave would surely read:

"When everyone is responsible for everything, no one is responsible for anything."

In psychology, there is the bystander effect—we are less likely to help someone in need when other people are present. It's why CPR instructors teach their students to never say *"Someone call for help"* but instead *"YOU, in the blue shirt, call 911."*

Yet in business, employees often cannot answer the question, *"Who's responsible?"* Making that answer clear is the cornerstone of a system of accountability, but also the foundation on which someone builds their sense of place and belonging in an organization. Without it, we can often hide from blame, but just as easily be left without the recognition and praise for a job well done.

Most businesses attempt to address this through organization charts, matrices for results, ownership, and accountability, or job descriptions. They are all documents that theoretically spell out who owns what. Yet these often fail in practice because they describe roles in abstract terms rather than actual decisions. A job description might read *"responsible for customer satisfaction"* without clarifying:

Who decides whether to issue a refund? Who owns the response when a customer escalates? Or, who makes the call when company policy conflicts with keeping the customer happy?

The result is what our earlier sales rep experienced: three managers giving three different answers with equal confidence, each assuming the decision falls within their domain. Or worse, everyone assumes it's someone else's call, and the decision simply doesn't get made. But most commonly everyone turns to the leader—because aren't they ultimately responsible for everything?

The question "*Whose decision is this?*" remains unanswered until something goes wrong. At which point it becomes a retroactive exercise in assigning blame rather than a proactive framework for taking action.

There's no one answer for every organization. Some businesses may benefit by using processes and functions as dividing lines; others should use geography or customer segment. It's part of why business is hard—our Horseman of entropy and the natural pull toward disorder. But finding the best answer for our organization is a necessary step on the expedition of business.

If decisions can be placed in our Pyramids of Decisions, then it stands to reason that the same structure can also hold **who** is responsible for each of those decisions.

The Lighthouse Board understood this instinctively. When they were organized, they created clear ownership at every level. And critically, at every level, there was **one** person ultimately accountable.

At the Goal level, the Lighthouse Board had members who deliberated collectively, but the **Secretary of the Treasury** held ultimate authority as president of the Board. And the Board elected a **chairman** to run day-to-day operations. It was not a committee where everyone had an equal say; one person owned the final call.

At the Strategy level, they divided the country into 12 lighthouse districts. Each district had **one naval inspector** as the responsible party. They may have been supported by an army engineer, but the inspector owned strategic decisions for their region: where to build new lights, which structures to replace, how to allocate resources. There was one person for one region, and there was clear accountability for the choices that were made.

At the Tactic level, each lighthouse had **one lighthouse keeper** responsible for that light. Each life-saving station had **one station keeper** who was responsible for a specific stretch of beach. If a ship went down off Cape Lookout, the Cape Lookout keeper made the call—not the crew collectively, not headquarters; one person owned the decision.

At the Execution level, the lighthouse keeper decided when to light the lamps, and the station keeper decided when to launch a rescue. They could consult others and reference the official documentation provided to them, but each keeper owned their outcome.

No ambiguity—at every level there was one name for each decision to be made; there was one person who got credit for success or bore responsibility for failure.

When a ship captain approached Cape Lookout, they weren't navigating a system of diffused responsibility. Every lighthouse had a lighthouse keeper. Every stretch of beach had a station keeper. Every district had an inspector. Every level had ***one person*** whose job it was ***to own that decision***.

If we want a member of our team to make better decisions without us, there may be nothing more important than making it clear that it is indeed ***their*** decision. And then to use both the fear of repercussions and the desire for appreciation as forces to drive their best decision-making. Then we can get out of their way and let them do their work.

Of course, exactly who we are charging with decision-making is not insignificant; it's also part of the constellation that leads us to more navigable waters.

MATCH THE PERSON TO THE ROLE

Before the Lighthouse Board was established, lighthouse keepers were political appointees. Often, as you might expect, the person selected for the role was a product of favors and backroom dealing. And just as when we hire someone using the wrong criteria, the caretaker of these important beacons was often ill-suited for the job at hand.

The Lighthouse Board cleaned things up. And while their selection process was still rudimentary compared to our nine gates in our Progression of Fit and our G.E.A.R. model, it still produced better results.

During "The Professionalization Era," one could not be a lighthouse keeper without being able to read and write, keep simple accounts, pull and sail a boat, make minor repairs, and maintain the premises. And everyone who started in the role was subject to a three-month probationary period.

It's easy to laugh at the simplicity of the requirements, but the point to be made remains the same. How "fit" someone is for the role we ask them to fill, and how capable they are of the tasks we need them to complete, has everything to do with how likely they are to make good and independent decisions.

Of course, even the world's best sailor would be hopelessly lost on a dark, foggy night off the coast of Cape Lookout in 1840. We all need some way to orient ourselves, and that brings us to the fifth of seven stars that orient us toward designing a better business.

PROVIDE CLEAR REFERENCE POINTS

If the first four principles were about putting the right person in the right position to use good judgment, the fifth is about them having the information they need to leverage it all into good decisions.

Any sailor knows that a lighthouse on the horizon means that land is near. On its own, it is nothing more than a high-level wayfinding point. Like the story, mission, or goal of a business, a single lighthouse can provide general direction. But the aforementioned rarely provide enough information to decide on the next step—the short- and medium-term actions that make up the bulk of business activity.

A customer is demanding a refund for a product they've clearly misused. The customer service representative handling the issue knows one of their company values is *"customer satisfaction,"* and that their goal is to *"build long-term relationships."* They know the general direction: keep the customer happy. But what exactly should they do next?

Issue the full refund? Offer store credit? Replace the product? Get a manager involved? At what dollar thresholds?

Without clear reference points, the rep makes a conservative guess—denies the refund and loses the customer, makes an expensive guess—gives away too much margin, interrupts their manager—the very thing we're trying to avoid, or freezes and does nothing—the situation escalates.

Meanwhile, their leader grows frustrated. *"Why can't they just use good judgment? We've told them we value customer satisfaction!"*

The navigable waters version looks different.

The rep knows there is a bias toward customer satisfaction; they see the lighthouse on the shore. But how exactly should they proceed?

On their computer screen is the customer service guide—a chart of the seas they're navigating. The company sells thousands of products each month, and someone wanting a refund related to their own misuse, along with dozens of other scenarios, was foreseeable.

A quick search for "Product misuse" triangulates their exact position and has them finding the following:

- *Under $50: Issue a refund or replacement at the customer's preference. Note in CRM.*

- *$50-$200: Offer store credit for 75% of value or full replacement. Note in CRM.*

- *Over $200: Offer store credit for 50% of value, escalate to CS Manager if the customer pushes back.*

- *Document all misuse cases in the weekly report. We review patterns quarterly to adjust policy.*

The decision wasn't about the refund or the amount thereof. It was, *"I don't know what to do here. Where can I look for more information?"* The reference points at their disposal answered the question, saved them from having to make further decisions, and their manager was saved from having to get back in the weeds to do *"someone else's job."*

The next call on their line was someone complaining that while they paid for the product at checkout, the bag was never handed to them by the cashier. Unfortunately, this time a search of the guide produced no results. And we're back to several unappealing options: bad decisions, customer escalation, or manager involvement. But while the guide may have omitted this specifically, it does provide some direction.

This scenario rhymes with the last one—customer unhappy, may have been our fault, maybe not, either way it's hard to prove. So, the rep defaults to the same criteria from "product misuse."

Was it a good decision? It's hard to argue it wasn't. They used the same judgment as before and once again sought the information available.

And here's what's easy to miss about taking the time to document information and making it accessible to our teams. It's impossible to cover every scenario, but the more of them we address, the smaller the gaps become between our lighthouses, buoys, and maps. With enough reference points, generalization and estimation become easier and more accurate—even without precise information.

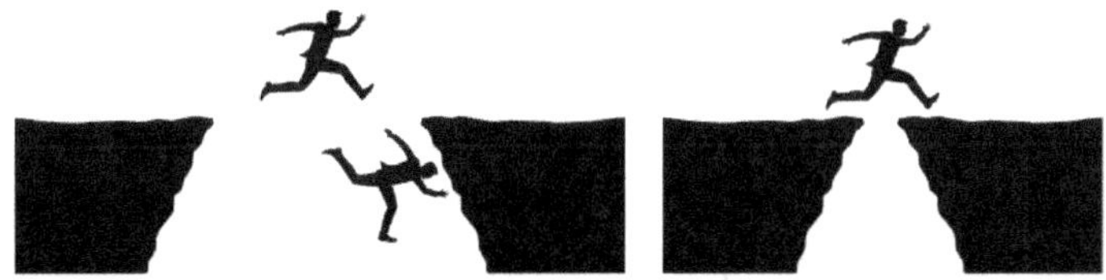

It's not necessary to provide people with everything.
If the gaps we leave are small enough, they can make the leap themselves.

Guides and written manuals are two types of wayfinding points, but they are hardly the only ones. Decision trees, flowcharts, FAQ documents, templates, and worked examples: as leaders, we're only limited by our imagination as to what assets we can create to help clarify how work should be done and how ***good*** decisions should be made.

The Lighthouse Board understood this principle. Before their work, a lighthouse was simply a warning: *"Don't run ashore."* But under the Board's direction, lighthouses became sophisticated navigation tools, ones that answered many critical questions.

Where am I exactly? By sighting two lighthouses and noting their bearings, a captain could triangulate their precise position. Cape Lookout visible at 045° and Cape Hatteras at 310° meant you could plot your exact location on the chart.

How far offshore am I? Each lighthouse had a known visibility range published in the "Light List." If Cape Lookout's light became visible, you knew you were within 19 miles of shore. The first sight of the light told you your distance.

Which lighthouse is this? The distinctive patterns—Cape Lookout's diamond checks, Cape Hatteras's spiral, Bodie Island's stripes—made each unmistakably identifiable during the day. At night, each had unique light characteristics. For example, Cape Lookout's white flash every 15 seconds was different from every other light on the coast.

What's my heading? By tracking your bearing to a known lighthouse, you could confirm you were maintaining course or calculate drift caused by currents.

The "Light List" itself was a masterwork of accessible information. Published regularly and available at every port, it told captains everything they needed: exact coordinates, light characteristics (color, flashing pattern, interval), visibility range, height of the light above water, and physical description. A sailor didn't need to memorize it all; they just needed to know where to look.

And that's where many companies go astray. The "Light List" was **one** book—not six or seven different files scattered in a drawer. There was no uncertainty about whether there were more documents to be referenced. Captains knew if they wanted information on lighthouses they should go to the "Light List." Once opened, they could then—via map, index, or table of contents—find the information they were looking for.

At my company, written information stemmed from one source: the "Operations Manual." It was our repository of wayfinding points. Other documents could be created, but they had to be referenced by and linked back to the "Operations Manual." Even our "Employee Handbook" of more generic information was a branch of the tree of which the "Operations Manual" formed the trunk.

If we want our organizations to be navigable waters for our team, then the way we set up and organize information must be equally navigable.

None of this is simple work, nor can it be accomplished without a significant investment of time—but that's what it takes to create an asset.

Many business leaders are great at activity—the doing, the jumping in, the explaining (and re-explaining). However, it doesn't scale. The results we get are symmetric to the time we invest, but that time is a limited resource.

To make the waters of our organizations more navigable, to create the conditions where more of our team can operate more often without our specific direction, we need the benefit to be asymmetric.

The work that goes into building our versions of the Lighthouse Board's systems is substantial, but once they are up and going, the benefits continue to accumulate. Those benefits free up leaders to move onto the next thing—to build new and better assets.

The entire process quickly becomes a flywheel of employee autonomy: leaders invest time to build better resources and systems—employees use those to make better independent decisions—time that leaders would have otherwise spent correcting, instructing, or demonstrating, is spent building even better assets—more employees use those to make even more good decisions—and the upward spiral continues.

On our climb up The Mountain of Why, clear and logical first principles include: a leader's time is more valuable than the time of those they lead, we all have limited time and mental capacity, and what is written down once can be read thousands of times. These principles are irrefutable, and the Lighthouse Board used them to build strategies, tactics, and executions that leveraged their efforts into outsized returns. We can do the same within our organizations.

It starts with building the right assets, but to overlook the improvement of those assets once developed would be a mistake. The Lighthouse Board didn't call it a day after the first wave of lighthouses and buoys were installed. They knew the flywheel to be had—that the better their systems functioned, the more people would use them, and the more scenarios they could foresee. Making upgrades was essential, and it's our next star.

OBSERVE, ADJUST, AND OWN THE SYSTEM

There are few things as frustrating for a business leader as putting time, energy, thought, and planning into systems and procedures, only to have their team either not use them or use them incorrectly. It's a feeling that's often followed by *"they know better," "I told them,"* or *"they need to show up and do what we pay them to do."* These are statements and feelings that are justifiable. But would we rather make a point, or would we rather have systems that actually get used?

If our teams aren't using the resources we've built, there are three likely scenarios:

1. They don't know or have forgotten that the resources exist. The solution to this problem isn't about reminding people—again. It's about embedding resources where people actually work: a template folder that gets automatically copied into every new project folder, pre-written notes in proposal templates that prompt the right questions, FAQ answers that pop up in the CRM when someone searches a common issue. What we want is information that appears in context and at the moment of need—not buried three folders deep in a shared drive someone has to remember to check.

If our teams need to actively remember that something exists, then we shouldn't be surprised when they forget. If it's right there when they need it, they're more likely to use it—and it's easier to hold them accountable when they don't.

As leaders, our job is to make the invisible resources visible—and even better, make them unavoidable.

2. The resources make one's work more difficult—not less. We know that people will default to doing things the easy way. If following the "right" process takes more effort and time than an alternative, we're in the danger zone.

Often, we bring this situation on ourselves. A seventeen-step checklist when eight would really do, a template so rigid that it takes longer to adapt than starting from scratch, an approval workflow that requires three sign-offs and two days when the customer needs an answer in hours: these systems don't reduce cognitive load. They create frustration, slow progress, and have even the best employees looking for workarounds.

Other times, we're justified in asking our team to do the extra, but necessary work. Completing a timesheet doesn't help get projects out the door, but it does give us the data we need to write better proposals in the future. A QC checklist may be completed a dozen times before finally, on the 13th use, it catches a serious issue. In total, the value of the system is there, but for an employee in the moment, it's easy to take a shortcut.

The answer isn't to guilt people into compliance or mandate that they "*follow the process*"—neither gets to the root of the problem. The solution is to keep our systems as lean and efficient as possible—lower the resistance—while designing the constraints that avoid common mistakes—raise the resistance.

The same way a fence keeps people from cutting across the grass at the corner of a sidewalk, we need systems that make the correct path the one of least resistance. Auto-save to the correct folder, required fields in the CRM that won't let you close a deal without notes, default settings to the most common correct options: they all help make it harder to do a task the wrong way than the right way.

If we're asking people to do more work than feels necessary in the moment, we can't rely on their discipline; we need to build guardrails that make the extra work unavoidable. The whole idea is to raise the "R" of real-time constraints in our G.E.A.R. model. Once it's high enough, their genetic wiring, enduring traits, or adopted narratives matter little. Like our dog eating collard greens, they're only left with the option that's available—the right one.

3. They don't see the resources as reliable or credible. This is the death spiral. A manufacturing supervisor checks the quality control procedures and finds they still reference equipment that has been gone for two years. An account manager follows the client escalation protocol and discovers that the "Senior Director of Client Success" who is referenced left the company six months ago—and the role was eliminated. A project manager uses the standard scheduling template but gets chewed out because it doesn't account for the new approval step—the one leadership added last quarter but never documented.

Once bitten, twice shy.

After a few experiences like this, employees stop trusting the "official" resources. They ask around instead. They rely on what the person next to them does. They make their best guess. The documented processes become historical artifacts, proof that someone once cared, but no longer are they tools anyone actually uses. And the whole system loses momentum.

When we observe how our systems are being used and the results they are producing, and when we collect feedback from those who are using (or not using) the resources at their disposal, we can make the necessary corrections to keep the flywheel going.

Making our companies more navigable waters is an iterative process, and one that rarely starts with things working just as we need them to. The Lighthouse Board made sweeping changes right after their inception, but things didn't stop there.

Critically, if captains were following the charts, using the "Light List" correctly, reading the lighthouses as designed, and ships were still running aground, the Board didn't blame the captains—they improved the system.

The continued credibility of the entire enterprise depended on captains actually using the resources provided and on those resources working as intended.

In business, this is where most efforts stall out. The initial energy goes into building the system, the guides, the templates, the processes, but the ongoing maintenance and improvement gets neglected. Nobody's job is to watch how the customer service guide is actually being used. Nobody updates the pricing guidelines when the business model shifts. Nobody reviews which questions keep getting asked despite the answers being "*documented*." The system slowly drifts out of sync with reality, credibility erodes, and we're back to document museums.

The alternative requires discipline. When people keep asking the same question, add it to the FAQ, make it more visible, or simplify the answer. When someone follows the documented process and gets a bad result, investigate what happened and update the process. When the business changes—new roles are added, positions are eliminated, approval thresholds change—update the documentation. When we notice people working around the system, ask why. Maybe they've discovered that the system doesn't work in practice. Maybe there's friction we didn't anticipate. Or maybe they have found a better way—and others need to know about it.

District inspectors regularly visited lighthouses, reviewed logs, and investigated groundings. When patterns emerged—lights dimmer than expected, buoys drifting, dangerous gaps in coverage—they made adjustments. New lights were built, inadequate structures replaced, and "Notices to Mariners" were regularly published and distributed so that captains had the latest information.

The system improved because someone was watching and responding, and it was clear whose job it was to do so. The **district inspector** owned their region's navigation system. They decided what needed updating and when changes should be made. One person was accountable for keeping resources up to date and improving or adding assets when needed.

In business, the systems that make our waters navigable often find themselves as orphans. Who owns the customer service guide? Who decides when the operations manual gets updated? Who's responsible for keeping the pricing guidelines current? Too often the answer is *"Everyone,"* *"Whoever wrote it originally,"* or worse, no one at all. Without clear ownership, even the best systems decay—our Horseman of entropy at work.

The solution mirrors our third star: assign ownership. The Operations Manager owns the operations manual. The Sales Director owns pricing guidelines and proposal templates. The Customer Service Manager owns the customer service guide. They don't personally write every update, but they own the decision of what gets included, when it's revised, and ensuring it reflects current reality. They get credit when the system helps people make good decisions. And they're accountable when it fails.

It's not about adding work to someone's plate; it's about preventing entropy and the slow drift into obsolescence that kills credibility and sends everyone back to asking the boss—and creates more work for everyone.

Someone needs to be watching, collecting feedback, adjusting, and keeping the system trustworthy. That's how navigable waters stay navigable.

However, navigable doesn't mean free from risk. No system is perfect, nor can any system accommodate the unexpected hurricanes or rogue waves—which brings us to our seventh and final star.

ACCEPT IMPERFECTION AND BUILD SAFETY NETS

Even with the Lighthouse Board's best and ever-improving efforts, some ships still went down off the North Carolina coast. Captains made errors in judgment, storms created conditions that charts were yet to reflect, equipment failed at critical moments: The "Graveyard of the Atlantic" became more navigable, but it never became perfectly safe.

The Board understood this. They didn't respond to every shipwreck by assuming the system had failed or that captains were incompetent. They investigated, they improved where patterns emerged, but they also accepted that sailing inherently involved risk. And they knew no amount of infrastructure could completely eliminate human error or acts of nature.

That's why the Life-Saving Service existed: stations positioned along dangerous stretches of coast, crews ready to launch when ships ran aground, rescue boats, life preservers, and emergency protocols. The system acknowledged it couldn't prevent all failures, so it built the capacity to respond when failure occurred.

In business, this is perhaps the hardest principle to embrace. After investing the time, energy, and thought into building systems, defining good decisions, reducing cognitive load, clarifying ownership, matching people to roles, providing reference points, and maintaining it all, we want those systems to work perfectly. We want our team to make good decisions every time.

They won't.

Even with everything in place, someone will misread the situation, someone will ignore the guide, someone will face a scenario no one anticipated—a customer will be lost, a project will fail, money will be wasted. And it will feel frustrating, maybe even infuriating, because you did the work—you built the navigable waters.

But here's the right question to ask: Was it worth the investment?

Are more good decisions being made independently more often? Are fewer things requiring our direct intervention? Can our teams operate with more autonomy than before? Are the mistakes that do happen less impactful, less frequent, or more contained?

If the answers tend to be "Yes," then it was worth it.

The standard was never perfection, and we can't lose sight of that. Because if we can't tolerate any mistakes, we're left with three options—all of them bad:

1. Do everything ourselves—which means we never scale beyond what we personally can accomplish.

2. Micromanage everything—which drives good people away and turns us into a bottleneck.

3. Move so slowly that nothing ever happens—which means our competitors win while we're still perfecting the process.

These are the only alternatives to accepting imperfection. And they're all worse than building the best systems we can and living with the fact that they won't be perfect.

But acceptance doesn't mean resignation. Just as the Life-Saving Service provided rescue when navigation failed, businesses need their own safety nets. Financial buffers, customer goodwill reserves, a reputation strong enough that one mistake doesn't destroy the relationship, redundancy in critical functions, documentation that survives someone's departure, a clear plan to replace any customers who may never return: fittingly, these are all fruits of a well-run business—a business of navigable waters for their crews.

Perhaps the most important consideration in designing our organization to be more self-sufficient is this: it's about the system, not the tactics.

The Lighthouse Board didn't transform the "Graveyard of the Atlantic" with any single innovation. It wasn't just the standardized buoy system, the distinctive lighthouse patterns, or the comprehensive "Light List"—it wasn't even the trained keepers or the district inspectors maintaining it all. The system was responsible, and the system was all of these elements working together toward a clear purpose: to enable competent sailors to navigate dangerous waters independently.

A captain approaching Cape Lookout in 1875 had what the 1840s captain lacked. They could triangulate their position using two lighthouses. They could confirm their distance from shore by when the light came into view. They could identify which lighthouse by its distinctive pattern. They could reference the "Light List" for exact specifications. They could trust the buoy system to mark the channel. And if despite all this they still ran aground, the Life-Saving Station stood ready.

None of these worked in isolation. Together, they created navigable waters.

Most businesses never achieve this. They create the individual tactics, the SOPs, the org charts, the job descriptions, the employee handbooks, but they miss the system. They document procedures without defining what "good" means. They clarify roles without reducing unnecessary decisions. They build reference materials without assigning ownership for keeping them current. They demand accountability without matching people to appropriate roles or providing the necessary resources.

The result is filing cabinets full of documentation nobody uses, and leaders still answering the same questions—making the same decisions, wondering why their team can't function without them.

The framework we've covered isn't complicated:

    1. Define what qualifies as a "good" decision.

    2. Reduce cognitive load and the number of decisions to be made.

    3. Make ownership clear. Answer, *"Whose decision is it?"*

4. Match the person to the role.

5. Provide clear reference points.

6. Observe, collect feedback, adjust, and own the system.

7. Accept imperfection and build safety nets.

But building the system does require the time and commitment to put all the pieces together—to take a break from the urgent and the hectic of the day-to-day, to work on the important, to build, maintain, and improve assets that will serve us and our businesses for years to come. The goal isn't to eliminate the need for navigation; it's building the infrastructure that makes navigation possible.

The story of an organization may be a North Star—the high-level direction that keeps everyone oriented toward the same destination. But the story alone doesn't navigate the ship. The direction from here to our goal is rarely a straight line, and there are a thousand decisions in between. Many of them, our teams must inevitably make without us present to guide them.

Setting north is about giving our crew the tools, information, and reference points to orient themselves along the way. Doing it well leaves us with an organization that is more self-sufficient, less dependent on its leader, and better performing—moving toward the intended destination on the expedition of business.

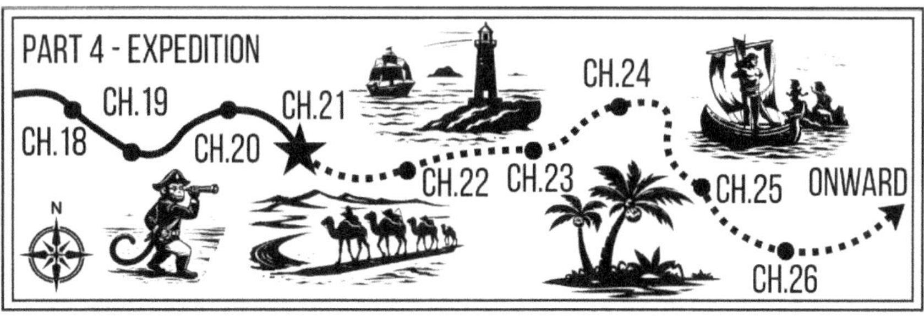

Providing navigable waters for our teams gives them a chance to succeed on their own. Developing the reference points forces us as leaders to be clear on the intended route.

But even the best buoys, lighthouses, and signal lights only prove useful if two conditions are met: we can see them, and we see them in time to act.

That's easy when conditions are calm and our vessel is small. But as visibility becomes limited or our organizations grow in size, the challenge intensifies.

Part of the craft of business is designing the assets and systems that allow our crews to make good, independent decisions. Another essential part is designing the systems of reconnaissance that alert us to those reference points—and deliver the other information we need while at the helm of our organizations.

Only then can we—or those we entrust—navigate a course toward our intended destination.

CHAPTER 22

NAVIGATION AND RECONNAISSANCE

In my business, opportunities and new projects came in waves. At times things were uncomfortably quiet and at others we were up to our eyeballs in promises to keep. Despite my best efforts to smooth out those ups and downs, it was the nature of the work. And we were in the midst of a busy stretch when I rushed to my car one afternoon—late for a meeting with a client.

I opened my phone to double-check the address. At the top of my inbox was a message from one of my most senior employees—an email packed full of all the complaints, frustrations, and unmet expectations that apparently had been simmering for some time. I sat in my car, bewildered at what I was reading—and even later for my meeting.

I had gone to lunch with the same individual earlier that day, and everything seemed fine. Obviously, it was not.

I don't know how Captain Smith felt when word of an iceberg dead ahead reached him, but I assume it was the much bigger brother of the helplessness I felt. There was no way he could turn the Titanic in time, and there wasn't much I could do to correct the course I was on with this employee.

I tried my best, but the damage had been done. A few months later they were gone, and I would have to replace a key member of our team.

As business leaders, we've likely all had similar moments. Our organizations are sailing smoothly along until ***BAM***—an iceberg gashes open the hull on our port side. A key member of our team leaves unexpectedly, an important and long-time customer doesn't renew their contract, or some new technology leaves us behind and scrambling to catch up: unfortunately, we must accept that some surprises are inevitable.

But part of the expedition of business is avoiding as many icebergs as we can.

After the Titanic disaster, the International Ice Patrol was established. It's a service run by the US Coast Guard that continually monitors and relays information about conditions to area vessels. After my email saga, I went from having "annual reviews" with my team to quarterly check-ins. Doing so increased my visibility of the seas I was operating in and helped avoid many future icebergs.

No one can say for sure whether Captain Smith was the utmost of professionals or derelict in his duty the night the Titanic sank. It's impossible to determine exactly what he knew and the decisions that were made. But one claim is safe to make: had he known the Titanic was on a trajectory to strike an iceberg, like me with my disgruntled employee, he would have changed course sooner.

And that brings us to a key component of both expeditions and business—navigation and reconnaissance.

We can leave port or start the year with the clearest of plans, but inevitably course corrections are soon needed.

To be better at those decisions, we learn from our experience, from others, from books, podcasts, peer groups, coaches, and consultants. We put in a lot of time and effort to listen, read, and consider—to hone the skills required for the craft of business.

But the best mental models, developed emotional control, and inventory of experiences are all for naught if we don't have the information we need.

Many regard Captain Smith's decision-making as sound—***given the information he had***. I don't fault my decisions regarding my soon-to-depart employee. My interactions with them in the office, at lunch, and in our conversations after their email: they were all sound decisions—***given the information I had***. The problem for each of us was a matter of perspective: what we could see and be aware of.

There are times in our businesses where we're at the top of a mountain on a clear day. As far as we can see, both forward and backward, the terrain crossed and yet to come is in view. When I first started my business, our small team shared a single room. It was nearly impossible not to see, feel, and hear the state of the business and the morale of the team.

However, one room becomes two, three people become six, then twelve, then more, and eventually the size and scale of the operation breaks the link between what we experience directly and the true state of the business. We find that we're no longer on the mountaintop, but down in the valley and mired in fog.

If Captain Smith had been at the helm of a small fishing vessel that night, the situation would have been different. His eyes would have been on the horizon, his ears on the radio, and his hands on the wheel to make the immediate course correction. But he was leading an organization—a team of people operating one of the largest ocean liners in the world. And his decision-making was beholden to the streams of information that made it, or didn't make it, to him on the bridge.

Getting the right information in business has become a popular topic in the last couple of decades: KPIs, scorecards, dashboards, and weekly metrics reviews—leading, lagging, and coincident indicators. These are helpful, but they can also be tactics in search of a strategy. If we lose the "why" behind these actions, then we lose the strategy they were meant to support in our Pyramids of Decisions. And if we lose the strategy, then we lose much of the benefit.

The strategy is simpler to state than to execute: get the perspective that we need. We seek a perspective that extends our vision beyond what we can personally observe. Because doing so gives us a truer picture of current conditions: where we are, where we've been, and where we're headed.

We know that too little information leaves us flying blind. What's less obvious is that too much information can be just as paralyzing. Captain Smith didn't benefit from certain messages his team withheld, nor from binoculars that were mistakenly locked away from his crew. But neither would he have benefited from hearing every radio broadcast in the Atlantic that night, nor an endless stream of direct reports entering his office with mostly banal information from their departments. He would have been awash in information, without the time or capacity to parse out what was important.

Getting the balance right is having enough information to see clearly, but not so much that we can't see anything. Only you can say exactly what information needs to make it to you on the bridge. But there are general principles that can guide us in building reconnaissance systems that replace unwelcome surprises with anticipated challenges.

If the most exchanged pleasantry in our society is *"How are you?"* then the most common in business certainly rhymes: *"How's business?"* It's a question that we've been asked hundreds of times, but one that's rarely answered with much detail. It raises the question, *"Just how is my business?"*

Maybe you're having your busiest year ever, so busy that you're working nights and weekends. So, is business good or bad? Maybe your revenue is running 10% below expectations for the year, but last month you were 20% behind—what's the answer then? Maybe you've got the best team you've ever had, but three of your senior people are all eyeing the promotion that only one will receive. Does that make you feel concerned or all warm and fuzzy?

Looking at one metric is rarely sufficient, and looking at too many muddies the water. As business leaders, answering *"How is business?"* really comes down to one key question. Do we need to change course, or is it *"Steady as she goes"*—sailing parlance for no change needed?

In sailing and in business, icebergs aren't the problem.
It's when we fail to change course before it is too late.

At 5:50 p.m. on the night the Titanic would sink, Captain Smith changed course slightly, a response to the warnings he had received about icebergs in the area. Around 7:30 p.m. he attended a dinner party, and before heading to bed, talked with the senior officer who had the next watch. The officer would later say:

"We remarked on the weather, about it being calm and clear. We remarked on the distance we could see. We seemed to be able to see a long distance. Everything was very clear. We could see the stars setting down to the horizon."

The captain's last instruction before he departed the bridge was, *"If it becomes at all doubtful, let me know at once."* His words implied that, for the moment, the course was *"steady as she goes."*

Available evidence shows that the rest of the crew agreed—at least until 11:40 p.m.

That's when the fatal iceberg was spotted. Then it was obvious a course correction was needed, and while a sharp one was made, it was too late—37 seconds later the hull of the ship was ripped open.

Captain Smith and I both sailed toward icebergs we didn't know about. We both answered *"fine"* to our versions of *"How's business?"* Neither of us was dishonest in our response—we just didn't know what we didn't know. And that's the challenge: how do we avoid being confidently wrong about the trajectory of our organizations—to not respond *"Steady as she goes"* when a course change is indeed needed?

The answer is partly the information we collect and partly how we make sense of it. Two leaders can look at the same monthly reports and reach opposite conclusions. One sees cause for celebration; the other sees warning signs. The difference isn't the data; it may be personality, but most likely it's the mental model they're using to interpret it. And mental models are what we use to turn information into decisions and action.

I've never piloted an ocean liner, but I have captained a boat. If you've done similar, you know that docking is often the trickiest part. It's the equivalent of pulling one's car into a parking space. But the task gets a little more challenging when it's not pavement beneath your wheels, but water below your hull.

As in business or expeditions, the destination is known: our vessel coming to rest safely in a slip or broadside to the dock—without crashing into something or someone along the way. But obstacles await: the wind pushing the boat in one direction, the current of the water in another, and the momentum of the boat itself. All are variables one tries to consider before pulling the levers at their disposal: forward, reverse, or neutral—throttle up or down—rudder to port or starboard—and fender bags (inflated pillows) to cushion any unfortunate collisions.

Perhaps the fanciest of boats have the equivalent of "auto-park," but for the rest of us, navigating the boat safely to dock starts with the information streams we have coming via our eyes, ears, and "feel." Next, we run those data points through our mental model of how we expect the boat to behave. The push of the wind and the drag of the current, the inevitable lag between a turn of the wheel or bump of the throttle and the boat actually responding: they are all the dynamics which translate information and our actions into outcomes.

It's a simplified version of trying to navigate our businesses. While in the aforementioned scenario we only need to consider the **trajectory** of the vessel and the **conditions** of the wind and water that surround it, in business we're doomed if we don't incorporate the condition of the **ship** itself and the **people** that we depend on into our model.

Paying attention to record revenues while infighting runs rampant through our teams, eyeballing new market opportunities while process bottlenecks are grinding production to a halt—both, and many other scenarios like them, are incomplete perspectives that will soon have us crashing into the dock.

For our models for navigation to be effective, they must consider and gather reconnaissance on all four dimensions that help answer *"How's business?"*

Trajectory – It's the easiest metric to see about the course we're on—revenue, profit margins, customer count, sales pipeline, project milestones, market share, or any other indicator that speaks to the results we're seeing.

Ship – Cash balance, equipment condition, system reliability, process bottlenecks, facility capacity: metrics, both qualitative and quantitative, that speak to the condition of the vessels that we and our teams operate.

People - Morale, turnover rate, workload levels, absenteeism, performance quality, and any other signs which show if a mutiny is brewing: these are the data points that tell us about our greatest asset.

Conditions - Competitor moves, market demand, regulatory changes, economic indicators, talent availability: these, and factors like them, are on par with the wind, weather, and currents our ship is sailing through.

Accepting that we need information on all four is the easy part. The harder part is building systems that actually deliver the data that we need. Because for every leader who's flying (or sailing) blind with too little information, there's another buried under dashboards and weekly reports that are hiding the signal in the noise.

The craft of business involves collecting information on these four areas, but also turning that information into something useful. What data is most valuable, how often to check, how to avoid the mistakes that quietly undermine even well-intentioned efforts: those are the questions we need to answer.

The best approach means moving higher on The Mountain of Why—leaving behind the camps of "W*hat everyone else is doing*" and generic dashboards or scorecards, and instead, thinking through our decisions from first principles.

When it comes to building the navigation and reconnaissance systems for our organizations, a useful principle is delivered by our Horsemen of human nature and limited resources: As leaders, our capacity to absorb and process information is only so large. So, when new information comes to us on the bridge, how much detail do we need, and how much detail clouds our view?

Let's say you're hiring for a new director of marketing. The candidate arrives, and you join them in the conference room. Here's what you know so far: this person exists, they have a résumé, and they're looking for a job. Everything else is TBD.

Are you ready to hire them? Of course not. Currently, the limited resource isn't your mind and how many details it can process; it's information about the candidate that's in short supply.

Next, you learn that they have some work experience. They've worked in sales before, apparently with some success, and they have a college degree.

Better, but the picture is still very fuzzy.

Next, you read through their CV and résumé.

They have a Bachelor of Science in Marketing—GPA 3.47, graduated in May 2021, worked 18 months at ThreeDucks Inc. (founded 2018, Series A, $4.2M raised, 23 employees at peak), performed well in an inside sales role—110.3% of quota in year one (Q1: 87%, Q2: 112%, Q3: 118%, Q4: 124%), 109.8% in year two, average deal size $8,400, 47 calls per day average, used Salesforce and HubSpot, are proficient in Excel (know VLOOKUP and pivot tables), they live 4.3 miles from office, have a cat named "*Mr. Socks*," and like their coffee black.

A new problem emerges: information overload. The picture is sharp, but your brain is in pain.

How about instead, HR puts a sticky note on the front of the file:

"Marketing degree from State University, spent two years at a tech startup doing inside sales with 110% quota attainment, left because the company folded, looking for a role with growth potential, available to start in two weeks."

Now you've got inputs that let the wheels of your mental model turn—without overloading the machinery of your brain. It's one of the prerequisites of a good navigation and reconnaissance system: the right level of detail—the right resolution.

"We have some money in the bank" isn't a very reassuring financial data point. Every transaction itemized by vendor, payment method, day of the week, and time of day isn't all that helpful either. The Goldilocks version—*"Just right"*—is knowing the current cash balance, burn rate, runway in months, upcoming major expenses, or similar details. That's information a leader can use. Informative but not overwhelming, that's our first principle at work, and what it means to get the resolution right.

------------◆◯◆------------

When looking at all the different metrics related to our businesses, it's often hard to pause, zoom out, and ask: *"What do I actually need to know?"*

Answering that question well means returning to our mental models and the variables that are in play. Which are important? And again, there's a parallel to playing captain.

If I'm docking a boat, the wind, the current of the water, and the speed of the vessel matter—what's playing on the radio, or whether the sun is out, do not. Though all are part of my information streams.

Once we zoom in on the necessary, there's the question of how those variables are presented.

That may be in their absolute value—knowing that my boat is 10 feet from the dock provides some detail. Or maybe their rate of change—knowing that my boat was 20 feet from the dock a few seconds ago provides more of the resolution I need.

How quickly our bank account is headed to zero, how quickly our reservation book is filling up, how much longer before a disgruntled employee finally blows their top: all are typically more valuable to know than a fixed reading.

But then sometimes, we need the rate of change...of the rate of change.

Knowing my boat is moving five miles per hour as it approaches the dock might be concerning—or maybe it's not. If a few seconds prior we were only moving at three miles per hour, that's cause for alarm. We're not slowing down but accelerating! If a few seconds prior we were moving at 10 miles per hour, then there's good reason to believe we'll soon be completely stopped—and out of danger. It's not just the distance from the dock, nor the current speed, but also the change. Are we accelerating or decelerating?

Customer churn was 5% this quarter. Last quarter it was 4%; the quarter before that it was 3%. We're not just losing customers; we're losing them at an accelerating rate! But if last quarter was 7% and the quarter before that was 9%, then that 5% looks a lot better. Retention efforts are working, and the trend is reversing.

But the nuance doesn't stop with the rate of change (speed), or even the rate of change of the rate of change (acceleration). Do we always need to be paying attention, or can we ignore some variables at times?

My boat might be speeding up or slowing down, but if I'm two miles from the dock, do I really care either way? It's not until I cross some threshold of speed or distance from the dock that those variables start to matter.

The percentage of time our staff spends on billable work might fluctuate between 70% and 80%. Every little change doesn't justify a reaction. But if it drops below 65%—not enough work to cover our costs, or if it climbs above 90%—people burning out and quality suffering, then the variable starts to demand our attention. Otherwise, it's a banal message to the bridge—one that dilutes the importance of others.

In the end, the specific variables that matter to you are unique to your organization—and your mental model of docking your boat. But chances are what you need to know for each falls into one of the categories in the table that follows: absolute value, rate of change, acceleration, and relevant thresholds.

WHAT WE NEED TO KNOW	SITUATION	EXAMPLE METRICS
ABSOLUTE VALUE (E.G. POSITION)	*Current state itself drives immediate decisions. We need to know exactly where we stand right now.*	*Cash balance, headcount, inventory on hand, days until deadline*
RATE OF CHANGE (E.G. VELOCITY)	*Trajectory matters as much or more than position. We need to know which direction things are moving and how fast to predict what's coming.*	*Revenue growth rate, cash burn rate, customer acquisition rate, deal velocity, churn rate*
ACCELERATION	*The trend itself is shifting. We need to know if a problem is getting worse or starting to improve, if momentum is building or fading.*	*Revenue growth accelerating/decelerating churn rate increasing/decreasing, cost creep speeding up/slowing down*
THRESHOLD ONLY (E.G. MAX/MIN)	*We don't need the exact number, just an alert when crossing a boundary that demands action. Protects attention by filtering normal from abnormal.*	*Utilization rates, customer concentration, debt covenants, critical milestones, minimum cash reserves*

Having a good mental model, understanding the variables we need to monitor, knowing the resolution we need for each—neither too high nor too low: these are many of the building blocks of a good navigation and reconnaissance system. But we still won't see the iceberg until it's too late if we ignore the most important variable: ***time***.

Time is what converts absolute values into rates of change, and rates of change into acceleration. It also likely sets our thresholds—when values begin to matter. But it matters in two other critical ways. It determines how often we need to refresh the information we have. And when that information tells us a change of course is needed, time dictates how much runway we have before our rendezvous with an ever-closer iceberg.

If our boat is 50 feet from the dock, checking our position every ten minutes is far too slow. If we're two miles out, checking every ten seconds is overkill. But what if our boat is 500 feet away? What's the right interval?

The Titanic's lookouts had their eyes on the iceberg 37 seconds before impact, but the ship needed minutes to turn.

We can dial in our mental models, understand the variables we need, the level of detail and resolution for each, but if we're not refreshing our information streams often enough, then we're making decisions in the past—and we should expect consequences in the future.

But if we're hit with a continuous stream of the latest data points, then we're back to our 3.47 GPA, black coffee drinking, cat-loving marketing candidate—lost in the fog, seeing everything, but understanding nothing.

Just as there are thousands of ships navigating an equally large number of seas and conditions, each business operates with their own rhythms and under their unique time pressures. It's impossible to say what getting the time scale right looks like for a specific organization without being on the inside, but chances are the following four principles give us time to make any necessary course corrections.

 MATCH FREQUENCY TO THE PACE OF CHANGE

Different metrics change at different speeds, and our monitoring rhythm should match.

As business leaders, we have a sense of how things progress in our business. Checking in with employees only once a year leads to some irate emails, while checking in twice a day would drive them to either suspicion or neurosis. Customer relationships, invoice aging, bank account balances, whatever the variable, the right frequency to refresh our information is proportional to the rate at which they change. It's the difference between how often a ship captain should be checking their compass (often) versus making sure there's not a tear in the mainsail (not as often).

 ALLOW ENOUGH LEAD TIME TO RESPOND

Even perfect information is useless if we don't have time to act. If it takes three months to hire and onboard a senior person, checking team capacity once a quarter isn't sufficient. By the time we spot the constraint and start recruiting, we're already weeks behind.

The same logic applies everywhere. Cutting expenses, pursuing new revenue streams, complying with new government regulations: the list is endless; there's always something we need to be doing. Part of the craft of business is working backward from *"How long does it take to change course?"* to figuring out *"How far ahead do I need to be looking?"*

 ## USE LEADING INDICATORS FOR EARLY WARNING

Leading indicators change before the variable we care about. They buy us the time we need to take action.

Employee engagement often drops quarters before turnover spikes. Sales pipeline velocity slows months before revenue declines. Customer support tickets increase weeks before renewal rates drop. Leading indicators aren't always perfect predictions, but like *"Red sky in the morning, sailor's warning,"* they often alert us to trouble ahead.

The value of leading indicators isn't hard to understand; they let us see the iceberg sooner. By the time turnover shows up in our numbers, people have already decided to leave. But if engagement scores are trending down, we can intervene before anyone walks out the door. Getting it right means building a mix of metrics: lagging indicators to know what happened, coincident indicators to know the current state of things, and leading indicators to see what's coming. If we do all three, we're in for *"Red sky at night, sailor's delight."*

 ## FILTER SIGNAL FROM NOISE

When we refresh our information streams frequently, we see variation. But not all variation matters. Daily revenue bounces around. Weekly utilization rates fluctuate. One customer complaint doesn't mean our service is failing. The challenge is distinguishing real change from normal noise.

This is where moving averages, trend lines, and seasonal adjustments become essential. Instead of reacting to every daily swing in reservations booked, meals sold, or widgets produced, what's the time window that paints a more accurate picture?

The answer is the amount of time we need to collect enough data to separate the signal from the noise. The scope of the math is beyond this book, and while there are formulas to determine the right time window for the variables that feed into our mental models, the important point is this:

Time is a river that brings information. If we're too impatient, we open the gates before we've put enough water behind the dam. If we wait too long, we're late to respond, the dam is overflowing, and the latest information is only reaffirming what we knew well before.

But when we get the time scale right, when we get the resolution right, when we don't fixate on any one element but keep our eyes on our ship, our team, and the conditions as well as the trajectory, we start to get the reconnaissance we need to put all our hard-earned judgment to effective use.

We stop being surprised by icebergs we should have seen coming. We gain the visibility to navigate with confidence, even as the organization grows beyond what we can directly see and feel. And we turn limited information from a Horseman working against us into a challenge we can manage better than our competition—and a competitive edge.

But it's an advantage we only realize if we return to a version of an earlier strategy: the best way to keep a system working is to foresee the reasons it often breaks.

———◆———

For all the principles that guide us toward navigating well and getting the reconnaissance we need, there are just as many ways to sabotage our efforts. Building a great system is essential, but so is being aware of what often wastes our efforts. And the following are five common culprits:

1. Metrics Aren't Reality – Data may tell us who, what, where, or when, but they rarely tell us why and how. A metric drops or spikes, the dashboard shows the change, but not the cause. The answer comes from talking to people, observing what's actually happening, asking questions, and being present. Leaders who only read reports miss the reality underneath the numbers, and without that narrative, we can't make sense of what we're seeing or know how to respond.

2. Wrong Units – Which is more useful, how many ***dollars*** a company has in the bank or how many ***months*** until they burn through that cash? With the right information, one can deduce the latter from the former, but expressing the metric in the most useful units upfront communicates the reality better.

Days of inventory on hand, debt coverage **ratios**, **percentage** of revenue: all are common, useful metrics that were made better by using the right units.

A good question to ask ourselves is: *"Does this metric, in these units, tell me something I can act on?"* If not, there's probably a better unit to be had—and a more usable way to communicate the information.

3. Tunnel Vision - The most dangerous trap in our reconnaissance is obsessing over one area while ignoring the others. Leaders fixate on where they're going while missing that their vessel is breaking down, their crew is exhausted, or conditions around them are shifting.

It's an easy mistake to make if we're working to fix a particular challenge. In that case, we understandably start to pay more attention to the associated metrics—the classic *"Squeaky wheel gets the oil."* And the limited resource of our attention runs dry before we get an update on the rest of the organization.

Another common mistake is letting comfort and our own G.E.A.R. model pull us off course.

A leader feels more comfortable in the realm of finance and strategy. It's work they enjoy, and they're happy to turn a blind eye to the state of their people and everyday operations. It's human nature, and something we must guard against.

4. Information Doesn't Flow – Captain Smith didn't benefit from his radio operator telling a nearby ship to *"shut up"* (true story), that he was too busy to deal with their messages. Of course, had the operator known the importance of the information to come, things would have been different.

But that's the problem. We don't know if something is a problem until we have the data, and we're less likely to collect the data unless we know it's a problem.

Engagement helps hold up our Tent of Comfort and is part of the "G" of Genetics in our G.E.A.R. model. And we make a fundamental error in the design of our organizations if we rely on people to consistently round up and transmit typically banal information—because it's boring work.

The best option is to remove people and our fickle human nature altogether—to automate data collection and transmission. When doing so is possible, those systems become some of the greatest assets of our organizations.

But often it's not, and we're back to one of our toughest jobs as leaders: getting people to do the important but non-urgent—and the boring. The "R" of real-time constraints in our G.E.A.R. model, and the topic of Chapter 11 can help with this task—as can the ideas and insights to come in the next chapter, "Lines of Communication."

5. Cognitive overload – We can't watch everything at once. Trying to monitor a hundred metrics in real time is a recipe for paralysis and mental exhaustion, not insight. We're back to the limits of human nature and our brains. Dump too much on them and nothing gets processed well. Again, it is why getting the resolution and timescale right is so important. Doing so helps eliminate excess information and distills information down to the most impactful to our mental models—and the course corrections we need to make.

But even then, it can be too much for one person. And once again we find ourselves needing to delegate and trust our team. With the right people and the right systems, we can let them monitor parts of our reconnaissance readings. They can shoulder part of the cognitive load, and like Captain Smith's crew, they can alert us *"if there is any doubt."*

It's easy to frame good reconnaissance as defensive: avoiding icebergs, preventing disasters, changing course with a key employee before they're ready to abandon ship. But that's only part of the benefit.

Good reconnaissance, and the precision navigation it allows, is also offensive. When we can see clearly and far enough ahead, when we have a firmer answer to *"How's business?"* we can move faster. We can take bigger risks because we'll spot problems early enough to correct them. And we can navigate tighter lines because we have a better idea of where we are and what's around us.

With the right systems and the right people in place, good reconnaissance allows us to pursue ambitious goals, enter new markets, and push people with less fear that they'll break. It's all because we have the visibility to know when we're drifting off course while there's still time to adjust.

While the leader without good reconnaissance must move cautiously, the leader with good reconnaissance can move decisively—confident they'll see what's coming (and their competition in the rear-view mirror).

Even better, the principles we covered don't just apply to leaders. Every level of the organization can benefit from the same thinking.

Our crews need reconnaissance too. They need to know how they're doing in their roles, whether they're on track, and what's changing around them. The salesperson needs visibility into their pipeline and performance. The project manager needs to see capacity constraints and timeline risks. The department head needs the same four-area view we've been discussing, just scaled to their domain.

The principles we've covered—getting the resolution right, matching timescale to the pace of change, monitoring all four areas, and filtering signal from noise—they all apply everywhere, not just at the bridge, but throughout the ship.

Good reconnaissance systems allow everyone to navigate their own responsibilities with the same confidence we're trying to achieve at the organizational level. And that's the goal: that when the time comes to change course or keep it *"steady as she goes,"* everyone can make good decisions—and early enough to avoid any icebergs.

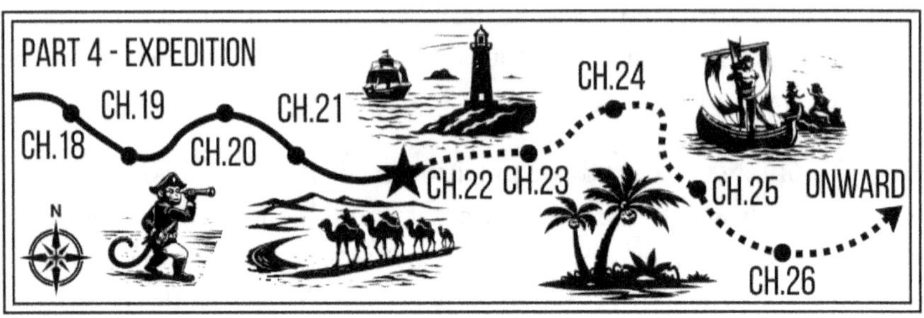

When Captain Smith and his crew needed to make a course correction, they had the wheel to control the one large rudder and the throttle to control the three engines at their disposal. Going to port or starboard on one and full ahead or full astern on the other were simple actions, but also the products of years of experience and calculated decisions.

In business, we have our Levers of Control to raise the energy, build unity, lower resistance, and achieve greater yield. But neither the actions we take nor the decisions we make are as simple. Both the vessel we captain and the waters we navigate are much more complex, and thus so are the movements of our levers.

It's why those who put in the work to build better systems, gather better reconnaissance, and develop better mental models are rewarded. Every organization has some form of navigation and reconnaissance system. The question is how effective they are.

If the goal that sits atop this Pyramid of Decisions is to have a system that allows us to safely sail tighter, more aggressive lines than the competition, then climbing higher on The Mountain of Why reveals a certain first principle that is key to better decisions around the strategies and tactics we need: the outcome of a decision is beholden to the information on which it was based.

Getting the right information starts with resolution—how much detail we actually need. Too little, and we're sailing blind. Too much, and we're buried under data points that crowd out the ones that matter.

But resolution alone isn't enough if we're neglecting certain information streams altogether. A complete picture means gathering reconnaissance across four areas: our trajectory, the condition of our ship, the state of our people, and the conditions we're sailing through.

And then there's the challenge of time and frequency. Check too often, and we're reacting to noise. Check too rarely, and the iceberg is already in our hull. Getting time right means matching how often we look to how fast things change, building in enough lead time to actually respond, using leading indicators that warn us before the damage is done, and filtering signal from noise so we're not mistaking a normal wave for a rogue one.

These principles guide us toward good reconnaissance. And when we avoid the common obstacles that get in the way, and we build systems that work up and down the ranks of our organizations, then we're well on our way to setting the right course.

But it's all dependent on one thing: information must flow. The best reconnaissance systems, the sharpest mental models, and the soundest principles are worthless if the information never makes it to us or the right members of our crews.

It may have been poor communication that sank the Titanic. It's certainly one of the chief frustrations within organizations. And that's why the next chapter is about establishing the lines of communication we need on the expedition of business.

CHAPTER 23

LINES OF COMMUNICATION

"Nobody told me..."

"I thought you said..."

"That's not what I meant..."

"We talked about this..."

"Did you not see my email..."

A strange noise from under the hood of your car, water dripping from the ceiling overhead, waking up with a scratchy throat: there are some occurrences in life that are just never good news. As business leaders, hearing certain phrases falls into that category. When we hear them, it's an unmistakable sign that things have gone off the rails. Poor communication is likely to blame, and there's a never-ending list of the problems that result.

Two team members spend weeks on the same deliverable. Neither knows the other is doing the same tasks as they are. When they finally compare notes, one person's work gets thrown away.

Someone makes a promise to a client. The team that must deliver never hears about it. The deadline arrives, the work is not done, and the client is furious.

Someone says, *"Let's meet Tuesday, the 19th."* But Tuesday is the 17th. Nobody asks for clarification—half the team shows up on Tuesday, the other half on the 19th.

We've all been burned by some form of these issues. As long as there have been leaders, they have been trying to improve communication within their teams.

Robert Falcon Scott's team installed 15 miles of telephone line across the Antarctic ice as part of their effort to reach the South Pole. Lewis and Clark held journal sessions at key points to allow their team to compare notes. Relay teams, message runners, buried caches of correspondence, color-coordinated flags, the earliest uses of radio: leaders of expeditions past tried nearly everything to keep information flowing.

Today, business leaders invest in instant messaging, message boards, or other collaboration platforms. They install video conferencing systems, adopt "open-door" policies, and enforce "core-hours." All are in addition to the phone lines, email inboxes, and "all hands" meetings that have been standard practice for decades.

We intuitively know how important good communication is, and how often bad communication costs us. And like our expedition counterparts, we go to great lengths to open lines of communication within our organizations.

Building and maintaining that infrastructure is a challenge, but the bigger problem is often how it's used—and the messages it delivers.

What's meant to provide clarity increases confusion. What's needed on time arrives late. And our efforts of more channels, more policies, and more people involved only produce more noise.

In the midst of everything, it is easy to overlook something. When we craft the tactics and execution that support the goal of good communication in this Pyramid of Decisions, there's a first principle that puts us higher on The Mountain of Why:

While good communication is undoubtedly an asset, the <u>need</u> for good communication is a liability.

Every conversation required, every message that must be sent, and every meeting that wouldn't be needed if the system was designed differently: these are points of failure waiting to happen. And unless leaders take steps to reduce these points of failure—to minimize the ***need*** for good communication—we will hear *"I assumed..."* or *"Didn't they know..."* and find our expeditions veering off course far too often.

The logic is straightforward: the more things that must go right, the more opportunity there is for things to go wrong.

As the need for communication grows, so does the liability.

I once had a boss whose answer to everything seemed to be, *"We have to communicate better."* A deadline is missed, *"We have to communicate better."* Client expectations become misaligned, *"We have to communicate better."* Someone's vegetarian spouse is served a T-bone steak at the holiday party, *"We have to communicate better."*

He wasn't wrong, but it was on par with *"We have to increase revenue,"* *"...cut expenses,"* or *"...turn straw into gold."* No one is questioning the benefits, but how? And it's a core question most business leaders wrestle with:

If making good decisions depends on having good information, then how do we ensure each member of our teams has the information they need—consistently and delivered in a way they can understand?

Finding the answer begins with an important step: know thy enemy.

In this case, it's me, it's you, it's our team members, it's humans in general. Our Horseman of human nature strikes again: we forget, we misunderstand, we're busy, we're distracted, and we assume that everyone communicates the same way we do.

We are the problem. But knowing that gives rise to certain strategies and tactics that can help.

When we craft the stories of our organizations, we eliminate the need for constant communication about purpose, direction, and challenges. The mission and the plan aren't secrets. They're documented, shared, and reinforced in clear language that only has to be written once to avoid being communicated individually hundreds of times.

When we make the waters of our organization navigable, we remove thousands of conversations that would otherwise be necessary. We replace them with reference points and information that people can seek themselves. They are no longer reliant on others to tell them what they need to know. Clear SOPs mean people don't have to repeatedly ask, *"How should I handle this task?"* Job descriptions and organizational charts eliminate constant communication about who does what.

When we establish better reconnaissance systems, we automate the flow of operational information. Dashboards show project status without someone having to remember to send an update. Metrics surface problems without someone having to notice and alert others. Data flows to those who need it, when they need it, without depending on human memory or attention.

Each of these steps eliminates entire categories of communication that would otherwise be necessary. The right systems move information from our heads to the infrastructure of our organizations. There it is accessible, consistent, and reliable. And there it is less prone to the inevitable "drift" or decay of accuracy that comes from (the liability of) person-to-person communication.

But while all those systems, and all the work that goes into getting them right, lower the resistance Lever of Control, they are not everything. We know that some information can't be systematized or automated. The decision that was just made in this morning's meeting, the problem that just surfaced on a project, the coordination between teams working on interdependent pieces: this is information that lives in people's heads, changes too quickly to document, or requires judgment about who needs to know.

And somehow, despite how prone we are to error, it's information that must reach the people who need it—and in a way that they can understand.

With the right approach, we can reduce the liability of our ***need*** for good communication. But there will always be certain situations where we have no option but to—once again—rely on our team to make their own good decisions. And in this case, they are decisions to communicate efficiently and effectively.

So, as leaders, we should do what we can to reduce the communication burden we put on our crew. And then, for what's left, for what we can't systematize, automate, or enshrine—we don't stop at *"We have to communicate better,"* but we help our teams improve their skills and abilities.

We can do so through specific, implementable practices. Just as expeditions used flags to relay critical information, we'll do the same here. There are seven flags in total, each one signaling how leaders can reduce the liability of communications that can't be avoided.

Some flags address who's on our team in the first place. Others shape how information flows once they're onboard. A few create the conditions where critical information can't be missed. But all of them recognize that better communication isn't about trying harder—it's about being better at the craft of business.

HIRE WELL

When it comes to hiring, we're often limited by how much we can see the person in action. While it's easy to see someone's typing speed, their ability to solve a problem on a worksheet, or whether their idea of "professional attire" matches our own, other qualities are more difficult to critique. Handling an irate client, keeping their files organized, being a team player: these are abilities that aren't gauged easily by a résumé and a few interviews.

Fortunately, when it comes to communication, the entire interview process gives us a front-row seat to see their skills in action. If the role we're looking to fill is communication-heavy, then we should be putting a candidate's relevant skills under the magnifying glass as part of our hiring processes.

Do they respond to emails promptly and clearly? Can they articulate questions when scheduling conflicts arise? During the interview itself, how do they provide their answers, but also how do they listen—do they ask clarifying questions, or do they jump to conclusions? We're gifted answers to these questions if we pay close enough attention.

The hiring process of my business included brief written exercises: drafting a response to a hypothetical customer complaint, summarizing a mock meeting, or asking a peer for missing information.

Even the small talk before and after formal interviews reveals whether they can build rapport, read social cues, and adjust their communication style to different audiences. By treating every touchpoint as a window into their communication abilities, we transform the hiring process from a simple interview into a comprehensive assessment of how well they can communicate.

The easiest time to head off communication shortcomings is before the problem comes aboard. For those already part of the crew, there's something particularly helpful we can do for them.

TELL YOUR TEAM WHAT THEY PROBABLY DON'T KNOW

We tend to think we're decent communicators. After all, we've been doing it our whole lives. And while we're always happy to assume a misunderstanding is the other person's fault, it's not until we put intentional thought into how we communicate—or someone else prods us into doing so—that we realize our "clear" messages are clouds of confusion.

We've seen a similar theme in both Part 2 and Part 3 of this book. Good communication is essential, but putting all the pieces together is hard.

The language that we choose, our *"um's"* and *"you know's,"* our eye contact, and our body language: there's a long list of what goes into being a good communicator. Fortunately, the gap between being ineffective and effective isn't innate talent; it's learnable skills.

Most organizations offer continuing education resources and professional development budgets. Technical certifications, industry conferences, and advanced degrees: all are supported and encouraged. Yet communication skills, which underpin nearly everything else, often get treated as something people should just figure out on their own—or not considered at all. It's the same mistake most educational curricula make: focusing on putting information into someone's head, but failing to give them the tools to get it back out.

When we make it our job as an organization to help people develop one of their most foundational skills, it tends to avoid a lot of headaches. But like most endeavors to improve, we don't start the journey until we see the gap between where we are and where we need to be.

 ## SET EXPECTATIONS

We give our teams reference points, access to materials, and the tools that allow them to make good decisions. But choosing when and how they communicate is a subset of the decisions we need them to make. And if we want those decisions to be *good* decisions, then we need to define what *good* communication looks like.

Job descriptions, SOPs, operations manuals: none of these or documents like them are complete without specific details on what communication is required. Without that information, we're failing to define what qualifies as a job well done.

But again, the more we expect our teams to remember or pay attention, the more our communication liability grows. Tactics are more likely to hold up our Pyramids of Decisions when we supplement written expectations with assets like templates, checklists, and example correspondence. They are assets because they help lighten the communication loads we put on our crews, and as a result, they provide more consistent results.

When we set clearer expectations around communication, we better orient our teams as to how they should proceed. And providing that orientation is most successful if we answer the questions many of us heard in Journalism 101:

Who needs to know? ***What*** needs to be included? ***When*** does it need to happen? ***Where*** should it occur? ***How*** should it be done—the medium to be used? And, perhaps most importantly, *why* does the communication matter?

 ## MAKE THE "WHY" CLEAR

Almost every morning, my wife asks me what the weather is supposed to be. Early on I'd say something like, *"I think it's supposed to be 55, and maybe some rain."* After a few years of marriage, I realized *"55"* wasn't landing, so my language evolved. *"Cool and rainy"* seemed to resonate better. It took me a few more years to realize my answer should be: *"Sweater, pants, and an umbrella."*

In every iteration, I communicated the information she asked for. But it wasn't until I understood the *why* that I became a good communicator. The question was never about the weather; it was about what she should wear that day. And my answer was only as good as how well it answered the real question.

When our teams understand what someone will do with the information they're providing, they communicate differently. Not just more accurately, but in a way that's more useful.

An estimator sends the cost breakdown for a project to a field superintendent. If they think they're *"handing off the file,"* they send the data and move on. But if they understand the superintendent uses it to brief crews and make real-time sequencing decisions, they just might include notes about risks, flag which assumptions were solid, and mention client sensitivities.

When people know the "why" of their communication, the "what" and the "how" often get better.

However, there's a reason this version of cognitive empathy is so valuable—because it's rare. It's unrealistic to think that we can get everyone on our team to have a "bird's-eye view" of the organization. Our Horsemen of human nature and limited resources keep any of us from seeing just how every part, piece, and person fits together.

So, we inform and instruct the best we can, but there's another powerful tactic to help "bridge the gaps."

 ## <u>CREATE "UNAVOIDABLE" MOMENTS</u>

For years, a blue 1ˢᵗ prize-like ribbon hung in my office. The embossed letters on the body of the ribbon read: *"I survived another meeting that could have been an email."*

Unfortunately, *"meeting"* has become a four-letter word in many organizations. And while we all know they can be a colossal waste of time, ***good*** meetings produce one of the keys to better communication: an unavoidable moment.

My company had two weekly all-hands meetings. You could be there in person, on the phone, or virtually—but you had to be there. Also, you had better hold on, because we were moving fast.

The Monday meeting was less than 25 minutes, and the Wednesday meeting rarely ran more than 15. They had the earmarks of all good meetings: structured format, required attendance, active participation—but most importantly, they were thick with information.

No one ever objected to these meetings because inevitably they made good communication unavoidable.

Chances are everyone in attendance could use the opportunity to share information they needed to share or receive information they needed to receive—all while knowing they had the other person's full attention. And even if the discussion seemed irrelevant, everyone was still being provided context on the state of the company, projects, and the challenges of everyone's job. In theory, all this information could have flowed through another channel, but a well-run meeting was the way to make these critical communications unavoidable.

These moments look different for every company. Maybe it's a routine "all hands" meeting, or more limited by department. Maybe it's training sessions, new employee orientations, or project pre- and post-mortems. Project handoff meetings, taking junior staff to meetings with clients, or having people from sales walk the factory floor (and vice versa): they all have similar benefits—unavoidable moments.

When everyone is heads down in their daily work, their horizon is just their feet and the trail in front of them. These moments force them to look out and see the wider landscape.

They also give people a platform. The field superintendent who's been dealing with a recurring vendor issue finally has leadership's attention. The junior developer who noticed a pattern gets heard by people who can finally do something about it. Information that would otherwise stay trapped surfaces because there's a structured moment for it to flow.

Maybe those in attendance see more than they need. Maybe others hear more context than is directly relevant to them. But it's often worth the trade-off: a little "wasted" time ensures important information gets to and from the key players—unavoidably.

Bad meetings deserve a bad reputation. Well-designed and purposeful meetings, along with any other scenario where we force people to show up and communicate, can be one path to an organization communicating better. They give people a better opportunity to speak and be heard—but how do we know the message lands as expected?

 ## FEEDBACK LOOPS

You walk up to an elevator; you hit the "down" button. What happens next?

The button lights up, and with that you know, *Message received.* For many elevators, there is an added bonus: a small display which reads "8" then "7" then "6." You are now doubly assured that the elevator is headed toward you.

The light glowing or the floors counting down might make you feel better—not having to question whether you hit the button hard enough or if the elevator is broken, but in the context of being a better communicator, they're doing something even more important.

They're freeing up your cognitive capacity—and you can move on to your next task.

For aviation, military, and medical professionals, these feedback loops are part of their everyday operations.

Air traffic control says: *"Cleared to land runway 27."*

The pilot doesn't just acknowledge; they read back: *"Cleared to land runway 27."*

Military radio has some form of "read back." And medical handoff protocols require the same: their version of *"I heard you, and here is what I heard."*

When someone tells us they *"got it"* or *"understood,"* all that we really know is that they **THINK** they got it or now understand. However, when they explain it back in their own words: *"So we need the budget numbers by Friday because finance is closing the books next week,"* then we know we're on the same page.

There's a psychological shift when someone acknowledges what we've communicated. For the sender, any anxiety about misunderstandings turns to relief—and their mind is free for what's next. For the receiver, they have moved from passive to active. Once they've confirmed, they've committed. They can't later claim they never got the message. Both parties now know that both parties know.

Part of mastering the craft of business is integrating the power of this sequence into our organizations' designs.

The language shouldn't be, *"Please confirm when you have a chance,"* but *"We cannot proceed without confirmation."* Feedback loops should be non-negotiable in our processes.

Of course, we can only see the elevator button light up if we're not drowning in other information—which brings us to our last, and perhaps most important, principle.

REDUCE NOISE

Every email, every meeting invitation, every Slack or Teams notification, every phone call, every pop-in to ask *"a quick question"*—all of them consume the same limited resource: our attention.

The problem isn't that these communications happen. It's that they happen constantly, indiscriminately, and without regard for whether right now is the right time.

The sender wants it off their plate, so they fire away immediately. Meanwhile, the receiver's day becomes a series of interruptions masquerading as productivity.

We know what it's like to give something our full attention.
We also know what it's like when we're drowning in noise.

Many organizations let their people drown in noise. They mistake activity for progress, see such exchanges as unavoidable, and then wonder why critical signals get missed.

When everything demands immediate attention, nothing gets proper consideration. The budget change that actually matters gets lost between the lunch order poll and the reply-all chain about parking spots. Recently, I was CC'd on an email including the president and two VPs of a 100-plus person organization. The topic: a question from the lady who cleans the office.

There are tactics organizations can use to save our brains from this constant bombardment. The immediate goal is part of a bigger strategy for better lines of communication: reduce the noise.

Some organizations set norms around response times, or instant messaging is reserved for genuinely urgent matters. Others create protected focus blocks where interruptions aren't acceptable except for real emergencies. My company had "do not disturb" lights on people's desks—red meaning *"Leave me alone,"* green meaning *"come on over."* Some establish regular rhythms for information sharing. If status updates happen every Monday at 10am, people can batch their communications instead of sending them the moment they think of it.

Shared documents where questions accumulate asynchronously rather than derailing someone's afternoon, end-of-day summaries instead of play-by-play updates, default-to-private channels instead of organization-wide announcements, no-meeting Wednesdays, core collaboration hours with protected deep work time outside them: they're all options to accomplish the same goal—communicate better by doing so more intentionally.

When the noise of our organizations dies down, people can better hear the communications that come their way. Their refocused attention can be directed toward important matters—like sending information that is critical to others. And suddenly, by cleaning up the backdrop against which work happens, all our other principles start working better. The result: better lines of communication—and by doing less, not more.

—◦—

When we systematically reduce the need for communication and build the resources to address the needs that remain, we get two benefits.

First, the communication that must happen—the communication that we have no choice but to rely on others for—it gets better. The information people need reaches them, and in a form they can understand. It does so more consistently—not by luck or heroic effort, but by design. We have fewer *"nobody told me"* moments, fewer *"I thought you said"* disasters, and fewer weeks of duplicated work. The baseline competence of our organizations rises as a result of our efforts: the environments we improve, the assets we build, and the skills we help others develop.

Second, and perhaps more importantly, we free people up.

When people aren't spending cognitive capacity wondering *"Did I tell Sarah?"* *"Where did I see that?"* or *"Who was I supposed to update?"* they can focus on what actually matters. The problem-solving conversations, the brainstorming sessions that generate the next breakthrough, the relationship-building that creates trust, even the socializing that makes people want to show up to work: we get more of those productive exchanges, and fewer of those that only generate noise.

Establishing better lines of communication is not just about preventing failures. It's about creating the space for communication that moves our businesses forward: the conversations that don't fit in templates or checklists, the creative collision of ideas, the *"what if we tried..."* discussions that lead somewhere unexpected. It's about funneling our limited time, and our limited memory and attention, to the conversations that matter most.

Success on the expedition of business is partly in the design: intentionally building systems that work with human nature—not against it, creating structures that make doing the right thing easier than doing the wrong thing, reducing reliance on our team's limited memory and attention, and taking steps to ensure we conserve these valuable resources. Because we can have all the technology in the world, but it's all for naught if our teams don't have the clarity and capacity to utilize it effectively.

Scott's telephone lines didn't save his expedition from disaster. The infrastructure and technology couldn't offset the problems with the design and operation of his organization. Meanwhile, Lewis and Clark's journal comparison sessions worked because they were part of a larger, designed approach. The difference wasn't the tool or the technology; it was thinking about how information needed to flow—and what stood in the way.

When we design communication systems that work, we're removing friction points within our organizations. We're lowering the resistance Lever of Control, and by doing so we raise the lever of energy and the lever of unity—because a team that can communicate more easily, and a team that contends with less noise, has more energy left to focus on the goal at hand.

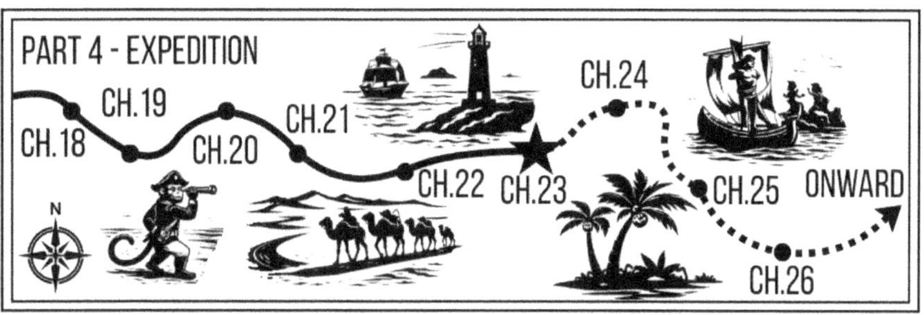

We can be certain of where we're going and why we want to get there. We can be clear on the challenges that await us, and we can have the right team to overcome them.

We can establish systems that let us and our people gather the information we need, and we can build the lines of communication which let us share that information throughout our organizations.

But none of it matters if we lose something along the way: the ability to make decisions on our terms.

While we've spent the last several chapters talking about how to think through certain challenges, and how to establish the infrastructure we need on the expedition of business, the next chapter pivots to the supply lines that keep our operations going—and the two resources a business can't do without: talent and customers.

CHAPTER 24

SUPPLY LINES

If leading a business is about making good decisions, then leading well means having the ability to make decisions on our terms. But too often, circumstances dictate our path.

Revenue is down, and we're forced to say "*Yes*" to messy projects and needy customers. Our team's working overtime, at risk of burning out, and we're forced to say "*Yes*" to questionable candidates—just to get some help in the door. Our decisions stop being a product of our best judgment and experience, but rather of the necessity of avoiding disaster.

It's uncomfortable, and it's our own G.E.A.R. model at work. The "R" of real-time constraints takes control and limits our options. The "G" of our genetics and most innate qualities has us responding to fear and uncertainty versus reason and analysis. And our "A" of adopted narratives is working hard to cook up any story we can to justify why the decision was indeed ours—and not forced upon us by circumstance.

However, the "box" we find ourselves in was a long time in the making. The scarcity may feel sudden, but the constraint was cumulative. It was the inevitable consequence of having supply lines which allow us to survive but are far from helping us thrive.

We may not have yet resorted to the business equivalent of scraping lichen from rocks and boiling shoe leather for our supper—the last option for many expeditions—but we know we would be better off with supply lines more akin to a steady stream of fresh-caught fish and wild pheasant.

As business leaders, one of the greatest powers we can have is the ability to say "*No.*"

"*No,*" to a long-time customer that's a large percentage of revenue but an absolute pain to deal with. "*No,*" to an employee who is highly productive but has unrealistic expectations around compensation. "*No,*" to a lucrative opportunity when we know there are red flags. "*No,*" to a candidate our competitors would love to hire, because saying "*Yes*" would mean lowering our standards.

The ability to say "*No*" to anything that might relieve near-term pressure, but at the expense of long-term performance: that's a power we want to have—and keep.

Expeditions need a long list of supplies to reach their destination: tools, equipment, polar suits, malaria pills. Whatever they may need, without it, their odds of success go down. Businesses are similar. Machinery, office space, point of sale systems, anti-virus software: we have an equivalent list of what success requires.

However, we know that not all supplies are as universal or critical. Whether we're summiting tall mountains or looking for lost treasure in the sands of Egypt, whether we're an industrial contractor or a B2B software sales firm, there is a shorter list of resources we can't do without.

For our expedition counterparts, it's food and water that are essential; for the business leader, it's customers and staff we can't do without. And the supply lines we establish for each dictate how often we are forced into decisions not of our choosing.

As a result, there may be nothing as important in business as keeping those two supply lines healthy and robust. There also may be no greater confluence of our Four Horsemen.

There's the **competition** that pursues the same talent and customers that we do. There are the **limited resources** of not only who is available, but also of the time, energy, and money we have to expend in our pursuit of them. There's our **human nature** that often has us putting off the important until it's urgent. And finally, there's the **entropy** that is always working to disrupt our efforts—the disciplined follow-up with prospects that becomes sporadic and the systematic outreach to candidates that reverts to an ad hoc approach.

If there's any consolation, it's that every organization fights a similar battle—including our competition. Thus, these headwinds also offer one of our greatest opportunities to establish a competitive advantage.

Step #1 to getting a "leg up" on the competition and building such robust lines: avoiding the trap of *"good enough."*

Imagine you and your team are completing a long journey across the Pacific Ocean. After weeks at sea, you are finally coming ashore on a remote, deserted island. You have some limited supplies, but only what you could bring along in your seafaring canoes. If you're going to last more than a week or two, you had better replenish your supplies, and fast.

But also imagine your new beachhead is a picture of abundance. Warm temperatures, consistent rainfall—waters teeming with fish, shrimp, and seaweed—land rich in birds, their eggs, edible plants, and tropical fruits: there are countless resources to be had by you and your team.

What you imagined was the experience of Chief Nanaulu when he and his small crew first set foot on what we now know as Hawaii. Though they were in a new land and had only what resources survived their 2,000-mile voyage, refreshing their supplies required little more than making routine trips down to the shore or into the bush. The surrounding abundance made establishing supply lines easy—ones that were more than *"good enough."*

Most businesses never have it so ideal, but there are parallels. Companies often start out as a smaller team, pursuing an opportunity or a market that dwarfs their organization in size. Being smaller means the need for talent and customers is more limited. And early successes have yet to attract the new competitors that are soon to emerge.

At this stage, getting supply chains to be more than *"good enough"* isn't hard. Leaders can do much of the work themselves; minimal effort produces an abundance, and saying "*No*" to the wrong people or the wrong opportunities is easy.

However, things can only get more difficult from there. Instead of having to meet the needs of 10 people, the crew expands. The number grows to 20, then to 50, and then more follow. Leaders can no longer round up all the talent and customers they need themselves—they must delegate the work to others.

To make matters worse, new expeditions soon come ashore. They've heard of this new land and market opportunity flush with potential—they want their share.

The new customers who used to come easily via word of mouth or network referrals are no longer a great fit—or there are just not enough of them. New hires are now needed twice per month, rather than twice per quarter, and good candidates have twice as many options.

The supply chains that the abundance of the "old days" kept flowing are breaking down. Efforts spent recruiting, interviewing, and onboarding seem to leave no time for making the process more streamlined, automated, and repeatable. The scramble to fill the sales pipeline means dialing in a better marketing plan will have to wait.

The land of abundance is now an island of scarcity, and it's all a business can do to keep their supply lines "good enough"—to survive.

The path to this point is similar for many organizations. Having a steady stream of talent and customers was never seen as unimportant; it just wasn't pressing. Things were "good enough"—until they weren't.

It's the classic struggle to work on the important when our days are filled with the urgent. When we're putting out fires right and left, it is easy to be content with supply lines that are sufficient and overlook the storms, or competition, on the horizon.

But then our need for new people hits the limit of our current talent pools, new competition emerges, and markets get saturated. Suddenly our tropical paradise feels more like a rock outcropping with winter soon approaching, and saying "*No*" to any resource feels more consequential.

And while it's easy to scold businesses of grasshoppers for lounging while times were good, behaving too much like ants—stockpiling resources to no end—creates new problems.

Double down on finding new talent, and a lean team of 15 becomes a bloated gaggle of 25. Keep dialing up marketing spend in the name of pipeline health and saying "Yes" to marginal fits "just in case," and the calendar fills with low-margin projects and difficult customers—all while onboarding and advertising costs erode profitability.

Finding the right balance, the middle ground between mere survival and over-preparedness, isn't easy. It's a fundamental challenge for a leader and part of the craft of business: building talent and customer pipelines strong enough that scarcity never forces our hand, while staying disciplined enough that abundance doesn't become its own liability.

It's tempting to have a bias toward running lean—to keep a close eye on where we invest our limited money and time. But there's an important consideration when it comes to our supply lines of talent and customers: things almost always get worse, not better.

Markets become more competitive, and talent pools get more strained. What was easy when we were 10 people becomes much more difficult when we're 50. The trends are rarely in our favor, and by the time it's clear we need to act—to improve our supply lines—the actual need has been there far longer.

Supply lines almost always have lead times exceeding those of the problems they are meant to prevent. It's an unfortunate reality that consumption is often immediate, while replenishment inevitably comes with some delay.

This calls for a bias toward improvement, toward investing in supply lines before we desperately need them. Not for obsession or drowning in worry, but simply to make the decision that talent and customer pipelines are key leverage points—that they preserve our power to say "*No*" and stop circumstances from dictating a "*Yes*" that we might soon regret.

The good news for us: many of our competitors live right at the survival threshold. Because of the dynamics outlined previously, they're stuck in the trap of "*good enough.*" It's the benchmark that keeps them from improving their supply lines when they are "good enough." And it's the benchmark they spend all their time and resources trying to reach when the flow of resources dwindles—when their supply lines are no longer "good enough."

If we can land anywhere in the middle, somewhere between paranoid over-preparedness and desperate scrambling, we will have an advantage.

But again, there's a cost. Taking time for the important-but-not-urgent, to beef up our supply lines before it's pressing—it's difficult to do. The time is valuable, the payoff is delayed, and there's always something more pressing demanding our attention. If we're going to pre-emptively expend our limited resources, we had better maximize the return.

Fortunately, there are certain approaches that benefit nearly every organization. Four questions and conditions that, if satisfied, keep our organizations feeling like lush tropical islands ripe with abundance. But more importantly, they maintain our power to make decisions on our terms. The first approach is about putting the right person in charge, not burdening them unnecessarily with other tasks, and it's one of the oldest principles in business.

WHO'S DOING THE FISHING?

Some 250 years ago Adam Smith popularized the concept of "division of labor," one of the most fundamental economic theories of modern times—the idea that by dividing up the tasks required to complete a project, people can better specialize and thus collectively be more efficient.

Yet, I still meet CEOs and presidents who are also their organization's main sales or business development person. And I come across many organizations that have a "seller-doer" model—often it's code for *"We just ask one person to do everything."*

When an organization is small, dedicated roles aren't always possible. And of course, owner-led sales or a "seller-doer" model can work—but only if they're able to primarily do the selling and very little of the doing. Otherwise, this all breaks down, and it's not hard to see why.

Too often businesses experience some form of this cycle. Work gets slow, so they double down on sales. Opportunities come in, everyone gets busy, and they dial back on chasing new business. Their pipeline declines as a result. Things get slow again, and the cycle repeats—over and over.

Recruiting talent can have a similar pattern. We get busy with work, so building a pipeline of people gets put on the back burner. Eventually, we can't put off hiring any longer and we scramble to find more help. That takes time away from work; it starts to pile up, and we're pulled away from our fishing for people.

In either case, we find ourselves oscillating between both sides of *"good enough."*

It's easy to assume the answer is a dedicated role, and while that may be the right decision for many organizations, there are other options. There is outsourcing—paying a service provider to ensure that someone is always working on our supply lines. There are part-time and fractional roles—a professional who splits their effort between keeping two or three expeditions well supplied.

But often, the best and most available option isn't about the right who at all. It's about reducing our supply lines' need for people—and their limited time—altogether. It's about leverage and automation. And it's about giving whoever we put in charge the means to make the most of their efforts.

ASSETS VS. ACTIVITY

I loved fishing when I was a kid—I still do. It's easy to say fishing is about patience. That's a nicer way of saying it takes time, a lot of time. Baiting the hook, casting, waiting, retrieving, walking or paddling to the next spot, over and over: fish or no fish, there's always lots to do.

Then, when I was 11 years old, someone gave me a fish trap. Add some bait, tie it to a tree, toss it in the river, come back the next day and collect your aquatic bounty—far less time, much less activity, many more fish.

Traditional fishing was an activity. Without expending my time and energy, there would be no fish fry. The trap was an asset, and with it I could decouple fishing from all the other important things an 11-year-old has to do.

In business, this looks different, but it rhymes.

Cold calling prospects, attending networking events, manually sending emails to follow up, giving sales presentations, creating proposals from scratch, setting up trade show booths: all of this requires time and effort. These tasks might make us feel productive and busy, but if we stop doing the activities, nothing gets done.

Assets are a different story. A website with SEO that brings in leads while we sleep, paid ad campaigns that run continuously once configured, email nurture sequences that guide prospects automatically, recorded demos and webinars that prospects can watch anytime, case studies and testimonials that do the selling for us, lead magnets that capture contact information: these work 24/7/365 no matter how busy we are.

The same is true for talent.

Posting job ads when a role opens, recruiting from your personal network, cold outreach on LinkedIn, manually screening resumes, attending job fairs: if we stop these activities because we're busy with other tasks, the candidate pipeline runs dry.

But the assets are a different story. Careers pages with content about opportunities, perks, and culture, employee testimonial videos, applicant tracking systems, university and community college partnerships, employee referral bonus programs: these keep working whether anyone is personally recruiting this week or not.

Assets don't have to be fully automated to be effective. They just need to produce results disproportionate to the effort required. A referral program needs management, but it leverages fifty people's networks instead of just ours. An employer brand needs tending, but once established, it pre-sells candidates before we even talk to them. Content needs occasional updates, but one great piece can generate leads for years.

Though perhaps the greatest asset of all is one we can't build directly: reputation.

When former clients tell prospects, *"You should work with them"* without being asked. When employees tell friends, *"You should apply here"* unprompted. When partners recommend us reflexively because we're the obvious choice. Reputation becomes the best asset we could hope for.

Of course, a good reputation comes easier with having solid supply lines.

The hardest part is getting started. It takes a mind shift to focus on the long-term and sustainability versus the demands of the urgent and the here and now. It takes dealing with the discomfort of delegating, outsourcing, dipping into our reserves, or forgoing profits to invest in the assets that will pay off for years to come—again, there's a cost to leadership.

Decoupling can stop unwanted cycles of feast and famine, building the right assets can leverage people's (limited) time, but both are built around a certain question: Just what should go in our supply lines?

The answer isn't *"everything,"* nor can it be *"only the absolute best."* The right path runs somewhere between the two. And it's our next condition for success.

BE AN OMNIVORE

Panda bears are some of the most remarkable creatures on earth: big, incredibly strong, and surprisingly good swimmers. They're also herbivores and beholden to finding more than 80 pounds of bamboo per day.

Lions are the *"kings of the jungle,"* fierce, athletic, and apex predators. They're also carnivores, and no matter how lush the savannah, only meat will keep them going.

These are two incredible animals. But once the bamboo runs out, or once the wild game is gone, so are they.

Humans, on the other hand, are omnivores. We can eat just about anything; as a result, we've come to spread to every part of the globe—and just about any food chain imaginable.

I talked with a recruiter recently who was having a very tough time finding candidates for one of her clients. There's a talent shortage in their industry, but the client wasn't helping the situation. They had become a devout believer in a popular personality assessment. Now, they will not, under any circumstances, entertain the idea of candidates that aren't identified as one specific "profile" out of the 15 or more that are possible. They've made themselves the pandas of the business world—they eat one type, and only one type, of food.

It's a common theme. We are burned by a bad hire or a problematic client. We put in new safeguards, new filters, and whatever it takes to not be *"fooled again."* Or we consume books, articles, and advice from gurus that help us identify *"A Players"* and *"Ideal Clients."* We are energized by finally knowing what a perfect fit looks like. But we fail to consider that knowing how to identify a unicorn doesn't mean we're likely to find one.

It's easy to adopt guidelines that help us avoid ***false positives***—not mistaking bad fits for good opportunities. But doing so comes with the cost of generating more ***false negatives***—saying "*no*" to customers and staff that we should actually consider.

I once talked to a competitor of my business about a mutual client. My competitor had decided to stop working with them. Apparently, they were put off by their stance on invoices—the client in question would only pay others once the owner of the project (their customer) had paid them.

My competitor's stern stance may have had them feeling like a lion, but they too were now limiting their food options—creating their own false negative.

I nodded along, listening to their rant, knowing that we didn't see the request as unreasonable. We were willing to adapt, to be an omnivore, and as a result, the client in question had become one of our most consistent, profitable, and ***best paying*** customers.

The extremes are clear, but where exactly do we want to land between them?

From the outside, it's impossible to know where any one business should be on the continuum. But, as a leader, if we're relating to one scenario more than the other, then we know the correct adjustment is to move more toward the middle—either less dogmatic or more adaptable.

The path forward isn't about lowering standards or averting disasters—it's about building capacity. Pandas can only eat bamboo because their digestive system can't handle anything else. Lions can only eat meat for the same reason. They're stuck with the systems nature gave them.

We are not. We get to build Pyramids of Decisions that define how our organizations operate, and a clear first principle that lets us move past the dogma of heuristics and frameworks, or mimicking someone else's "canned" approach, is this:

Scarcity only exists relative to what a system requires. Expand what the system can use, and scarcity diminishes.

The tactics that support such a strategy are unique to the organization they serve, but the aim remains the same—to build an organization that's capable of turning more "*C*" talent and opportunities into more "*B's*," and more "B's" into "*A*'s."

What we want is a business that's capable of adapting to the quirks and nuances of more candidates and customers. Because if we can do so, we enjoy the returns we'd expect from more ideal fits—and we'll leave the pandas and lions of our competitors behind.

Anyone can be successful with "rockstar" employees and the perfect customers. We're often sold the dream of finding plenty of both, but it is indeed a fantasy. They're "unicorns" because there are so few of them. The real world requires us to adapt. It's best to be an omnivore—knowing, somewhat poetically, that the more we can say "*Yes*" to the correct range of supplies, the more we protect our ability to say "*No*" to the people and customers who are likely to cause problems.

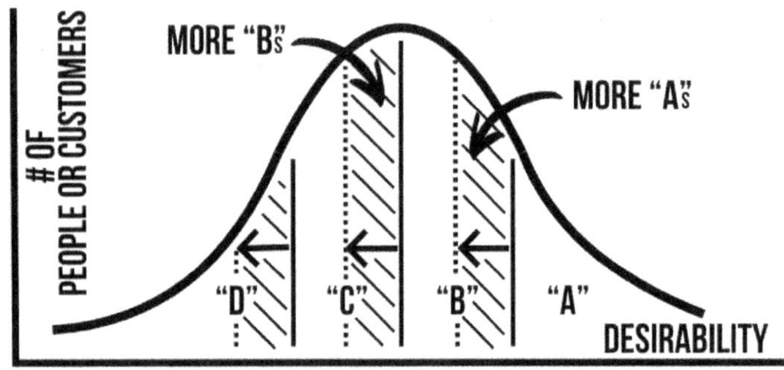

The "fit" of talent and customers for a business both form a distribution. The "average" are in the middle; the exceptionally good (and bad) are at the tails. Each leader defines their own A, B, C, or D. But the better the organization is designed, the more they can push the lines left, and the better options they have.

There's one more way to make our supply lines better. We can have the greatest dedicated sales and recruiting force, possess top-tier assets, and be able to spin straw-like talent and customers into gold—but if we're fishing in the same pond, the same way as everyone else, our supply lines are likely to remain only "*good enough.*"

BE (TRULY) DIFFERENT

"Our people are our greatest asset."

"We want clients who value the relationship."

"We're not the cheapest."

"We're focused on customer service."

I have a unique perspective: I spend most of my working hours talking to people about their business. Most business leaders spend the bulk of their time focusing on one business, their own.

There's a hard truth that people often don't want to hear. How they describe their business—their approach to people, customers, and recruiting—may sound unique to them, but often it is not. What they tell me may be an accurate description, and it's likely not a bad approach, but chances are it's the same thing I hear from their competitors.

Being different is hard. It requires time and energy to come up with new ideas—money and resources to make them a reality. There's also the element of risk—yes, of failure, but also of blame. There's an old saying that *"no one ever got fired for choosing IBM."* It's the safety of the known, the defensible decision. And there's a version of that truth in every business.

Posting job openings on LinkedIn, running banner ads on Facebook, creating marketing materials that look, feel, and use the same language as "big brands"—there's an endless number of ways to play it safe. They may keep us from getting fired; they may have us sleeping a little better at night, but they keep us at the bottom of The Mountain of Why—and we won't be catching any more fish than the competition.

To transition our supply lines of talent and customers from *"good enough"* to the flows of resources that let us thrive often takes being different. Maybe that means packing up and setting off for a less crowded island, or maybe it's finding a new way to fish before our competition does. But once again, the only thing certain is that the trend is rarely with us. Without intentional effort, our supply lines are likely to get leaner, not more robust.

So, what does truly different look like?

Zappos is famous for offering new hires $3,000 to quit after one week of training—believing the short-term expense is cheaper than someone who doesn't want to be there in the long-term. Menlo Innovations pairs up candidates at "mass auditions" and requires them to complete tasks together—the goal being to make their partner, not themselves, look good. It's a filter for collaboration over self-promotion, the idea being that ego-driven hires are costlier than an unconventional hiring process. And Dyson recruits bright high school students and lets them earn a college degree in-house—bypassing the competition for new graduates.

These may be good tactics, or they may be bad ones. For every idea that became a success story, there are likely many more that their creators would like to forget. But they are all truly different. They're the type of ideas that make us squirm in our seats a little. And that's what we're after. Because if they don't, if we're totally comfortable with a new idea, then chances are our competitors are too.

The annals of successful expeditions are filled with explorers who took a different route, who used dog sleds to cross new terrains instead of horses that had carried them across the familiar ones, who sourced what they needed from the land versus the traditional stockpiling of supplies. It took being different to find success, to find more resources and make better use of what they had—to maintain their own power to say "*No.*"

Having a better-thought-out expedition allowed them to say "*No*" to pushing ahead when the weather was bad, to say "*No*" to a shortcut that carried more risk, to say "*No*" to putting plants and critters of questionable edibility on their dinner plate. And these "*No's*" meant that the leaders, not circumstances, would dictate their decision-making.

If we want to do the same, it takes avoiding the stagnation that can occur when companies don't differentiate. And that stagnation is a feature, not a bug, of the marketplace. It's a product of an ecosystem finding its balance when all the players are similar. Everyone's close to the same, so no one can ever get a huge advantage—but also no one can ever fall that far behind. It's hard to outright lose because it's equally hard to outright win. As a result, we get mired in competition and mediocrity—everyone thinking they're different while doing the same.

Talent and customers are the supply lines no business can do without. When we keep them healthy—and well beyond "good enough"—we preserve our power to make the most important decisions on our terms.

But the same dynamics apply to most of the supply lines that our businesses depend on. Capital, partnerships, innovation, expertise: whatever it is that we need to replenish regularly, chances are the same Four Horsemen that thwart our pursuit of people and opportunities await.

To get ahead, we must separate from the pack—continue to gather our resources when the competition pauses to get back to their doing, build the assets that let one hour of our time be worth multiple hours of theirs, make use of the false negatives that our competitors overlook but our omnivore organizations can utilize. And as much as anything, we must be a little daring—not reckless—but be willing to take the risk of being truly different.

If we can do all of that, we'll find what we need to thrive. We won't be slowed by a lack of resources and supply lines that are only *"good enough."* We will maintain the ability to say *"No"* when we should and *"Yes"* when it makes sense.

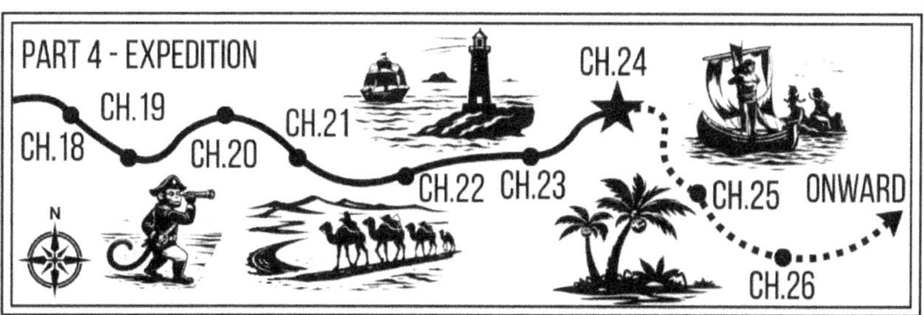

This chapter focused on the defensive nature of good supply lines. And while it's true that having robust systems for acquiring the talent and customers our organizations need often keeps us out of trouble—just like being able to sail more aggressive lines with better navigation and reconnaissance systems—there's an offensive advantage to having a steady stream of opportunities.

When we have more alternatives, we find ourselves with better leverage in setting terms and charging higher prices. Knowing that we can handle more "No's" from our customers and clients allows us to adjust one of our Levers of Control. We can raise our yield lever—asking for more money and more favorable conditions, knowing that if it costs us an opportunity, there are "plenty of other fish in the sea."

Similarly, but perhaps more uncomfortably, having a reliable stream of talent allows us to be less tolerant of underperformers. While much of this book has been devoted to building conditions where people can thrive, there still comes a time when we must take people to task if they're not pulling their weight. When a replacement for a problem employee is more readily available, we can act sternly—but fairly—without as much fear of someone jumping ship.

But an upper hand with customers, clients, or underperformers will not be had if we don't first do the work of building robust supply lines. And then once they are established, they join the ranks of our process for building our coalitions, the way we craft and communicate the story of our organization, our systems for orienting and "setting north" for our crews, and our reconnaissance, navigation, and communication systems in that they too must be maintained—if not improved.

It's true of all the structures, systems, and routines that we need on the expedition of business—and it's true of the organization as a whole. Occasionally, we need to hit pause, zoom out, and take stock of our situation.

So, while most of Part 4 has been about preparing for and setting out on our journeys, the next chapter is about establishing beachheads. They are moments when we slow down to go faster—to go together.

CHAPTER 25

BEACHHEADS

Midnight – Meteorological observations. Instrument readings logged.

8:00 a.m. – Awaken crew. Breakfast. Log entries of night observers.

9:00 a.m. – Instrument maintenance. Workshop tasks.

11:00 a.m. – Mandatory snowshoe training and readiness drills.

5:00 p.m. – Evening meal, informal discussion, and planning.

8:00 p.m. – Formal daily inspection of engine room. Fire safety check.

If you were part of Fridtjof Nansen's expedition to the North Pole, something close to this was your day—day after day, for three years from 1893 to 1896. Your ship, the *Fram*, was intentionally frozen into the polar ice to drift from Siberia to Greenland—hopefully passing near enough to the North Pole that a quick jaunt there and back would be possible.

The routine was intentional: collecting vital information, avoiding breakdowns, making small repairs, staying in shape, keeping morale up.

In business, we find similar stringent routines. A former employee of mine once worked for an aircraft parts manufacturer. It was a high-precision environment. Each day concluded by packing up your desk, putting all your items in a box, and placing your box on a shelf. The next day started similarly: take your box, pick a desk, get to work—no stacks of papers, no empty cans, no dried splatters of coffee.

Restaurant staff scrubbing every square inch of kitchen equipment at the end of each dinner service, construction crews sweeping the job site "broom clean" at the end of each day, garage mechanics putting every tool back in the right drawer before punching out: the routines run parallel to those of the *Fram*. They correct and prevent what would otherwise be an inevitable accumulation of disorder.

Most businesses aren't as meticulous, but they have their own cadence: regular work hours, weekly meetings, the cleaning crew that comes in once a week. We intuitively know that these cycles are important. We brush our teeth each morning and every night. We try to go to sleep and wake up around the same time each day. And many of us wouldn't dare jump in the car without our morning cup of coffee.

As individuals, as businesses, and like expeditions past, we benefit from such routines. They are frequent; they become the pattern of our every day, and they are always top of mind—because we just did the same yesterday.

The problem arises when the cadence becomes less frequent. The time between repetitions increases. And what was easy to remember a few days or a few weeks after the last occurrence vanishes from our minds. We forget to clean the accumulated disorder from our forest floor, and conditions are set for a disastrous fire to ignite.

One morning, our eyes glance down at the odometer, then up at the sticker on our windshield, and we realize we're 2,000 miles overdue for an oil change. We lose some important notes—swept up in the avalanche of the paper mountain on our desk. And I get an angry email from an employee I haven't sat down with in several months.

These episodes are not a product of laziness—but the opposite—we seem to always be busy.

For many expeditions past, the pattern was the same—push, battle, find a way forward, only stopping to pause when weather or conditions made advancement impossible. And as a result, we find records of mutinies, dwindling supplies, accumulations of disorder, and destinations never reached.

Many businesses operate under a similar model. Like Nansen's crew, they may have a solid short-term routine, but the gears turn day after day, week after week. Weekends provide a structural respite, as do holidays and the occasional vacation, but otherwise momentum and the grind have them on an inevitable course toward breakdown.

Nansen's team survived three years floating with the ice partly because their routine occasionally called *"time-out."* Once a season they re-rationed food, performed supply audits, and adjusted daily routines to deal with the Arctic extremes of daylight and darkness. Once a year, they reviewed the ship's course and drift with the ice, discussed the viability of completing the expedition, and re-prioritized scientific observations. They were all steps to interrupt the momentum of the day-to-day and opportunities for course corrections before it was too late.

Many businesses try to establish similar cadences. Annual planning sessions, quarterly offsites, leadership retreats: the idea is the same—an opportunity to rest, regroup, and make changes for the better. The intent is to avoid the default cycle of pushing until something breaks. But often, the efforts fall flat.

I once attended a company's annual planning meeting. The next day, I was surprised by one participant's sarcastic view of the session. We were making small talk before dinner when he said, *"Some meeting, yesterday"*—eye roll included.

"I thought it was pretty good," I said.

"The topics were good," he said. *"But they were good last year, and the year before that. Every year it's the same meeting, but nothing changes."*

More recently, I was told of a company retreat where the first rule was *"No talking about work."* Everyone was too burned out, too exhausted, to even consider how they might not end up in the same condition next year.

A feeling of intrigue, but also disappointment followed each conversation. The wasted time, the lost potential—it was obvious what benefits could be had from the events. But it's also obvious why they often don't deliver.

Poor agendas (that aren't followed), talking in circles, the same old office politics, outside facilitators that have you reading chapters of a book, no clear takeaways or action items, *"trust falls"*—there are dozens of manifestations that leave leaders and employees jaded about what could be the most impactful days of their business's year.

They provide evidence that while any savvy leader wants to avoid the default of short-term routines with long-term consequences, it takes more than just carving out the time.

The worst renditions of these meetings merely go through the motions. The best versions re-center our teams; they remove the accumulated disorder, and they provide a solid base to move forward from. They establish a beachhead.

Beachheads were originally a military concept—forming one means establishing a secure position in enemy territory. But the idea has become familiar in both business and expeditions. The intent is to routinely pause and regroup, consider the terrain we've crossed, and question what can be better. When done well, the exercise allows us to set off on the next leg of our journeys with clarity—refreshed and energized that we have found better ways forward.

But these results won't be achieved if we see strategic pauses as just another meeting. If we treat them that way, then the same patterns and dynamics that dominate our day-to-day activities are carried over. Short-term thinking, focusing on pressing problems, personal dynamics, egos, and attitudes: they all can sabotage what is supposed to be a chance to reset.

To get the results we want, a beachhead must cause us to do four things: to **shift our thinking**, to **revisit our story**, to **engage and energize the team**, and to **turn insights into action**.

All four are required. They're an integrated system of organizational renewal—a longer-term cadence that breaks the momentum and clears up the accumulated disorder of the day-to-day and week-to-week grind. Remove one element, and we may compromise the entire process—and leave those who are jaded by the whole idea justified in their skepticism.

Without the ability to **shift our thinking**, organizations become prisoners of their own existing mental models. Innovation dies, perspectives narrow, and the team becomes trapped in incremental thinking that prevents breakthrough ideas.

When our teams fail to **revisit our story**, they lose connection with their fundamental strategy. The combination of character, goal, challenge, and resolution that originally inspired and united the team decays and drifts. The story fails to receive the updating and refreshing it needs to stay effective.

Skipping **engaging and energizing the team** leaves unresolved tensions and accumulated organizational stress unaddressed. Team members become hesitant to speak up, hidden frustrations build, and the collective energy that drives results begins to dissipate.

And without **turning insights into action,** reflection becomes an academic exercise. Powerful discussions and breakthrough insights feel great in the moment but never translate into tangible movement. The team becomes increasingly cynical, losing faith that strategic conversations can actually change anything. Each meeting becomes another iteration of the same unproductive conversation. *"Every year, it's the same meeting."*

Achieving all four looks different for every organization, and it's up to you as a leader to craft the routines and agendas that best serve the needs of your business. And doing so takes putting in the intentional time and effort to make it all happen.

Simply put, on the expedition of business, occasionally, we all need to circle up around the campfire.

SHIFT OUR THINKING

It's late 2021, and a mid-sized construction firm finds themselves in a precarious situation. The crisis stage of the pandemic has passed, but the aftershocks are in full force. Government stimulus and record low interest rates have them sending out more bids and booking more work than ever.

However, there's another side to the story. Supply chains are snarled, and lead times for equipment and materials that used to be 8 weeks are now 8 months—or more. Local governments and municipalities are overwhelmed and short-staffed. Permitting new projects and inspecting ones under construction are happening at a snail's pace. And the entire industry is facing a labor shortage like never before.

The company is at the biggest inflection point in its history. Will it take advantage of the unprecedented demand for their services, capture market share, and build repeat clients for years to come? Or will it collapse under the stress of too many obligations, slow supply chains, missing inspectors, and overworked staff in desperate need of reinforcements?

The specifics may be unique to them, but many of the pressures are familiar to most business leaders. You're in the heart of the storm, and the decision to change course or keep it *"steady as she goes"* has rarely been as important.

For the construction company, their quarterly leadership meeting couldn't have come at a better (or worse) time. They were slammed, busy, working nights and weekends, but they also knew something needed to change.

Early in the meeting, the instruction was given—put away the phones, put away the laptops. The day already felt different—meeting offsite, getting out of the office—but now the familiar dings, buzzes, and pop-ups were gone as well.

It was by design. Under sustained stress, our attention narrows. The brain prioritizes immediate threats and quick resolutions. It becomes harder to slow down, harder to question assumptions, and harder to consider alternatives. Not because leaders aren't capable, but because the environment keeps pulling them back into reaction mode. No one can do their best thinking while being drowned in notifications.

On expeditions, crews learned to separate moments of movement from moments of orientation. You don't check your position while hauling gear. You stop, secure things, and take your bearings. This meeting was starting to serve that purpose.

With the pace slowed, the next shift came from information that hadn't been looked at together in a long time.

They reviewed projects currently underway, not as individual jobs but as a portfolio. Lead times, staffing levels, permitting delays, change orders—none of it was new on its own. Everyone in the room had touched some part of it already. What was new was seeing it all at once, stripped of the usual explanations and workarounds. It was the "big picture."

A new perspective was gained, and patterns emerged that were hard to ignore.

Jobs that looked profitable on paper were consuming disproportionate leadership attention. Schedules were technically intact, but only because teams were absorbing delays personally: working longer hours, cutting corners on recovery time, and quietly carrying risks the business had never explicitly agreed to take on.

The data didn't accuse anyone. It just didn't fit the narrative that many believed about the state of the business. That opened the door to a different kind of conversation.

Someone asked how another firm had handled similar conditions. Another wondered aloud how industries with tighter margins dealt with volatility when they couldn't just *push harder*." Comparisons surfaced, not as prescriptions, but as contrasts.

The energy in the room shifted again.

As viewpoints broadened, people were asked to explain things they usually assumed were understood. Why a certain type of project was always considered a win. Why growth had been treated as the primary indicator of health. Why saying *"No"* still felt more dangerous than overextending.

Some answers came easily. Others stalled halfway through. A few sounded less convincing when spoken out loud than they had when left unexamined.

That friction was useful. It forced clarity.

Beliefs that had lived comfortably in shorthand now had to survive full sentences. Ideas that had been inherited rather than chosen were suddenly visible.

At one point, someone posed a simple constraint: "*If we could only pursue half the work we're currently bidding, which half would it be?*" The question wasn't hypothetical for long. It immediately surfaced tradeoffs that had been avoided: what they valued, what they were willing to protect, what they were willing to give up.

The constraint didn't limit thinking. It focused it.

By the time they broke for lunch, the conversation had moved well beyond tactics. The way they saw their situation had changed. They weren't done deciding. But they were no longer stuck in the same frame.

The change in environment, some new information, the forcing of constraints, asking the right questions, and nudging people to articulate what they "*knew*" to be certain: these aren't random. They're some of the most effective techniques to get us thinking better. They get our brains off of autopilot, out of the weeds and the noise of the day-to-day, and into seeing things in a new light.

REVISIT OUR STORY

After lunch, the construction team was able to step back and revisit a more fundamental question: "*What are we actually trying to build here? And what is yet to be completed?*"

In the rush of day-to-day work, that question rarely surfaced. Everyone was too busy solving the next problem. But without it, decisions were made while detached from a shared destination.

They started with who they believed themselves to be as a company.

"Reliable" had always been the word they came back to—reliable to clients, reliable to partners, reliable to each other. It was a point of pride, and one that had differentiated them in a crowded market. But when they held that ideal up against current reality, the picture was mixed.

They were still delivering. Projects were getting done. Commitments were being met. Yet, the way those results were achieved mattered. Increasingly, reliability was being propped up by individual effort rather than by systems. Long hours, constant adjustments, and personal sacrifices were filling the gaps.

That wasn't what they had set out to build, but it had become the default way of moving toward their goal.

Growth had been their "North Star" for years. More work meant more opportunity, new roles, better projects, and a stronger position in the market. Until recently, growth and health had moved together. Now, they weren't so sure.

They looked honestly at where growth had taken them. Which parts of the business were stronger as a result, and which were stretched thin? Which wins were worth repeating, and which had quietly created fragility?

The goal itself wasn't immediately discarded. But it was no longer taken for granted. Growth, they agreed, only mattered if it moved them closer to the kind of company they wanted to be—the company that some metrics showed them close to achieving, while others showed them with much work to do.

Where the gap was large, it came back to challenges: some familiar, some new and emerging.

Supply chains, labor shortages, permitting delays: all were real, and all were outside their direct control. But beneath those was a more central challenge they hadn't fully named: the gap between how much work they were taking on and how much the organization could absorb without breaking its own standards.

Currently, both were a problem. And if the story of the organization was going to have a happy ending, their approach and their resolutions to challenges needed some adjustment.

For years, the answer had been straightforward: say yes, work harder, and figure it out. That approach had built the company. It had earned loyalty and trust. But when they tested it against the present environment, its limits were clear.

Endurance alone was no longer enough, and some new ideas were needed.

Revisiting their story wasn't about abandoning what had brought them here. It was about acknowledging where the story had advanced and where it needed to evolve if it was going to carry them forward.

They were taking stock of current conditions: their progress so far, the "gap" that existed between where they were and where they wanted to go, and if their current trajectory would get them there.

That shared understanding changed the tenor of the room. They weren't debating preferences. They were ensuring that they all wanted to be part of the same story.

The re-orienting was grounding for everyone, but it was also motivating. Like cleaning our desk or reorganizing our room, it felt like a fresh start. And with new ideas on how to move forward, there was hope that better results with less stress and strain were soon to come.

If nothing else, a message was made clear: we are an organization that learns and adapts; we refuse to keep grinding it out the same way month after month. We will always work to be better.

However, building the momentum didn't stop there.

ENGAGE AND ENERGIZE THE TEAM

Before talking about what needed to happen next, time was spent acknowledging what had already happened: the hours people had put in, the adjustments teams had made on the fly, the quiet problem-solving that had kept projects moving when plans broke down.

This wasn't ceremonial. It was making things right.

In the pace of day-to-day operations, effort had been assumed rather than named. Stress had been normalized. Pausing to recognize the work already done helped reset the tone. It made it possible to talk honestly about change without implying failure.

Just as importantly, it allowed the group to see not only the gap they were facing, but the gains they had already made: what had improved, what they were now capable of handling that would have overwhelmed them a few years earlier. The distance already traveled mattered, especially before asking people to go further.

From there, the conversation widened again. Today was a day where people were invited into decisions rather than informed of them.

Leaders asked where the pressure was showing up first, what was working despite the strain, and what ideas had been considered before but never brought to light because there hadn't been room to discuss them.

Some of the ideas fit. But even when they didn't, they were acknowledged and explained—not dismissed. People understood why certain paths wouldn't be pursued, which mattered almost as much as having their ideas accepted.

Shared discussions didn't slow decisions down; they clarified them. When people understood the constraints and participated in shaping choices within them, commitment followed naturally. Not because everyone agreed, but because the process felt fair and visible.

By the end of the discussion, the room felt different from that morning—not lighter, but steadier. The work ahead was still hard. The constraints were still real. But the burden was shared, and the direction felt intentional.

It spoke to something that we as leaders intuitively know to be true, but we may struggle to articulate. The most powerful moments of organizational renewal aren't about grand motivational speeches, but they are about creating genuine spaces of recognition and shared understanding.

Nansen kept his team together and moving forward because he understood their expedition wasn't just about technical competence or their grand strategy; it was also about maintaining collective psychological resilience.

His routines were deliberately designed to engage and energize the team. Mandatory snowshoe training, shared mealtimes with informal discussions, routine all-hands briefings: these weren't just survival tasks, but mechanisms for maintaining team cohesion. Nansen created an environment where every team member's contribution was visible, where challenges were collective, and where the burden of survival was consciously distributed. His leadership wasn't about heroic individual action but about creating a shared narrative of survival and potential.

As leaders, we can do the same. By deliberately pulling specific psychological levers—acknowledging individual efforts and the challenges overcome, creating transparent decision-making, providing platforms for people to be heard, and reminding everyone of progress and their part in it—teams can transform from collections of individuals to aligned purposeful groups. They all become characters in the same story, in pursuit of the same goal.

Of course, all our thinking, all our story editing, and all our course corrections—all the enthusiasm, all the buy-in, and all the commitment—it's all an exercise in futility unless our strategic pause accomplishes and our beachhead provides our final objective.

TURN INSIGHTS INTO ACTION

The temptation at this point was to leave feeling good.

They had stepped out of the noise, seen the situation more clearly, re-grounded themselves in what they were trying to build, and reconnected as a leadership team. That alone was more progress than most organizations make in a year of busy, reactive work.

But on expeditions, there's a difference between morale and movement. A crew can share a good meal, tell stories, and feel renewed; then walk back into the same conditions and have the same prevailing winds push them off course once again.

Nansen's routines mattered because they were paired with decisions: ration adjustments, changes to routines, and re-prioritized observations. The pause only earned its keep when it changed what happened next.

For the construction firm, the same rule applied. Insight without action would decay into *"same as last year"* cynicism. People would return to their projects, open their laptops, and within a day be right back inside the old frame. The meeting would become one more well-run conversation with no downstream effect.

So, the final portion of the day narrowed deliberately.

They acknowledged what everyone already knew: time is limited, and people are busy. Not everything could be fixed. Not every opportunity could be pursued.

That reality forced the question that mattered most: "*What is worthy of our full attention right now?*"

They went back to the story they had just clarified: reliability, durability, a healthier kind of growth. And they used it as a filter. Opportunities that once looked like obvious wins were reconsidered. Projects were evaluated not only by revenue, but by what they would cost the organization in schedule risk, staffing strain, and leadership bandwidth.

They made tradeoffs explicit: fewer bids, tighter criteria, willingness to say "*no*" even when it hurt, commitment to protect certain standards even if it meant slower expansion, and a focus on reinforcing capacity—hiring, training, and creating processes—rather than assuming heroics would continue to cover gaps.

Then came the part that separates intention from commitment: ownership.

Each priority needed a person attached to it. Not a committee, not "the team," not a vague "*we*." Each needed someone who would carry it forward, coordinate the next steps, and report back at the next meeting and at points in between. Accountability wasn't punitive; it was structural. Without it, priorities would dissolve into good ideas, polite agreement, and things would stay "*the same as last year.*"

They also decided how follow-up would work.

Not as an afterthought, but as part of the commitment itself. When would they check progress? What did "progress" even mean? How would they know if the changes were working, or if they needed to adjust again? The point wasn't to create bureaucracy. The point was to make sure the beachhead didn't erode, that the next strategic pause didn't include an all-too-common phrase: "*we talked about this last time.*"

In the end, the outputs were simple and few: a small set of clear objectives, a short list of immediate actions, a handful of decisions that would change what happened on Monday morning. The measure of success wasn't how much they discussed. It was whether the organization could feel the difference in the weeks that followed.

On expeditions, you don't leave a beachhead with a speech. You leave with a heading, an intended route, and a shared understanding of who is responsible for what. Otherwise, you're just camping.

For this leadership team, turning insight into action was what made the entire day worth the time. It turned reflection into movement, alignment into execution, and renewed energy into something durable.

And when they returned to the storm—the emails, the calls, the delays, and the shortages—the goal wasn't to avoid the pressure. The goal was to face it with a clearer plan, tighter priorities, and a cadence strong enough to keep them from drifting back to the default.

And that is the purpose of a strategic pause. Not to escape work, but to do it better. Not to reach our goal all at once, but to make sure we keep moving forward.

⬥

It's easy to view strategic pauses as just a break from the day-to-day, or a beachhead as just a recap of the past quarter. However, they can be much more.

Just like robust supply lines, reconnaissance systems, and navigation beacons, strategic pauses and the beachheads they create are a form of organizational infrastructure. They are a reliable way of dealing with the inevitable accumulation of disorder in our businesses. They are an opportunity to pause and re-orient our team, to hear the ideas of others, to express our own thoughts, and to head out on the next leg of the journey with more clarity and enthusiasm.

The immediate benefits are visible: teams think more clearly, assumptions get challenged, priorities get sharpened, and energy returns. But the deeper value lies in what happens after the meeting ends—the second-order effects that quietly reshape how the organization functions day to day.

When teams regularly practice **shifting their thinking**, they don't just generate better ideas in the meeting room. Over time, they loosen their attachment to a single way of seeing the world. People become more willing to question inherited beliefs, surface uncertainty, and explore alternatives earlier, before options narrow. The organization becomes less brittle. Perspective becomes a renewable resource rather than a rare event reserved for quarterly or annual meetings.

When organizations routinely **revisit their story**, they maintain a living relationship with their strategy. Purpose doesn't calcify into slogans. Goals don't drift unnoticed. Teams develop a shared language for talking about who they are, what they're trying to build, and how current decisions move them closer, or farther from that ideal. This creates coherence, especially during periods of stress, when it's otherwise easy for short-term decisions to erode long-term intent.

When leaders intentionally **engage and energize the team**, something subtle but powerful occurs. Psychological load is reduced. Effort is acknowledged. Tensions that would otherwise leak out sideways are addressed directly. Over time, people stop carrying unresolved concerns alone. Trust increases, not because everything is easy or agreeable, but because the system proves it can hold honest conversations without breaking.

And when organizations consistently **turn insights into action**, credibility compounds. People learn that reflection leads somewhere—that decisions stick, that ownership is real, and that priorities are chosen, not endlessly postponed. Cynicism loses its footing because the pattern changes—strategic conversations stop feeling performative and start feeling consequential.

These effects don't show up directly on a dashboard. But they fundamentally alter how work gets done between pauses.

We and our teams become more willing to "park" improvement ideas—neither rushing to implement them nor losing them to the busyness of the everyday. Day-to-day anxiety decreases because not every issue has to be resolved immediately to be heard—there will be a time and place for certain discussions. Feedback becomes timelier and less emotionally charged—small problems are addressed before they harden into crises. The organization develops a rhythm that absorbs stress rather than amplifying it and clears accumulated disorder rather than adding to it.

Like Nansen's expedition, which survived partly thanks to deliberate routines of observation, maintenance, and course correction, organizations that build intentional pauses into their cadence move from a rhythm of reactive survival to purposeful adaptation and continual improvement. It's how they make progress and find success on the expedition of business.

In Chapter 12, we discussed why businesses have employees, that our crew is the source of energy that propels our organizations forward. And while much of this book has been focused on tapping into and directing the power of that resource, there is more than energy to be had. The people who make up our teams, especially those who share the responsibility of leadership, are also repositories of experience, wellsprings of ideas, and the eyes and ears that see and hear far more collectively than we ever could as individuals.

"Synergy" is perhaps an overused word in business circles, but that doesn't mean there's no value to be realized by pooling our observations, insights, and ideas. When we take a collaborative approach to building our Pyramids of Decisions, we utilize one of the truest first principles of any organization: the whole can indeed be greater than the sum of the parts.

And so, strategic pauses and efforts to establish a beachhead are by default the result of decisions made high on The Mountain of Why—they are first principles at work. But the opportunity to re-center our teams, have mean-ingful conversations, and hear feedback, thoughts, and ideas from others becomes that much more valuable when we consider the other dynamics at work.

Collaboration feeds the "G" of genetics in our G.E.A.R. model—providing the certainty of the path forward, the autonomy of having a voice, and the relatedness of working closely with others to chart a better path forward. And the outcomes of these meetings improve when we leverage the diversity of personalities and perspectives—both the "E" of enduring traits and the "A" of adopted narratives in our model.

But maybe most importantly, taking a hiatus from the grind and the busyness of the day-to-day relieves us all of the "R" of real-time constraints. When we finally get a break from the "fires" we must put out, and the constant stream of messages we have to respond to, our minds settle down and the picture of the road ahead becomes clearer.

And it's the latter that keeps resurfacing in our effort to design, build, and lead a better business. Our thoughts and our actions are often, if not always, influenced by the circumstances and the environment we find ourselves in. It's an inconvenient truth, but reality nonetheless.

So, just as we craft plans to do battle with our ever-present Four Horsemen, we need to look ahead to another headwind we're sure to face. It's the future storms and turmoil that will have us wanting to change course, tempted to go back on certain decisions even if our original thinking and judgment remain solid.

And it's in those moments that the ship and the crew we've worked so hard to build are at risk. It's then that we may run aground on a rocky shore. Avoiding disaster means seeing the storm of circumstance approaching, and crafting a plan before the weather turns.

CHAPTER 26

ANCHOR BEFORE SETTING SAIL

When you start a business from nothing, taking on your first full-time employee is a big deal. It's an achievement, but the cost and the responsibility weigh heavily. So, it's not too surprising that I remember interviewing the first person to join our crew—but one detail stands out for a different reason.

We were wrapping up our conversation when he asked about the timeline for my decision.

"Check back in with me Monday afternoon," I said.

"Sure thing," he replied. Then he did something that—though simple—still sticks in my mind years later.

He pulled out his phone and set a reminder for Monday afternoon. And it showed me more than any resume or interview ever could.

Here was someone who was self-aware, a realist about their abilities. Someone who had learned what might seem easy at the time was going to be much harder later—a person who was willing to act in the present to ensure the future outcome that they wanted.

Today he is still part of the organization I founded and has been an essential part of the team all along. It's not surprising for someone who displayed one of the greatest abilities we can have:

The ability to act today to pre-empt a foreseeable failure in the future.

It might seem like I'm making too big of a deal about a simple calendar reminder, but how many times in business has your desired outcome been derailed by an *"I forgot,"* *"I didn't remember,"* or *"I know we talked about it, but...."*

Our memories letting us down creates enough issues, but that's only the tip of the iceberg.

There are dozens of ways our Horseman of human nature causes us problems. Short-sightedness, temptations, and impatience: they all stand ready to tear a hole in the side of our ship of good intentions.

My good hire and longtime team player demonstrated something that, though small, all business leaders can learn from. He knew where his mind was likely to fail him. He foresaw the gap between the outcome he wanted and the one his mind, unassisted, was likely to produce. The alarm going off on his phone wouldn't force him to check back in, but it would create an environment where he was more likely to do so—and at the right time. He took control of his future conditions and narrowed that gap.

I imagine he learned this lesson the hard way—forgetting important "to-do's" despite his best efforts. How he operated previously was producing undesirable results, and he—unknowingly—took the words attributed to W. Edwards Deming to heart:

"Every system is perfectly designed to get the results it gets."

To get a better result, he needed a better system—and his phone alarm, an outsourced extension of his memory, was part of that system.

Making New Year's resolutions, starting a weight-loss plan, trying to stop smoking, or vowing to cut down on screen time: we've likely all found ourselves in some repeating cycles of frustration. They lead us to double down on commitment and intention, only to find ourselves right back where we started a few weeks later.

We tell ourselves we need to want it more, put in more effort, or remember better, but we rarely respond by redesigning the system—changing the environment we operate in.

Much business advice reflects this same misplaced instinct. We are urged to adopt better mindsets, increase discipline, shift beliefs, and hold people accountable—as though awareness or motivation alone were enough to overcome human nature.

But knowing what to do has never been the problem. If it were, gyms would be as busy in September as they are on January 2nd, tobacco companies would be a thing of the past, and strategy plans would execute themselves.

We know from Chapter 11 that we over-attribute outcomes to character and under-attribute them to circumstances. Of the genetic wiring, enduring traits, adopted narratives, and real-time constraints of our G.E.A.R. model, it is the "R" we overlook most often.

It is true of the members of our crew. But it is equally true on an organizational level, and for us individually as leaders. We hold tight to the belief that if we only devoted additional time, understood more, or just put in that extra effort, doing so would improve *"who we are"* and we'd get the results we want.

It's the same mistake over and over: well-intended plans and intentions made in the clarity of the present moment are derailed by the distraction, pressure, and noise which arrives later—all because we didn't see it coming. We failed to consider the likely possibility that at some point in the future our minds would fail us.

If we want a different result, we need a better system. We need an approach that decouples the circumstances under which we think and act from the later, less tranquil times when we need to carry those plans through. The idea is to protect our decisions made in moments of clarity from our later second guessing—and the bad decisions that occur when the stress of the moment has us more short-sighted.

My first hire knew how to protect his intention, but he was hardly the first. The battle between our past self—of better judgment—and our present self—mired in circumstance—is as old as time, and so are those who found solutions.

We can learn from the example of Ulysses—hero of the *Odyssey* epic, one of the first expedition leaders on record, and pioneer of not letting future circumstances derail good decisions made in the here and now.

"First you will come to the Sirens who enchant all who come near them. If anyone unwarily draws in too close and hears the singing of the Sirens, his wife and children will never welcome him home again, for they sit in a green field and warble him to death with the sweetness of their song."

That was the warning from the sorceress Circe to Ulysses on his long journey home from Troy. He and his crew would soon sail past an island inhabited by the Sirens—half-bird, half-human creatures whose singing was so beautiful and so irresistible that sailors would steer their ships toward the rocks in a desperate attempt to get closer.

Nobody had ever heard the Sirens' song and lived to tell of it; all who came before had crashed and drowned upon the rocks.

Ulysses faced a choice. He could sail far around the island, avoiding the danger entirely but adding time to an already decade-long journey, or he could devise a system—one that would allow him to shorten the trip, hear the Sirens, and survive it all.

He chose the system, and Circe told him how to build it.

"Therefore, pass these Sirens by, and stop your men's ears with wax that none of them may hear. But if you like you can listen yourself, for you may get the men to bind you as you stand upright on a cross-piece halfway up the mast, and they must lash the rope's ends to the mast itself, that you may have the pleasure of listening. If you beg and pray the men to unloose you, then they must bind you faster."

Before they came within earshot of the Sirens, while his mind was clear and his judgment sound, Ulysses gave his crew those instructions. The plan worked exactly as designed.

When the Sirens' song reached Ulysses, it was as irresistible as promised. He strained against the ropes, shouted orders to his crew to release him, and pleaded with them to turn the ship toward the rocky shore. But his crew, unable to hear either the Sirens or their captain's desperate commands, simply rowed on.

Ulysses' present self, the one thrashing against the mast, had been saved by his past self—the one who knew what was coming and built a system that would survive the coming storm of desire. When they finally passed the island, he returned to his senses.

The episode provided the world's first "Ulysses Contract," a freely made decision that binds our future self to a course of action our present self knows is right—the **right** course that we'll desperately want to change for the **wrong** reasons.

Like only ordering half a glass of wine or intentionally leaving our phone in the car, it's the recognition that the person we are in moments of clarity is not the same person we'll be when temptation, pressure, and our Horseman of human nature strike.

My first hire understood this instinctively when he set that alarm. Ulysses understood it nearly three thousand years ago. The question for us as leaders is:

What are the Sirens in our business, and what systems have we built to keep ourselves and our teams lashed to the mast when we're desperate to turn the ship toward the rocks?

Most business leaders know their Sirens. We can name them in moments of clarity.

There's the Siren of the urgent drowning out the important. There's the Siren of the customer crisis that demands immediate attention while our strategic initiative sits untouched for another week. There's the Siren of the employee drama that consumes our afternoon while the job descriptions that would prevent such ordeals remain unwritten.

There's the Siren of comfortable mediocrity. We know we need to have that difficult conversation with an underperformer—but today's *"not the right time."* We know our pricing is too low, but this isn't the quarter to *"risk upsetting customers."* We know we need to invest in new scheduling software, but we'll wait *"until things calm down."*

There's the Siren of doing it ourselves: we know we should delegate, train others, and build systems that don't require our constant involvement, but it's faster to *"just get it done"* this time—and the next time, and the time after that, until we've become the bottleneck in our own business and trapped by our own competence.

Here's what makes these Sirens so dangerous: they don't sound like Sirens at all. They sound reasonable—responsible, even.

The song is beautiful because it's not obviously wrong; it's just incomplete. It's the truth without context, the right thing without consideration of cost, the urgent masquerading as the important, the near term over the long term, and the circumstances of the moment versus the character of who we and our organization want to be.

And like Ulysses, we know all this. Right now, reading this, some of the aforementioned likely hit home—how we've been pulled away, distracted, or talked ourselves into putting things off for a few weeks more.

But we have it a little tougher than Ulysses. He only had to bind **himself** to the mast. As leaders, we're not just trying to keep ourselves from trying to swim to shore. We're responsible for an entire crew, each with their own Sirens calling.

The sales team hears the Siren of the easy "*Yes.*" They know they should qualify prospects carefully, turn away poor-fit clients, and protect the operations team from impossible promises. But in the moment, with quota looming and a prospect ready to sign, the song is irresistible: "*Just say yes, we'll figure it out later.*"

The operations team hears the Siren of the workaround. They know the system is broken, and that the temporary fix from six months ago is now causing daily problems. They know they should stop and rebuild it properly. But there's work to be done today, and fixing the system means everything stops. So, they'll keep patching, keep working around it, and keep singing, "*Just one more time.*"

Our teams have sat through the training, nodded at the strategic plan, and agreed with the priorities. They have the character and the competence to do excellent work. But character and competence aren't enough when real temptation comes knocking. Our best people, with the best intentions, may still steer toward the rocks, not because they're weak or careless, but because they, like us, are human.

And this brings us to one of the greatest skills in mastering the craft of business. It's one thing to come up with a clear strategy, to build all the systems and infrastructure we need for the journey, but it's another to step back and look at it all, our team, and ourselves, and ask:

It all can work, but how are we most likely to screw it up?

For expeditions attempting to reach the South Pole, one of the most common tactics was to stockpile supplies at pre-arranged depots along the intended route. This was partly to ease the burden of traveling with extra weight, but it also had an "Ulysses Contract" element.

Along the way, exhausted crews would face the temptation of unproven shortcuts, unexplored routes that might save time—or end in disaster.

Taking such a risk is easy to dismiss as foolish when we're warm and well-fed, plotting our course in comfort. But weeks into the brutal reality of polar travel, it's easy to rationalize bad decisions.

The pre-positioned supply depots made the choice simple: deviate from the route, lose your lifeline.

In business, the sequence is similar. Removed from the heat of battle, we can foresee how things might go sideways. But do we guard against the emotions that are to come later?

A CEO knows he'll be tempted to raid the marketing budget when operational fires emerge. So, at the start of the year, he has the CFO divide the relevant funds and lock the amounts into separate accounts. Using marketing funds to deal with other issues is no longer the CEO's liability alone; it now requires formal board approval.

A founder knows that if she's desperate to fill a critical role, she'll be tempted to overlook red flags and rationalize a mediocre hire. So, she creates a scorecard with the nine entry gates of our Progression of Fit. She then publicly announces a rule with her leadership team: she can't extend an offer unless two other team members independently review her assessment and agree there are no red flags. The hiring bar is set before desperation can lower it.

A manufacturing company knows that when cash gets tight, their maintenance team will be tempted to stretch equipment replacement cycles. *"Just another six months,"* becomes a year, then two. So, they create a capital reserve account that auto-funds based on equipment age and usage hours. When a machine hits the predetermined threshold, the funds are already set aside. The decision to reinvest was made when the equipment was new. The funds were moved automatically—all before the reality of breakdown risk could battle against the emotions of budget pressure.

We know there are moments when we make good decisions, and moments where circumstances impact our judgment. The more we can use the former to plan for the latter, the more successful we will be.

The specifics will look different for every leader and every business. Your Sirens aren't mine. Your supply depot locations won't match those of polar explorers. And how you lash yourself to the mast will be unique to your expedition.

But the principle remains the same: the decisions that matter most shouldn't be left until the moment when they're most impactful. Often, that is when we're tired, pressured, tempted, or convinced that *"Just this once"* makes sense. Part of the expedition of business is figuring out how we and our teams can make certain decisions preemptively—and bind ourselves to them.

We spent Part 1 thinking about how to make a fair and rational assessment of our efforts, Part 2 understanding people and how to align them to our organizations' benefit, Part 3 seeing how to be an effective leader, and Part 4 building out the systems, infrastructure, and strategy that help both businesses and expeditions succeed.

But here's the hard truth: without what we've covered in this chapter, most of it won't matter.

My first hire understood this when he set that alarm. Ulysses understood this when he instructed his crew. Great expedition leaders understood this when they strategically placed supplies.

It's part of the craft of business: placing the constraints that keep us and our teams on course—not just knowing what to do, but ensuring it actually gets done.

The Sirens will always sing. The question is: Are we prepared?

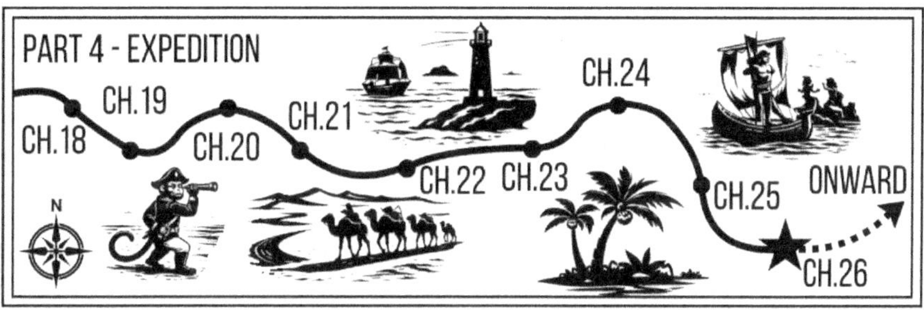

Much of the expedition of business is about doing our best to predict and plan for what lies ahead. It's about being aware of factors outside our control, of having a deeper understanding of our crew so we can avoid them veering off course, and of knowing there's a cost to leadership—knowledge that keeps us from retreating when our climb up promising new routes gets steeper and less certain.

And much of our craft is about designing and building the systems, structures, and routines that form our defenses against the Four Horsemen that too often cause us to violate Rule #1—to come up well short of our destination.

Ulysses Contracts run in the same veins. They are a powerful tactic to support the strategy of foreseeing trouble ahead—of winning by avoiding all the forces that often have us losing.

And while there's undeniable value in answering the question of what might go wrong, there are also benefits to be had from another question:

What happens when things go right?

That's where our journey takes us next—a chapter that shows us the rewards that await.

ONWARD

New Zealand is a country of striking natural beauty. With coastlines of deep, rocky fjords and white sandy beaches—crystal-clear lakes, blue snowmelt-fed rivers, ancient wildlife, and 2,000-year-old trees—today it feels like stepping into another world. One hundred years ago, even more so—but it was in that place and time that a certain young man lived a rather mundane life.

Every day he woke up early and rode his bike to the local train station. The ride would take him from his rural home and the central hub of his family's beekeeping operation to the second leg of his commute. Next, a train would take him some 40 miles north to Auckland, and a short walk would put him at his school—the closest one meeting his mother's approval.

To pass the time on the train, he read any adventure book he could find. They were accounts of distant lands, both real and imaginary, and escapes from a life of routine hardship with a strict, discipline-minded father.

While he shared a country with some of the most impressive mountains on earth, they lay hundreds of miles to the south. And in a time before highways and automobiles, it was no surprise that by the age of 16 he had never ventured far above the coastal lowlands he knew as home.

But that all changed on a school trip and a visit to Mount Ruapehu. His climb to over 9,000 feet turned cold, snow, and altitude from imagined landscapes into a real-life experience. And, as he would later say, *"returned home in a glow of fiery enthusiasm."*

But his reality didn't change. He was still, by his own admission, a *"tall, bony, clumsy-looking youth"* and living in what felt like the middle of nowhere. Two years spent at university would soon be a dead end, and a brief stint at a law firm had him resigned to returning home and working on the family farm.

How this young man and his climbing partner, Tenzing Norgay, would become the first to summit Mount Everest 18 years later is a story of honing one's craft and a lesson in how great accomplishments are a long time in the making.

The lanky teenager buried in his reading was not yet someone capable of climbing the world's highest peak. Nor was the 20-year-old who later climbed Mount Ollivier—a notable effort, but at only 6,000 feet, well short of Everest's 29,000.

Reaching the tallest peak on Earth would require the elevation of his capacity, knowledge, and experience. The heights he could reach would be dictated by his craft as a climber.

The ascent of Sir Edmund Hillary started rather unintentionally. Working long days and hauling heavy beehives on the family farm increased his physical strength and stamina. "Tramping" with his university club, carrying heavy packs on long hikes through the bush, had a similar effect. And taking up boxing was great preparation for the rugged conditions of the Himalayas—it was controlled exposure to discomfort and fear.

While time in the ring, long days in the sun, and early ascents may have made him tough enough for serious climbing, the official government biography of Hillary notes *"he lacked technical mountaineering proficiency."*

His physical capacity and natural talent had taken him as far as they could, but well short of Everest.

That all changed when he began climbing with Harry Ayres, an experienced and respected mountaineer. Under Ayres' tutelage, Hillary would see different terrains, become familiar with new tools and techniques, and practice them all while climbing some of New Zealand's most challenging peaks. It was a period of growth from a young man with potential to one of his country's best climbers.

Yet, no one had ever reached the top of Everest, nor would Hillary through mimicking others alone. To do what hadn't been done before, he had to take the craft of climbing where it had never been.

A few years prior to summiting Everest, his own approach to mountaineering took shape: whether to use tents or dig snow caves, how to use bottled oxygen, the correct use of skis, slow staged ascents versus rapid climbs, and the role of sherpas.

Everest remained elusive; there was no *"right way"* to climb it. Others had their opinions, but it was Hillary who decided how he and his team would make their ascent. And, like the actual path they would chart to the top of the mountain, he found a better way forward.

Building his capacity, learning from others, practicing new tools and techniques: they all helped Hillary improve his craft. But mastery came when he found his own first principles and what he himself believed to be true about climbing. Doing so allowed him to climb like no one had before, and as a result, we all know his name and his accomplishment.

Reaching the top of Everest started with one thing: potential. There was the potential for Hillary to be a better climber, the potential for the craft of climbing to be advanced, and the potential for men and women to reach the world's highest point. Hillary saw that potential and used his craft to manifest it all into reality.

And that's where any craft begins. A woodworker starts with an empty workbench but can see the potential for the table that will soon rest upon it. A painter looks at a blank canvas but feels the potential for a great work of art to emerge. An entrepreneur finds an underserved market and knows the potential for a new business to succeed.

They give it their best shot, but the resistance emerges. The gap between what they can do and what they believe is possible becomes obvious. So, they turn to a different type of potential: the potential within themselves.

We all know Hillary for climbing Everest, but it was a long road that led him to that point. Ernest Shackleton and his polar expedition may be famous for enduring years stranded in the Antarctic, but it was the countless voyages before that prepared him. And our friend Amundsen would not have been the person to lead his team through the Northwest Passage if not for all his experience and the past guidance from others.

The craft and expedition of business are no different. It's an ongoing pursuit to do better, but it all starts with seeing the potential to be a better leader, to design a better organization, to operate it better—and as a result—provide better for our team, our families, and ourselves.

In time, we learn we share something else with leaders of expeditions—our journeys never really end.

Hillary would climb Everest but then go on to reach the South Pole. Later he would trace the Ganges River from where it emptied into the sea to its headwaters in the Himalayas. And he would dedicate the rest of his life to building schools, hospitals, and infrastructure to support Sherpa communities.

But he was hardly alone in moving forward until the end.

Shackleton would become a national hero for saving the lives of his crew, serve in World War I, and spend the rest of his life devoted to exploration. Fittingly, he would pass away from a heart attack during his final expedition south.

And Amundsen would become the first person to reach the South Pole, pioneer aviation exploration of Arctic areas, and disappear during a rescue mission. He would lose his life while attempting to save another.

It's likely our business careers will end well before our time on Earth is up, but pursuing mastery of our craft doesn't end with a particular role or position. Like Hillary and the route up Everest, it was always about finding a better path forward—manifesting more of the potential of our organizations into reality, but also turning more of the potential of ourselves into better leaders.

I certainly don't compare the ascent of my business career to climbing Everest, but there are portions of Hillary's story that ring familiar—and that's probably true for all of us.

For me, I can relate to a childhood in a quiet setting, and neither of our fathers was ever nominated for "Dad of the year." Hillary's dreams of new opportunities and a different life are also relatable. He thought of adventure and exploration; I just knew better was possible—a world where people realized more of their potential, me included.

And whereas Hillary's ascent started with boxing and beekeeping, it was hard for me to see how growing gardens, playing basketball, and days spent fishing were preparation for what lay ahead.

But the biggest parallel was how the level of our craft dictated the heights of success.

Like Hillary, I started with natural ability, but it didn't take long to realize that talent alone would never be enough. Pulling all-nighters, working on weekends, packing my laptop for every vacation: they were all signs of one trying to replace the craft of business with brute force.

They were also evidence of one paying the opportunity cost of time with friends and family. And they were signs of a leader who needed to provide better for his team—a team that deserved better than confusion, being surrounded by some bad hires, and going without the resources they needed for their own climb.

Thankfully, finding the right mentors was part of my journey as well. Hillary had Harry Ayres to help him develop his craft. Mine was not a single individual, but a collection of dozens. The majority I never met; I only read or listened to what they had to say. But the result was the same: better success, and better realization of potential, through being better at one's craft.

The hours got shorter, no more working weekends, and vacations became devoted to friends and family. My team grew faster, did better work, and found a better environment in which to thrive. The ascent of my craft was well underway, but it took escaping the cycle of busyness to climb high enough to get a better view of what was really happening.

Like Hillary, my highest heights were reached when I could form my own views on how to succeed on the expedition of business. Hillary developed his thoughts on skis, oxygen tanks, and sherpas. I developed mine around decision-making, people, leadership, and organizational design.

And they are what have filled the pages of this book—a book that began with a question: What is the journey that's brought you to where you are today?

I share my experience not because it's unique, but because it is common. The exact path, details, and summit of my journey were different from Hillary's. Yours is or will be different still. But they're also the same.

Showing potential, trying and failing, learning, developing our own way—it all has us ascending higher. It's the path of mastering any craft, and of those who leave their unique impression on the world.

<hr>

"Amundsen Reaches South Pole!" "Lindbergh Does It!" "Everest Conquered!" "Men Walk On Moon!"—some are from the New York Times, others the Chicago Daily Tribune, but they're all headlines of great expeditions coming to a successful end. Those who completed these journeys returned to great fanfare—but why?

There was little direct benefit to those who cheered the success of Amundsen, Hillary, and others like them. Their expeditions ending in success didn't provide more prosperity, freedom, or security to anyone reading or watching at home.

It's a fair question to ask why anyone cared at all. Why are we drawn to men and women we don't know who are taking on risks we might not understand in places we've never been?

We care because they expand what we know to be possible.

We cheer for them as individuals, but just as much we're celebrating the expanding frontier of human capability. And the latter is the benefit: an increase in potential, a bigger idea of what we ourselves could do given the right opportunity.

So, it's understandable why the famous explorers of history may grab the headlines, but there's an argument that business leaders like you are equally worthy of praise.

Summiting tall mountains and reaching new frontiers might inspire and intrigue those who cheer, but it's the business leader who has a more direct impact on the world in which those people live and work.

The customers and clients you serve, the goods and services provided to your communities—all have a tangible impact on the lives of others. For those inside your organization, it's the leadership you display and the environments you craft for your team. These are the conditions under which they can be at their best—like my dad and his trim carpentry, doing work they can be proud of. It all provides for a better life for them, for their families, and for all the lives they impact.

It's also how great businesses are built.

Leaders of great expeditions deliver the idea that we are capable of more. Leaders of great businesses do the same for those in their charge. ***But they go further***; they help their teams see the potential in themselves, ***and*** they create the opportunities to turn that potential into reality.

Providing these conditions isn't just the right thing to do—it's the strategic choice that separates remarkable organizations from average ones. It's the dividing line between organizations that see people simply as they are and those that see people as what they could be. The latter know that making the climb between those two points benefits everyone—the individual, the business, and the world at large.

But doing so isn't easy. Just like our expedition counterparts, the paths we forge are often new, and the risks are uncertain.

Early in this book, we took on the idea that only so much is in our control—that often, despite our best efforts, the results we achieve fall short of what we may deserve. We followed that idea with plenty of warnings and cautions about the difficulties of business: the Four Horsemen who await us along the trail, our crews who are our greatest asset but also our greatest liability, and that our biggest enemy is often ourselves. We considered that our greatest challenges are often our own natural limits, our own undesirable tendencies, and our own ability to sabotage our best efforts.

But while these cautions are warranted, and there's value in asking what could go wrong, there's another side to the story: the question of what happens when things go right.

There are great rewards to be had when we work hard at our craft—when we not only set meaningful goals but also build the Pyramids of Decisions and define the strategies, tactics, and execution that support them.

We find greater success when we make our climb up The Mountain of Why—when we move beyond copying others and plant our flag on the peaks of the first principles that we hold to be true. Because it's those that help us move the Levers of Control—to build and unify the energy in our organizations, to lower the resistance, and to maximize the yield of the work to be done. And when we do so, we receive a greater return for our efforts.

Things go right when we come to understand people better and all that goes into the G.E.A.R. model that drives them. Things go right when we use that insight to avoid them being the anchors that hold our businesses back and align them to be the wind in the sails that push us forward. Our frustration diminishes, and our hope rises.

It all starts when we understand our job as leaders and are ready to pay the cost of what's required. It's then we can do the work of designing an organization that's better prepared for the expedition of business. It's then that we hone our craft of building the systems, structures, and routines that are essential. And it's then we become a better leader of people—providing the clarity and order our crews require.

It's then that things go right.

In the end, we make better decisions, we do things our way, all our hard work meets good fortune and we manifest all the potential of what we knew was possible—our own version of the perfect business becomes a reality.

But along the way there will be plenty of voices to the contrary. There will be others who tell us to play it safe, to follow the well-trodden paths, or to be content with "good enough."

It may be the voice in our own head—the one that tells us that we can't, that we shouldn't, that reminds us of all the consequences of failure.

It's hard to know the exact discouragement that awaits, or who ***they*** will be. But I know this: Whoever ***they*** are can go to hell.

For the leader who has set off on an expedition, for the craftsman intent on mastery, and for you who know that better is possible, there's only one direction to be concerned with:

Onward.

ABOUT THE AUTHOR

Zack Tomlin lives in Raleigh, North Carolina with his wife Jackie, their two daughters, Hadley and Abilene, and one furry degenerate son, Bruce the dog.

He works with business leaders of small and midsized companies, both in person and remotely across the country.

If you enjoyed this book, Zack would love to hear from you.

EMAIL: ZACK@HARNESSING.ENERGY

PREPARE FOR THE REST OF YOUR JOURNEY

You've reached the end of this book, but also the beginning of the next leg of your expedition.

No leader plots a course forward until they understand their current position.

The Expedition Assessment will help you compare your current business against the principles covered in this book and identify where to focus your efforts next.

Scan the QR code or visit the link below to begin:

WWW.THEEXPEDITIONOFBUSINESS.COM/ASSESSMENT

NOTES & REFERENCES

The following notes provide sources and additional context for references made throughout the book. They are organized by chapter and keyed to phrases from the text (shown in bold).

CH. 1: THE PERFECT BUSINESS

"The average age of winners of major golf tournaments is 32"

According to PGA.com, the average age of a golf major champion is 32 years old. Joe Posnanski's analysis for Golf Channel confirmed this, finding the average and median age for major champions is 32 going back to 1960. See: pga.com/archive/average-age-of-golf-major-champi on-32-years-old and Posnanski, "Does Age Really Matter in Golf? Yes, It Does," golfchannel.com, September 27, 2018.

"making him 11 years older than any prior major champion"

The previous oldest major champion was Julius Boros, who won the 1968 PGA Championship at age 48. Had Watson won at 59, he would have broken the record by 11 years. Phil Mickelson has since surpassed this, winning the 2021 PGA Championship at age 50.

"landed right where I wanted it to" / "I like it"

Watson's post-round remarks and subsequent interviews about the 72nd hole of the 2009 Open Championship at Turnberry. Watson described his confidence in the shot as it was in the air ("I like it") and confirmed the ball landed on target ("landed right where I wanted it to"). See: "Tom Watson: A Tale of Two Shots at Turnberry," theopen.com, March

9, 2023; Watson's first-person account in *Golf Digest*, October 2009 (reprinted at golfdigest.com/story/tom-watson-turnberry).

"several spectators telling him that as the ball hit the green, a gust of wind...blew through"

From a later Watson interview. See: "Tom Watson: Open Heartbreak Still Haunts," *The Guardian*, July 13, 2010. Also recounted at forethe goodofthegame.com.

CH. 2: THE MOUNTAIN OF WHY

"SPIN Selling, Porter's Five Forces, EOS, Scaling Up, The 4 Disciplines of Execution"

Neil Rackham, *SPIN Selling* (McGraw-Hill, 1988). Michael E. Porter, *Competitive Strategy* (Free Press, 1980), which introduced the Five Forces framework. Gino Wickman, *Traction* (BenBella Books, 2011), the foundational text for EOS. Verne Harnish, *Scaling Up* (Gazelles, 2014). Chris McChesney, Sean Covey, and Jim Huling, *The 4 Disciplines of Execution* (Free Press, 2012).

"As one historian later recounted..." / "According to the testimony of several trustworthy writers..."

The account of Abbas Ibn Firnas's flight attempt is commonly attributed to the 17th-century historian Ahmed Mohammed al-Maqqari in *Nafh al-Tib min Ghusn al-Andalus al-Ratib*, drawing from earlier medieval sources. Al-Maqqari compiled histories of notable figures from Moorish Spain, including Firnas's attempted flight in Córdoba, c. 875 CE.

CH. 3: PYRAMIDS OF DECISIONS

"Strategy is our philosophy of becoming." — Seth Godin

Seth Godin, *This is Strategy* (Portfolio/Penguin, 2024).

CH. 4: THE FOUR LEVERS OF BUSINESS

The Wright brothers / Wilbur had won a coin toss / Orville would be at the controls / the plane started bouncing down the launch rail

The Wright Flyer's first powered flight took place December 17, 1903, at Kill Devil Hills, North Carolina. Wilbur won a coin toss for the first attempt on December 14 but stalled on takeoff; Orville flew successfully three days later. The aircraft used wooden launch rails and landing skids rather than wheels. See David McCullough, *The Wright Brothers* (Simon & Schuster, 2015); Smithsonian National Air and Space Museum (airandspace.si.edu).

CH. 5: PADDLE DOWNSTREAM

"Jerry Jones going $50 million in debt before finally striking it rich buying the Dallas Cowboys"

Jones's pre-Cowboys debt and oil strike are recounted in the Netflix docuseries *America's Team: The Gambler and His Cowboys* (2025), directed by Chapman and Maclain Way. In the first episode, Jones describes being "really good at borrowing money," which left him more than $50 million in debt before an $800,000 oil well purchase turned into a $100 million windfall. See also: "Coin Flips, Death Threats, and Oil Money," wfaa.com, August 2025.

"Roughly 250 people operate the Hoover Dam"

As of 2014, Hoover Dam's workforce was approximately 250 employees, per the Bureau of Reclamation. See: "Hoover Dam Is Solid, but Its Workforce Is Aging," Las Vegas Review-Journal, February 23, 2017.

"generates enough power for 1.3 million people"

Per the U.S. Bureau of Reclamation, Hoover Dam generates about 4 billion kilowatt-hours of hydroelectric power annually—enough to serve 1.3 million people in Nevada, Arizona, and California. See: usbr.gov/l c/hooverdam/faqs/powerfaq.html.

"one employee could be between 25% and 200% more productive than a peer in similar circumstances"

McKinsey research has found that superior talent can be up to 800% more productive in highly complex roles and up to 400% more productive across a range of fields. A study of more than 600,000 researchers, entertainers, politicians, and athletes in *Personnel Psychology* confirmed the 400% figure. See: "Attracting and Retaining the Right Talent," mc kinsey.com, November 2017.

"If you could get all the people in an organization rowing in the same direction..." — Patrick Lencioni

Patrick Lencioni, *The Five Dysfunctions of a Team* (Jossey-Bass, 2002). The exact wording varies across sources; this version is consistent with the book's central argument.

CH. 6: VANTAGE POINTS

"nearly 60% of us overestimate how effectively we communicate"

Gilovich, Savitsky, and Medvec found that people overestimate how apparent their internal states are to others—a phenomenon they termed the "illusion of transparency" (*Journal of Personality and Social Psychology*, 1998). Keysar showed that speakers systematically overestimate listener comprehension (*Current Directions in Psychological Science*, 2007). Economist Intelligence Unit research found that inefficient communication increased stress (52%), delayed projects (44%), and lowered morale (31%).

"'That's right' are the best words you can hear in any negotiation."

Chris Voss with Tahl Raz, *Never Split the Difference* (Harper Business, 2016). Voss, a former FBI lead international kidnapping negotiator, argues that "That's right" signals genuine understanding, as opposed to "You're right," which often signals dismissal.

CH. 7: UNDERCURRENTS (G.E.A.R.)

"Creative Blindness" / "You don't start with what you want people to do; you start with what people want to do."

David Trott, *Creative Blindness (And How to Cure It)* (Harriman House, 2019). Trott, a veteran advertising creative director, argues that effective persuasion begins with understanding what your audience already wants, not with imposing your own agenda.

"People don't understand the nature of their own motivation, so when they are unhappy at work, they ask for more money."

Susan Fowler, *Why Motivating People Doesn't Work...and What Does: The New Science of Leading, Energizing, and Engaging* (Berrett-Koehler, 2014).

"A lot of times, people don't know what they want until you show it to them."

Widely attributed to Steve Jobs, commonly cited from a 1998 *Business-Week* interview. The exact wording varies across sources; this version is consistent with Jobs's well-documented philosophy on product design and consumer research.

CH. 8: WIRED FOR SURVIVAL

"As descendants of these successful ancestors..." / "Psychological mechanisms are information-processing devices..." / large-game hunting / genetic variation

David M. Buss, *Evolutionary Psychology: The New Science of the Mind*, 6th ed. (Routledge, 2019). Multiple passages in this chapter are drawn from Buss: "As descendants of these successful ancestors..." (p. 33); "Psychological mechanisms are information-processing devices" (p. 62); "It is virtually impossible to hunt large game alone" (p. 61); "Modern human populations show an exceptionally low amount of genetic variation" (p. 23).

"these make up the famous 'Flow' state"

The concept of "flow" was introduced by Hungarian-American psychologist Mihály Csíkszentmihályi. While researching the creative process in the late 1960s, Csíkszentmihályi noticed that artists became so absorbed in their work that they ignored hunger, fatigue, and discomfort—yet only while the work was going well. He went on to study artists, athletes, chess masters, surgeons, and others who pursued activities for intrinsic satisfaction, and found a common underlying experience: a state of deep, effortless concentration in which people lost track of time and felt fully in control. Because so many of his interviewees described the feeling as being carried along by a current, Csíkszentmihályi named it "flow." He first presented the concept in *Beyond Boredom and Anxiety* (1975) and later expanded it in his landmark book *Flow: The Psychology of Optimal Experience* (Harper & Row, 1990). Csíkszentmihályi is widely regarded as one of the founding figures of positive psychology; he died in 2021 at the age of 87. See also Csíkszentmihályi's 2004 TED talk, "Flow, the Secret to Happiness."

"First, Break All the Rules" / "80,000 managers across 400 companies"

Marcus Buckingham and Curt Coffman, *First, Break All the Rules* (Simon & Schuster, 1999). Based on Gallup research involving over 80,000 managers across more than 400 companies and over one million employee interviews over 25 years.

CH. 9: MADE DIFFERENT

Myers-Briggs Type Indicator, DISC, The Enneagram Institute / "Big Five" personality scale / NEO Personality Inventory

The MBTI was developed by Isabel Briggs Myers and Katharine Cook Briggs (first published 1962). DISC is based on William Moulton Marston's *Emotions of Normal People* (1928). The Enneagram is documented in Don Richard Riso and Russ Hudson's *The Wisdom of the Enneagram* (Bantam, 1999). The "Big Five" personality traits (Openness, Conscientiousness, Extraversion, Agreeableness, and Neuroticism) emerged from decades of factor-analytic research, with key contributions from Lewis Goldberg, Paul Costa, and Robert McCrae. The NEO Personality Inventory was developed by Costa and McCrae as a standardized measure of the Big Five; see Costa, P.T. & McCrae, R.R., *Revised NEO Personality Inventory (NEO-PI-R) and NEO Five-Factor Inventory (NEO-FFI) Professional Manual* (Psychological Assessment Resources, 1992).

"Research by DeYoung, Quilty, and Peterson found that the various manifestations of each of the 'Big Five' naturally cluster into two related but distinct aspects"

DeYoung, C.G., Quilty, L.C., & Peterson, J.B., "Between Facets and Domains: 10 Aspects of the Big Five," *Journal of Personality and Social Psychology*, 93(5), 880–896 (2007). The study used factor analysis to identify two distinct aspects within each of the Big Five traits.

Jim Collins, made famous by his book "Good to Great," got the business world talking about people and seats

Jim Collins, *Good to Great: Why Some Companies Make the Leap...and Others Don't* (HarperBusiness, 2001). This specific three-part formulation—the right people on the bus, the wrong people off the bus, and the right people in the right seats—also appears in a video discussion on jimcollins.com, "Getting the Right People in the Right Seats Over Time."

CH. 10: INTERNAL MAPS

Anthony de Mello / "The shortest distance between truth and a human being is a story."

Widely attributed to Anthony de Mello, S.J. (1931–1987), an Indian Jesuit priest and psychotherapist known for his books on spirituality and awareness. The quote is consistent with the parable-driven approach of his works, including *One Minute Wisdom* (Doubleday, 1985) and *The Song of the Bird* (1982).

George Loewenstein / information-gap theory / fMRI research on curiosity

Loewenstein, G., "The Psychology of Curiosity: A Review and Reinterpretation," *Psychological Bulletin*, 116(1), 75–98 (1994). Loewenstein proposed that curiosity functions as a form of cognitively induced deprivation arising from the perception of a gap in one's knowledge. fMRI research: Kang, M.J. et al., "The Wick in the Candle of Learning," *Psychological Science*, 20(8), 963–973 (2009), finding that curiosity activated caudate regions associated with anticipated reward—the same brain areas that respond to food, sex, and addictive substances. See also Gruber, M.J. et al., *Neuron*, 84(2), 486–496 (2014).

Will Storr / "The Science of Storytelling" / Loewenstein's four mechanisms

Will Storr, *The Science of Storytelling: Why Stories Make Us Human, and How to Tell Them Better* (Abrams Press, 2020). Storr synthesizes Loewenstein's information-gap theory with neuroscience to explain how storytelling exploits the brain's curiosity-driven reward system.

CH. 11: NARROW TRAILS

Lee Ross / "The Intuitive Psychologist and His Shortcomings" (1977)

Ross, L., in L. Berkowitz (ed.), *Advances in Experimental Social Psychology*, Vol. 10 (Academic Press, 1977), pp. 173–220. This paper introduced the "fundamental attribution error": the tendency to overemphasize personality-based explanations for others' behavior while underestimating situational factors.

CH. 12: HARNESSING ENERGY

It's 1812 in Philadelphia / Each pays $5 admission / Charles Redheffer / an old man in the attic

The Redheffer perpetual motion hoax is documented in Arthur W.J.G. Ord-Hume, *Perpetual Motion: The History of an Obsession* (St. Martin's

Press, 1977). Ord-Hume documents Redheffer's 1812 Philadelphia exhibition, the city commissioners' inspection in January 1813, the discovery that the gear teeth were worn in a way suggesting the machine was being driven rather than producing power, and the exposure by Nathan Sellers and engineer Isaiah Lukens. Contemporary accounts also appear in *Niles' Weekly Register* (1810s).

The most common business size in the United States is one.

According to the U.S. Census Bureau's Nonemployer Statistics program, the majority of all U.S. business establishments are nonemployer firms. The SBA's 2024 FAQ reports 28.5 million nonemployer firms, with 86.3% being sole proprietorships. See: census.gov/programs-surveys/nonemployer-statistics.

CH. 13: BUSINESS LEADERSHIP DEFINED

"Leadership is influence — nothing more, nothing less." — John C. Maxwell

John C. Maxwell, *The 21 Irrefutable Laws of Leadership* (Thomas Nelson, 1998). Maxwell calls this "The Law of Influence" and devotes an entire chapter to the concept.

"Leadership is the art of getting someone else to do something you want done because he wants to do it." — Dwight Eisenhower

Recorded at the Eisenhower Presidential Library (eisenhowerlibrary.gov) and originates from "What is Leadership?" *Reader's Digest*, June 1965. See also Bret Baier, "Seven Business Leadership Lessons from Dwight Eisenhower," *Forbes*, January 31, 2017.

"As we look ahead into the next century, leaders will be those who empower others." — Bill Gates

Widely attributed to Bill Gates. Cited in Marcel Schwantes, "Bill Gates Explains What Separates Successful Leaders from Everyone Else in 2 Words," Inc., 2020. No primary source document has been identified.

"Leadership is not about being in charge. It is about taking care of those in your charge." — Simon Sinek

Simon Sinek, *Together is Better* (Portfolio/Penguin, 2016).

"[Great] Leaders display a powerful mixture of personal humility and indomitable will." — Jim Collins

Jim Collins, *Good to Great* (HarperBusiness, 2001). Collins describes this as a defining characteristic of "Level 5 Leadership."

Heaven's Gate / On March 26, 1997 / 39 members

The Heaven's Gate mass suicide in Rancho Santa Fe, California. The group was led by Marshall Applewhite, who convinced members to end their lives to reach a spacecraft they believed was following the Hale-Bopp comet. See, e.g., "Mass Suicide Involved Sedatives, Vodka and Careful Planning," The New York Times, March 27, 1997.

Gene Kranz / "failure is not an option" / "go or no go" / "over 86 hours"

Gene Kranz, *Failure Is Not an Option* (Simon & Schuster, 2000). Kranz was lead flight director during the Apollo 13 crisis, which began on April 13, 1970, when an oxygen tank explosion crippled the spacecraft approximately 200,000 miles from Earth. The "go or no go" quote is from Kranz's public remarks describing his role (see, e.g., PCMA Convening Leaders, 2019). The phrase "failure is not an option" was written for the 1995 Ron Howard film; Kranz later adopted it as his memoir's title. The rescue lasted approximately 87 hours from the initial explosion to splashdown on April 17, 1970.

CH. 14: WHAT LEADERS PROVIDE

Peter Drucker / "Leadership is defined by results, not attributes." / "It's not about attributes."

Widely attributed to Peter F. Drucker. The fuller version—"Effective leadership is not about making speeches or being liked; leadership is defined by results not attributes"—appears across multiple compilations of Drucker's work. See Drucker, P.F., *The Effective Executive* (Harper & Row, 1967) and *The Daily Drucker* (HarperBusiness, 2004).

Richard Fuld / "Gorilla of Wall Street" / Lehman Brothers bankruptcy and Global Financial Crisis

Richard S. Fuld Jr. served as CEO of Lehman Brothers from 1994 until the firm's bankruptcy filing on September 15, 2008—the largest in U.S. history at the time. His aggressive, risk-heavy leadership style earned him the "Gorilla of Wall Street" nickname. See Andrew Ross Sorkin, *Too Big to Fail* (Viking, 2009); also Lawrence G. McDonald with Patrick Robinson, *A Colossal Failure of Common Sense* (Crown Business, 2009).

Elizabeth Holmes (Theranos), Adam Neumann (WeWork), Sam Bankman-Fried (FTX), Jeff Skilling (Enron)

Well-documented leadership failures. See: John Carreyrou, *Bad Blood* (Knopf, 2018); Reeves Wiedeman, *Billion Dollar Loser* (Little, Brown, 2020); Michael Lewis, *Going Infinite* (W.W. Norton, 2023); Bethany McLean and Peter Elkind, *The Smartest Guys in the Room* (Portfolio, 2003).

On average, a business in the United States has 24 employees

Per the U.S. Census Bureau's SUSB, the average firm size is approximately 24 employees. The SBA reports that 98.2% of employer firms have fewer than 100 employees, and the vast majority have fewer than 50. See: census.gov/programs-surveys/susb; SBA Office of Advocacy, 2024.

"With malice toward none, with charity for all..."

Abraham Lincoln, Second Inaugural Address, March 4, 1865. Full text available at the National Archives (archives.gov) and the Library of Congress.

"This is Day 1 for the Internet..." / relentless focus on customer satisfaction

Jeff Bezos, 1997 Letter to Shareholders, Amazon.com, Inc. Publicly available via the SEC (sec.gov). Bezos attached the original 1997 letter to every subsequent annual shareholder letter as a reminder of Amazon's founding principles.

the average driver is only involved in three to four crashes in their lifetime

Widely cited in driver safety and insurance publications. Some analyses place the figure at three to four reportable crashes over approximately 50 years of driving. See NHTSA crash statistics at nhtsa.gov.

CH. 15: WHY LEADERS ARE CHOSEN

warmth and competence / over 80% of the variance

From the Stereotype Content Model by Susan T. Fiske, Amy J.C. Cuddy, and Peter Glick. Key references: Fiske et al., "Universal Dimensions of Social Cognition: Warmth and Competence," *Trends in Cognitive Sciences*, 11(2), 77–83 (2007); Fiske et al., *Journal of Personality and Social Psychology*, 82(6), 878–902 (2002); Cuddy, A.J.C., Fiske, S.T., & Glick, P., "Warmth and Competence as Universal Dimensions of Social Perception," in *Advances in Experimental Social Psychology*, Vol. 40, 61–149 (2008). Abele and Wojciszke (2014) found these two dimensions account for more than 80% of the variance in individual impressions; some analyses report figures above 90%.

William Queen / "Under and Alone"

William Queen, *Under and Alone* (Random House, 2005). Queen spent over two years undercover with the Mongols motorcycle gang under the alias Billy St. John.

we make decisions based on emotion and rationalize the decision later

Jonathan Haidt's "social intuitionist model" argues that moral judgments are driven by rapid intuitive reactions, with reasoning occurring after the fact; see *Psychological Review*, 108(4), 814–834 (2001). Daniel Kahneman's System 1/System 2 framework supports this; see *Thinking, Fast and Slow* (Farrar, Straus and Giroux, 2011). Antonio Damasio's somatic marker hypothesis also demonstrates the role of emotion in decision-making; see *Descartes' Error* (Putnam, 1994).

CH. 16: WHO LEADERS ARE

"First, Break All the Rules" by Buckingham and Coffman

See Ch. 8 notes.

"If each of us hires people who are smaller than we are, we shall become a company of dwarfs." — David Ogilvy

David Ogilvy, *Ogilvy on Advertising* (1983). This statement reflects a principle Ogilvy practiced earlier in his career. He famously illustrated it by placing Russian matryoshka (nesting) dolls at executives' seats during a board meeting, each containing a message about hiring people "bigger than we are." The anecdote dates to the 1960s, though the quote itself is documented in his 1983 book.

John Maxwell's "Law of the Lid"

John C. Maxwell, *The 21 Irrefutable Laws of Leadership* (Thomas Nelson, 1998). The "Law of the Lid" is the first of Maxwell's 21 laws: an organization's effectiveness is capped by its leader's ability. As leadership ability rises or falls, so does the organization's potential.

"Mount Stupid" / Valley of Realization / Slope of Improvement

Draws on the Dunning-Kruger effect, first described in Kruger, J. & Dunning, D., "Unskilled and Unaware of It: How Difficulties in Recognizing One's Own Incompetence Lead to Inflated Self-Assessments," *Journal of Personality and Social Psychology*, 77(6), 1121–1134 (1999). The specific labels "Mount Stupid," "Valley of Despair," and "Slope of Enlightenment" come from popular visualizations of the effect, sometimes attributed to internet adaptations of the Dunning-Kruger curve.

Apollo 11 / Neil Armstrong / nearly one-fifth of the world's population was watching

NASA estimates that approximately 600 million people worldwide watched the live broadcast of Armstrong's first steps—roughly one-fifth of the 3.6 billion world population in 1969. See nasa.gov.

the curse of knowledge

Introduced by Camerer, C., Loewenstein, G., & Weber, M., *Journal of Political Economy*, 97(5), 1232–1254 (1989). Popularized by Chip and Dan Heath in *Made to Stick* (Random House, 2007).

"executive function" / prefrontal cortex

Well-established in cognitive neuroscience. See Diamond, A., "Executive Functions," *Annual Review of Psychology*, 64, 135–168 (2013).

The urgent versus important matrix

Widely attributed to Eisenhower. Stephen R. Covey popularized the concept as a four-quadrant matrix in *The 7 Habits of Highly Effective People* (Free Press, 1989), Habit 3: "Put First Things First."

CH. 17: THE COST OF LEADERSHIP

"Suppose one of you wants to build a tower. Won't you first sit down and estimate the cost…"

Luke 14:28–30 (New International Version). The passage continues: "For if you lay the foundation and are not able to finish it, everyone who sees it will ridicule you, saying, 'This person began to build and wasn't able to finish.'"

CH. 18: RULE #1: DON'T DIE ALONG THE WAY

Lindbergh / four crashed planes / fuel tanks, periscope, no radio, no parachute, wicker chair / Clarence Chamberlin

See A. Scott Berg, *Lindbergh* (Putnam, 1998) and Charles A. Lindbergh, *The Spirit of St. Louis* (Scribner, 1953). The Spirit of St. Louis was a custom-built Ryan NYP monoplane with a single Wright Whirlwind engine. Multiple competitors vied for the $25,000 Orteig Prize; prior attempts resulted in several crashes and fatalities. The forward fuel tank placement, periscope for forward visibility, absence of radio and parachute, and lightweight wicker seat are described in both sources. Clarence Chamberlin flew from Roosevelt Field, New York, to Eisleben, Germany, approximately two weeks after Lindbergh's May 20–21, 1927 crossing, covering a greater distance but receiving far less recognition.

Apollo 13 CO2 crisis / "make Filter A fit into a hole for Filter B"

See Gene Kranz, *Failure Is Not an Option* (Simon & Schuster, 2000) and Jim Lovell and Jeffrey Kluger, *Lost Moon* (Houghton Mifflin, 1994). After the explosion damaged the command module, the crew moved to the lunar module, whose lithium hydroxide canisters were a different shape from those in the command module. Mission Control engineers improvised an adapter using materials available on board—cardboard, plastic bags, and duct tape—to make the square command module canisters fit the round lunar module receptacles. The "Filter A / Filter B" framing is the author's summary of this famous engineering improvisation.

CH. 19: COALITIONS AND CARAVANS

"start with why"

Simon Sinek, *Start with Why* (Portfolio/Penguin, 2009). Sinek's concept, popularized by his 2009 TED talk, argues that inspiring leaders and organizations communicate from the inside out—starting with "why" (purpose) before "how" or "what."

Lewis and Clark / Darwin's voyage on the HMS Beagle

The Corps of Discovery (1804–1806) included approximately 33 members of diverse backgrounds. York, enslaved by William Clark, and Sacagawea played significant roles. See Stephen E. Ambrose, *Undaunted Courage* (Simon & Schuster, 1996). Darwin's voyage on HMS Beagle (1831–1836) is described in *The Voyage of the Beagle* (1839).

OCEAN dimensions

See Ch. 9 notes.

CH. 20: TELL THE TALE

Stephen King's mentor / "When you write a story, you're telling yourself the story..."

Stephen King, *On Writing: A Memoir of the Craft* (Scribner, 2000). The "mentor" was John Gould, King's editor at the *Lisbon Weekly Enterprise*.

Will Storr / "The Science of Storytelling"

See Ch. 10 notes.

Sir John Franklin's expedition / Fridtjof Nansen / Amundsen and the Northwest Passage / Nansen's ski jump, skating record, and skiing championships

The Franklin expedition (1845) and the loss of all 129 men aboard HMS Erebus and HMS Terror is one of exploration's most infamous disasters. Amundsen's biography—reading about Franklin at age 8, watching Nansen return from Greenland at 17, his eventual navigation of the Northwest Passage aboard the Gjøa (1903–1906)—is drawn primarily from Roland Huntford, *The Last Place on Earth* (Modern Library, 1999). Nansen's exploits—the ski jump at age 10, breaking the world skating record at 18, winning Norway's national cross-country skiing championship 12 times, and his east-to-west crossing of Greenland (1888)—are documented in Huntford, *Nansen: The Explorer as Hero* (Abacus, 2001).

"A person's toothache means more to them than a famine affecting millions." — Dale Carnegie

Dale Carnegie, *How to Win Friends and Influence People* (Simon & Schuster, 1936). The exact wording varies across editions; the underlying point—that people are most concerned with their own problems—is a recurring theme throughout the book.

"culture is the stories we tell ourselves about ourselves." — Clifford Geertz

Clifford Geertz, *The Interpretation of Cultures* (Basic Books, 1973). Geertz, an anthropologist at the Institute for Advanced Study in Princeton, argued for an interpretive approach to culture, viewing it as a web of meanings that people spin and within which they are suspended.

"The great enemy of clear language is insincerity." — George Orwell

George Orwell, "Politics and the English Language," Horizon, April 1946. The essay argues that political language is designed to make lies sound truthful and that vague, pretentious writing is a symptom of unclear or dishonest thinking. Widely reprinted and available in most Orwell essay collections.

CH. 21: SETTING NORTH

Lighthouse Board history / over 5,000 vessels / "Graveyard of the Atlantic" / Cape Lookout, Cape Hatteras

The waters off Cape Hatteras earned the "Graveyard of the Atlantic" nickname due to thousands of shipwrecks caused by Diamond Shoals, the collision of the Gulf Stream and Labrador Current, and shifting sandbars. In 1851, a congressional review led to the creation of the U.S. Lighthouse Board, which professionalized operations, standardized equipment (including Fresnel lenses), established keeper qualification requirements, and published the Light List and Notices to Mariners. Cape Lookout's distinctive white flash and Cape Hatteras's black-and-white spiral pattern were part of this effort. See David Stick, *Graveyard of the Atlantic* (UNC Press, 1952); U.S. Lighthouse Society (uslhs.org); National Park Service; NCpedia (ncpedia.org/lighthouses). The "over 5,000 vessels" figure reflects cumulative estimates of shipwrecks along the Outer Banks dating to the colonial era.

"wearing too many hats" and "too busy working 'in' the business to work 'on' the business"

Based on survey research conducted by Steve Van Remortel and MyTalentPlanner, Inc. (mytalentplanner.com). Van Remortel is the Founder and CEO of MyTalentPlanner and of Stop the Vanilla, LLC, and is an award-winning author, speaker, and recognized thought leader in strategy and talent planning. MyTalentPlanner surveyed thousands of small and medium-sized business (SMB) leaders to identify the top challenges hindering business growth. Among the most frequently cited pain points: leaders reported being stuck in the day-to-day, spending too much time working "in" the business rather than "on" it, wearing too many hats, and struggling with a lack of accountability and productivity. See also Van Remortel, *Stop Selling Vanilla Ice Cream* (named one of Soundview Executive Book Summaries' Best Business Books of 2013); mytalentplanner.com.

Bystander effect / CPR instructors

First described by Darley, J.M. & Latané, B., *Journal of Personality and Social Psychology*, 8(4), 377–383 (1968). The CPR training practice of pointing to a specific individual is standard AHA and Red Cross training to counteract diffusion of responsibility.

CH. 22: NAVIGATION AND RECONNAISSANCE

Titanic / Captain Smith / iceberg 37 seconds / radio operator / International Ice Patrol

RMS Titanic struck an iceberg on April 14, 1912, and sank in the early hours of April 15, with the loss of more than 1,500 lives. The "37 seconds" interval between the lookout's warning and impact derives from trials conducted on Titanic's sister ship Olympic and testimony before the British Wreck Commissioner's Inquiry (1912). Wireless operator Jack Phillips told the nearby Californian to "shut up." Captain Smith's standing order, "if it becomes at all doubtful," was reported in testimony by Second Officer Charles Lightoller. The International Ice Patrol was established in 1914 and operates today under the U.S. Coast Guard. See Walter Lord, *A Night to Remember* (Henry Holt, 1955); the British

Wreck Commissioner's Inquiry (1912); the U.S. Senate Inquiry (1912); Encyclopedia Titanica (encyclopedia-titanica.org).

CH. 23: LINES OF COMMUNICATION

Robert Falcon Scott / 15 miles of telephone line across the Antarctic

Edward Wilson's diary from the Terra Nova expedition (1910–1913) records the installation and use of telephone lines connecting Cape Evans to Hut Point and observation stations. See also David Crane, *Scott of the Antarctic* (Knopf, 2006).

"Cleared to land runway 27" / military readback / medical handoff protocols

Aviation readback protocols are governed by the Federal Aviation Administration (FAA) and the International Civil Aviation Organization (ICAO). Military communication procedures, including readback and "I say again" protocols, are documented in U.S. military field manuals. Medical handoff protocols such as SBAR (Situation, Background, Assessment, Recommendation) were developed to reduce communication errors during patient transitions; see the Joint Commission's patient safety standards.

CH. 24: SUPPLY LINES

Chief Nanaulu

Chief Nanaulu is a figure from Hawaiian oral tradition, credited with leading a Polynesian voyaging expedition of over 2,000 miles across the open Pacific more than 1,000 years ago. The story is preserved in Hawaiian cultural accounts and reflects the remarkable navigational achievements of Polynesian seafarers. See Ben Finney, *Voyage of Rediscovery* (University of California Press, 1994).

Adam Smith / "division of labor"

Adam Smith, *An Inquiry into the Nature and Causes of the Wealth of Nations* (1776). Smith's famous pin factory example in Book I, Chapter 1, demonstrated how dividing production into specialized tasks dramatically increased output. The concept predates Smith but he popularized it as a foundational principle of economics.

80+ pounds of bamboo per day

Giant pandas consume approximately 26 to 84 pounds of bamboo daily. See the Smithsonian's National Zoo (nationalzoo.si.edu) and the World Wildlife Fund (worldwildlife.org).

"no one ever got fired for choosing IBM"

A widely known business adage from the 1970s and 1980s, reflecting risk-averse corporate IT purchasing during IBM's mainframe dominance. Not attributed to a specific individual.

Zappos $3,000 quit offer / Menlo Innovations mass auditions / Dyson recruits high school students

Zappos's practice of offering new hires money to quit after initial training (the amount has varied over the years) is described in Tony Hsieh, *Delivering Happiness* (Grand Central, 2010). Menlo Innovations' collaborative hiring process, including paired auditions, is described in Richard Sheridan, *Joy, Inc.* (Portfolio/Penguin, 2013). Dyson's apprenticeship-style program for young recruits is documented at the Dyson Institute of Engineering and Technology (dysoninstitute.com).

CH. 25: BEACHHEADS

Fridtjof Nansen's Fram expedition / drifting from Siberia to Greenland / three years frozen in the ice / routines, re-rationing, supply audits, course reviews

Nansen's Fram expedition (1893–1896) deliberately froze the ship into the Arctic pack ice north of Siberia, drifting with the current toward Greenland over approximately three years. The crew's survival depended on disciplined routines of observation, supply management, and periodic review of the ship's drift and course. See Fridtjof Nansen, *Farthest*

North (1897); Roland Huntford, *Nansen: The Explorer as Hero* (Abacus, 2001).

CH. 26: ANCHOR BEFORE SETTING SAIL

"Every system is perfectly designed to get the results it gets."

Often attributed to W. Edwards Deming, though the IHI has noted the exact quote does not appear in Deming's published works. Variants attributed to Arthur Jones and Paul Batalden. Consistent with Deming's philosophy in *Out of the Crisis* (MIT Press, 1986).

"First you will come to the Sirens…" / "the world's first Ulysses Contract"

Homer, *The Odyssey*, Book XII. A "Ulysses contract" (also called a "Ulysses pact") is a decision made freely by a person to bind their future self against anticipated temptation or weakness. The term derives from the Sirens episode. The concept is discussed in behavioral economics; see Jon Elster, *Ulysses and the Sirens* (Cambridge University Press, 1979).

South Pole supply depots

Pre-positioning supply depots was critical for both Amundsen and Scott in 1911–1912. Amundsen laid depots at every degree of latitude; Scott's less systematic placement contributed to the fatal outcome. See Roland Huntford, *The Last Place on Earth* (Modern Library, 1999).

ONWARD

"returned home in a glow of fiery enthusiasm"

Edmund Hillary, *High Adventure* (Hodder & Stoughton, 1955).

"tall, bony, clumsy-looking youth"

Hillary's self-description, also from *High Adventure* (1955).

controlled exposure to discomfort and fear

An analytical characterization of Hillary's boxing experience. The Te Ara biography (Shaun Barnett, 2010) and NZ History note that boxing helped the shy schoolboy gain physical confidence.

"he lacked technical mountaineering proficiency"

Shaun Barnett, "Hillary, Edmund Percival," *Dictionary of New Zealand Biography* (Te Ara, 2010), citing Alexa Johnston, *Sir Edmund Hillary: An Extraordinary Life* (Penguin, 2005), p. 73. This changed when Hillary began climbing with Harry Ayres from 1946 onward; under Ayres's tutelage he became one of New Zealand's best climbers.

Ganges River / Amundsen / Shackleton

Hillary led a jetboat expedition up the Ganges from its mouth to its source in the Himalayas in 1977. Amundsen reached the South Pole on December 14, 1911, and later pioneered Arctic aviation, disappearing during a rescue flight over the Barents Sea in June 1928. Shackleton died of a heart attack on January 5, 1922, at South Georgia island, at the start of his fourth Antarctic expedition. See the respective biographies cited in Ch. 20 notes; also Alfred Lansing, *Endurance: Shackleton's Incredible Voyage* (McGraw-Hill, 1959).